Nigeria and the UN Mission to the Democratic Republic of the Congo

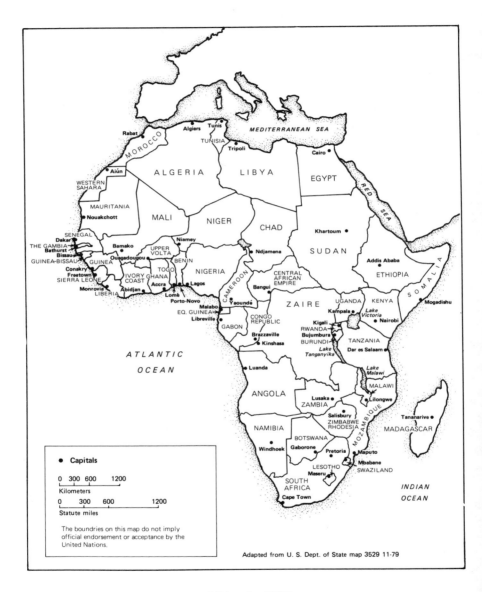

Africa in 1980

FESTUS UGBOAJA OHAEGBULAM

Nigeria and the UN Mission to the Democratic Republic of the Congo

A Case Study of the Formative Stages of Nigeria's Foreign Policy

A UNIVERSITY OF SOUTH FLORIDA BOOK

University Presses of Florida
Tampa / St. Petersburg / Sarasota / Fort Myers

DT
515.8
O346
1982

Library of Congress Cataloging in Publication Data
Ohaegbulam, Festus Ugboaja.

Nigeria and the UN Mission to the Democratic Republic of the Congo.
"A University of South Florida book."
Bibliography: p.
Includes index.
1. Nigeria—Foreign relations—1960– Case studies. 2. Zaire—History—Civil War, 1960–1965—Diplomatic history. 3. United Nations—Zaire. 4. United Nations—Nigeria. 5. Zaire—History—Civil War, 1960–1965—Participation, Nigerian. I. Title. II. Title: Nigeria and the U.N. mission to the Democratic Republic of the Congo.
DT515.8.O346   1982   327.669   82–11193
ISBN 0–8130–0709–7

Contents

List of Maps and Tables   vi

Acknowledgments   vii

Introduction   1

1. Preparations for Independent Nigeria's Foreign Policy   8
   Training for Foreign Service, 9. Emergence of public awareness
   of foreign policy issues, 14. Declaration of broad outlines of
   sovereign Nigeria's foreign policy, 16.

2. The Congo Crisis: A Summary of Its Causes
   and the Course of Its Resolution   20
   Causes of the crisis, 24. Highlights in the course of the resolution
   of the crisis, 43. The summit conferences of Congolese leaders in
   Tananarive and Coquilhatville, 49.

3. Nigeria's Policy on the Congo Crisis   53
   Responsibility for the crisis, 58. The Nigerian policy: objectives,
   principles, and major tenets, 62. Nigeria's policy in relation to those
   of the power blocs and the other African states, 69.

4. Formulation of Nigeria's Congo Policy:
   Factors and Determinants   72
   The process of policy formulation, 72. Summary, 83.

5. Avenues of Policy Implementation: The United Nations   85
   General Assembly debates on the Congo situation, 86. The UN
   Conciliation Commission for the Congo, 91. Nigerians seconded to
   the United Nations for service in the Congo, 96. Congo
   constitutional reviews, 99. The Royal Nigerian Army with the UN
   Operations in the Congo, 106. The Nigeria Police Force
   contingent with the UN Operations in the Congo, 111. Nigeria's
   financial contribution to the UN Operations in the Congo, 114.
   Nigeria, the United Nations and the Congo: An appraisal, 116.

6. Avenues of Policy Implementation: Bilateral Aid   119
   Medical aid, 121. The Congo Relief Fund, 121. University and
   secondary-school scholarships, 122. Modernization of the
   Congolese police force, 123. Summary, 126.
7. Congolese Appraisal of Nigeria's Role   127
   Resulting Nigeria-Congo relations, 131. Nigeria-Congo relations
   from conclusion of the UN Operations in the Congo to December
   1965, 136.
8. Conclusion   138
   Effect on the Congo of Nigeria's participation, 140. Effect on the
   collective interests of African states, 141. Effect on Nigeria's
   external relations and domestic conditions, 144. Significance of the
   study, 146.
Notes   151
Selected References   171
Index   185

Maps and Tables

Africa in 1980   FRONTISPIECE
Map 1.1 Nigeria in 1960   12
Map 2.1 The Congo and Its Neighbors, 1960   22
Table 2.1 The Congo's Provinces:
            Economic and Geographic Analysis   23
Map 2.2. Deployment of UN Forces in the Congo, 31 July 1960   46
Table 5.1 Nigerian UN Troops:
            Chief Areas of Deployment in the Congo   108

Acknowledgments

I AM INDEBTED to many people for their assistance in the preparation of this book. I acknowledge the help of officials of the Africa Division of Nigeria's External Affairs Ministry. I am deeply grateful to both the Honorable Dr. Jaja Wachuku, formerly Nigeria's minister of external affairs, and Dr. T. O. Elias, formerly Nigeria's attorney general and minister of justice, for their generosity in granting me extensive interviews and the benefit of their knowledge of Nigeria's Congo policy. My gratitude goes to Chief S. O. Adebo, formerly Nigeria's ambassador to the United Nations, who allowed me to interview the secretaries at Nigeria's UN Mission in New York. The press officer of the Nigeria Police Force and a number of other Nigerian policemen supplied material on the activities of the Nigeria Police Force contingent in the Congo. Captain O. Alily, formerly of the Nigerian Army, was especially helpful in providing detailed accounts of the work of the Nigerian Army in the Congo. The late Dr. Ralph Bunche supplied vital leads at the initial stages of the study. To him I am grateful. I thank Dr. Robert C. Good, formerly U.S. ambassador to Zambia, for the benefit of his insights into Nigeria's bilateral relations with the Congo.

Dr. Louis Perez, chairman, Department of History, University of South Florida, read the manuscript at least twice and offered critical stylistic and contextual comments. One of the readers for the University of South Florida Press editorial committee provided lengthy and objective comments which have materially enhanced the quality of the work. For the help of both these scholars I am very grateful. For whatever the work still lacks, the responsibility is mine.

Finally, I thank my wife Emma and my children, Emeka and Adanna, for their understanding during the days when I literally neglected them in order to write this book.

Tampa, Florida   F. U. O.

Introduction

NIGERIA BECAME a sovereign and independent state on 1 October 1960, three months after a crisis of major proportions had erupted in the Democratic Republic of the Congo. The political independence and the territorial integrity of the republic in the heart of Africa were gravely threatened from within and without five days after the proclamation of its independence on 30 June 1960. The two events—Nigeria's achieving independence and the crisis in the Democratic Republic of the Congo—occurred at a time when the international atmosphere was particularly tense. In fact, in May 1960, about a month prior to the political independence of the Congo, East-West relations had become very tense as a consequence, among other reasons, of the shooting down of an American U-2 aircraft over Soviet territory and an alleged earlier violation of Soviet airspace by an American U-2 plane. In addition, the world had already split into ideological factions competing for the allegiance of the new states of Asia and Africa.

The Congo episode was a crisis that affected the interests of the West, the Soviet bloc, and African states. Its eruption at the height of the cold war gave it special significance and added enormously to its complexity. The United States and its Western allies were apprehensive about Soviet penetration of Africa in the wake of the termination of European colonial rule in the continent. Amidst U.S. bipolar perspectives on international politics there was a great deal of concern that the interlinked economies of the United States and Western Europe, insofar as they were dependent on African natural resources, might be jeopardized by any severe breakdown of order following the withdrawal of the European colonial powers from Africa. This concern—and the belief that the Soviet bloc "prospers" in chaotic situations and has a special knack for fishing in troubled waters—encouraged Western interventionist and neocolonialist policies toward Africa in general and areas of conflict and tension in particular. Thus the implications of the Congo crisis for both Africa and the world were considered to be very grave, and Nigeria was called upon to participate with the United Nations in the rescue of the new republic and in forestalling thereby the dangerous international consequences of the crisis. The resolution of that crisis was by far the most complex operation that the United Nations has ever undertaken.

The circumstances in which political self-rule came to the Congo were among the fundamental causes of the crisis of independence. Nigeria, however, came to independence under circumstances different from those under which the Republic of the Congo became a sovereign nation. Unlike the Congo's experience, the road to self-rule had been peaceful for Nigeria, which entered independence with political leaders whose names had become household words throughout the country, who had exercised the responsibilities of office for almost a decade, and who had become associated with the actual workings of government at many levels prior to the day of independence. Nigeria's political leaders had had more experiences in common than had the Congolese leaders. Even the credit for Nigeria's achievement of independence they tended to share more equitably than did the Congolese leaders. Under the prevailing international situation of intense competition for dominance or advantage in Africa, the political circumstances of the Congolese peoples attracted the world's opportunist powers.

In the complex of events and policies that comprised the Congo crisis, the leading powers of the world strove for advantage. The United States, the Soviet Union, the United Kingdom, and France obviously were more concerned with their own economic interests or with the ideological struggle for geopolitical hegemony and control over the minds and actions of men than with the political interests of the Congolese people and their new republic. The Western European powers were particularly concerned about events and developments in the Congo from the eve of the republic's independence.

First, Belgium had a definite interest in the security of its nationals, who were the majority of about a hundred thousand Europeans employed in the Congo. Those persons had expected long careers in relatively comfortable material circumstances in the Congo. They had a private stake, which they expected their national government to protect. Belgium also had an obvious interest in safeguarding the legal status of its private and corporate enterprises in the Congo, for example, the Société Générale de Belgique, which controlled directly or indirectly 70 percent of the Congolese economy.[1] Loss of this control would be extremely damaging to the Belgian economy and national budget. To protect all these interests therefore became a political imperative for the Belgian government of the day. Belgium was propelled into deep involvement in and aggravation of the crisis in its former colony.

Britain and France as colonial powers had a stake in preserving their freedom of action in Africa. It was their policy to oppose and resist in subtle ways the desire of Afro-Asian nations to use the United Nations as an instrument of rapid decolonization. They were, together with West Germany and Italy, consumers of minerals from the Congo. British investments in the Congo, particularly through Unilever and Tanganyika Concessions, were second only to those of the Belgians. In addition the British government at the time of the crisis was sensitive to developments that might affect existing white-black political relations in the British Central African Federation.

American interests were at once ideological, political, and economic. At the period of the crisis the newer and developing nations of the world had become the major arena of the ideological struggle between the United States and the Soviet Union. Thus American policymakers, who viewed the Congo through a prism of the cold war ideology, were very alert in that context to the opportunities in a significant and strategically located new state like the Congo. They believed that a pro-Communist Congo would not only jeopardize Western sources of strategic raw materials—uranium, cobalt, copper, industrial diamonds, for example—but would also create a base for the Soviet subversion of Central Africa. They were determined to preserve the status quo in Central and Southern Africa and to ensure that Western Europe's economic and strategic advantages in the Congo and its neighboring states, crucial to Europe's economic health and so of material and strategic interest to America, were maintained against any onslaught of Soviet penetration.

It was these Western concerns in their entirety, more than any opportunistic actions by the Soviet Union, that aggravated the Congo crisis. There is no doubt that the Kremlin wanted footholds in Africa, but its interests in the Congo crisis were mainly aroused by the actions of the Western powers. It seems the United States and its Western allies failed to appreciate a fundamental fact: that Africans, no matter how politically inexperienced, had not struggled so hard for their freedom only to surrender it so quickly to the Soviet Union.

In Africa there was a definite interest in successful decolonization. Even so the new states were so new that they found themselves with little power to deal effectively with the crisis in the Congo, a crisis that was of great concern to every African country. African nationalists, however, saw immediately that the crisis spotlighted a new dimension of imperialism, the menace of "neocolonialism"—the return of foreign political domination through the back door of economic and ideological control. According to this interpretation the Belgian government, which for economic reasons precipitately intervened in the Congo, had granted the Congolese people a "pseudo-independence" with the concealed intention of making the former colony a "client state" and thus controlling it effectively by means other than political ones.

Through this neocolonialist strategy, Moise Tshombe, the secessionist president of Katanga Province, had become, in the eyes of some of the African political elite, a tool in the hands of Belgian officials—the neocolonialists. His regime, at the time, was viewed by African nationalists as dependent entirely on Belgian arms, men, and money. Without that support his government in all probability would have quickly disintegrated from within or have been overrun from without. The outline of Belgium's emergency policy for Katanga at that time, said London's *Daily Telegraph* (27 July 1960), was "to protect the great Belgian financial stake [there] and hold a political bridgehead in the hope of a Congolese union amenable to Belgium and the West." Certainly, after Belgium was forced at a Brussels Round Table Conference in January 1960 to promise to grant independence to the Congo five months later, it planned to retain traditional politico-economic hegemony over its former colony through economic ties. Since it planned to do so, Belgium obtained enormous support from its allies—the United States, France, and Great Britain. These, particularly the United States, through bribery and manipulation of professed Congolese leaders, political assassination plots, and pressures on the less powerful members of the United Nations and the organization's secretariat, were able to achieve their ideological and neocolonialist objectives in the Congo and Central Africa[2]—and thus decisively affect the outcome of the Congo crisis.

The crisis immediately posed three pertinent problems to all African states: the extent to which the newly independent African states could consider themselves their own political masters; the extent to which Africa was to become involved in the ideological struggle between the Western and the Eastern power blocs; and whether independent African states would adopt similar policies toward the crisis or would splinter into groups pursuing differing, perhaps opposing, policies and objectives. In fact, it was not long before the independent African states found that they were acutely divided in their views and consequently on their policies concerning the Congo problem.

For Nigeria, on the threshold of independence, two questions in particular appeared pertinent. What would be its evaluation of the crisis? Would its preindependence evaluation of the crisis remain the same or would independence change the Nigerian outlook on the Congo? Immediately upon gaining its independence, Nigeria was put to the test about what policy it would pursue in the continuing crisis. Would it toe the line of the former colonial administrator—Great Britain—or adopt its own independent policy?

Moreover, the Congo crisis was taking place in a republic with both population and natural resources as diverse as those of the Federation of Nigeria. Both Nigeria and the Republic of the Congo have a multitude of ethnic groups of varying sizes and distinctive cultural traditions. To some extent both countries have an uneven geographical distribution of economic resources and opportunities as well as an uneven political awareness among their constituent populations. Indeed, the Democractic Republic of the Congo is a vast country where conditions differ from area to area as they differ in the vastness of Nigeria itself. The Congolese political parties were numerous, as were those of Nigeria, even when the tendency in most African countries was toward a one-party system. Some of the Congolese political parties were lineal descendants of ethnic and cultural associations, as were the Action Group of Nigeria and to some extent the Northern (Nigeria) Peoples' Congress. The few elections the Congolese had held—the 1957 and 1958 municipal elections and the May 1960 national elections—were contested, as were similar elections in Nigeria, on the basis of ethnic interests and were influenced by ethnic loyalties rather than by national issues. In the Congo, just as in Nigeria, not ideology but personal and sectional interests were the major issue of political debates.

Although Nigeria's progress toward nationhood had been comparatively less abrupt and more definite than that of the Congo, objective political observers were aware of the ominous similarities. The independent *Observer* (London), commenting on the qualities of Sir Abubakar Tafawa Balewa, prime minister of Nigeria, on the occasion of Nigeria's independence, said, "One thing is certain, Nigeria has fundamentally the same type of problems that produced the Congo crisis. But there is, happily, small chance of its going that way." At any rate, for both the Federation of Nigeria and the Republic of the Congo, conditions of peace and orderliness were and remain essential for national unity, planning, and prosperity. Therefore, whatever happened in the Congo, and in fact in other parts of Africa, could not fail to be important to Nigeria. Sir Abubakar himself constantly maintained that Nigeria belongs to Africa and so Africa had to claim first attention in Nigeria's external affairs. Jaja Wachuku, the federation's first indigenous Speaker of the House of Representatives, later to become Nigeria's minister of External Affairs and Commonwealth Relations until 1964, declared in Nigeria's House of Representatives debates in January 1960 that Nigeria would not "abdicate the position in which God Almighty has placed us."

Dr. Nnamdi Azikiwe, first Nigerian governor-general of Nigeria, had also stated earlier that Nigeria could not be neutral in anything affecting the destiny of Africa. Furthermore, in his criticism of the Afro-Asian states for their failure to invite Nigeria to the Bandung Conference (1955), Dr. Azikiwe had stated that he might say

> without fear of contradiction that any decision made at Bandung on the future of this [African] continent that does not take into account the fact that every sixth person in Africa is a Nigerian, is bound to be like a flower that is born to blush unseen and waste its sweetness in the desert air. . . . The powers will do well to appreciate the historic mission and manifest destiny of Nigeria on the African continent.

What then was the reaction of this new state of Nigeria, as conscious as its peoples were and are of their own menacing differences and of their place and potential role in Africa, to the Congo crisis—and to the United Nations' mission to the Republic of the Congo? What was Nigeria's interpretation of the crisis—its causes and implications? What was the policy it adopted toward the crisis? What considerations went into the making of the policy? How was that policy executed? What overall role did Nigeria play in bringing the crisis to an end? Was such a role commensurate with Nigeria's size as the most populous African country and with the belief, universally held by its political leaders and its elite class, that Nigeria had a "historic mission" in Africa?

This study is an attempt to answer these questions. It is an attempt to examine the Congo crisis (1960–June 1964) and to evaluate Nigeria's role in the resolution of that crisis. It is both a case study in the international mediation of a national conflict and an attempt to ascertain what effective use Nigeria made of the United Nations as an instrument of its maiden foreign policy.

I am fully aware of the changes in nomenclature (the name of the nation itself, names of the national capital, cities, provinces, and provincial capitals, for example) that have taken place in the Republic of the Congo, formerly the Belgian Congo, since the late 1960s and particularly since President Mobutu Sese Seko's "authenticity drive" in the early 1970s. But since these name changes occurred after the events dealt with in this work, I have used the names that were contemporaneous with the UN mission to the Congo. Doing so, in my view, gives the work and the events described a special flavor of authenticity and facilitates further research into the sources on the period.

The frontispiece map shows Africa in 1980. The following list clarifies the changes in nomenclature since the 1960s.

Former name	*Present name*
Republic of the Congo	Republic of Zaire
Congo River	Zaire River
Coquilhatville	Mbandaka
Elizabethville	Lumumbashi
Katanga Province	Shaba Province
Léopoldville	Kinshasa
(national capital)	(national capital)
Luluabourg	Kananga
South West Africa	Namibia
Stanleyville	Kisangani
Joseph Desire Mobutu	Mobutu Sese Seko
British Central Africa	Federation of . . .
Nyasaland	Malawi
Northern Rhodesia	Zambia
Southern Rhodesia	Zimbabwe

1

Preparations for Independent Nigeria's Foreign Policy

IN A STATE WHERE a unitary system of government operates, it is taken for granted that the conduct of the state's foreign relations is the exclusive preserve of the chief executive. But in a federation such as the First Republic of Nigeria, which is made up of states endowed with considerable autonomy and prone to pursue their sectional interests, it is necessary to delimit the component units' spheres of competence and that of the national government as well. The Nigerian Federal Constitution (1960), the "independence constitution," undertook this delimitation as part of a conscious effort to harmonize Nigeria's strengths and weaknesses for the overall advantage of its domestic and foreign policies. The details of the constitution were worked out largely by Nigerians themselves with the deliberate and invaluable help of the British Colonial Office in London after a series of conferences and consultations among representatives of Nigeria's political parties, special interest groups, and every shade of public opinion.

The independence constitution enumerated the powers that were the exclusive authority of the national government and others that the national government shared concurrently with the component regional governments. It conferred competence over residual matters on the regional governments. Thus the constitution placed the following matters relating to foreign relations under the exclusive competence of the federal or national government: external affairs; public relations of the federation; borrowing of moneys outside Nigeria for purposes of the federation or of any region; defense; deportation, immigration, passports; and treaty-making power.[1] However, Section 69(2) limited the treaty-making power of the federal government particularly with regard to residual matters in which the regional governments had competence. Furthermore, because of conventions allowed by the constitution, the federal prime minister had to brief the regional premiers on matters of foreign policy.

Under these constitutional provisions, therefore, the Congo crisis came under the exclusive responsibility of Nigeria's federal government. The prime minister, who undertook the responsibility, advised the regional premiers on the tenets and objectives of his policy toward the crisis. This briefing helped to ensure that Nigeria's voice on the Congo crisis was essentially unified. This state of affairs contrasted vividly with that on the eve of independence when, although Nigerians were not yet fully in control of their own foreign affairs, the regional premiers and governments, in their extensive activities and frequent missions abroad seeking good will and investments, had made uncoordinated and unauthorized statements relating to Nigeria's foreign policy.[2]

Again, the manner in which these provisions of the Nigerian constitution relating to the conduct of foreign policy and other matters had been worked out by Nigerians themselves affected Nigeria's interpretation of the Congo crisis. Although Britain's role in drafting the Nigerian constitution that led to independence had been more subtle and pervasive than Nigerians could admit at the time, Nigeria's political leaders felt that the Congo's crisis was partly due to the Congolese constitution, which, they believed, was a Belgian imposition designed to protect Belgian interests in the Congo and not an instrument formulated by the Congolese people themselves for the orderly governance of their own country.

Training for Foreign Service

With few exceptions—Nigerian students' affairs, consular matters, and labor matters—the interests of Nigerians outside their own country were represented until 1 October 1960 by the Foreign Service of the British government. But so much importance did Nigerian politicians attach to the conduct of independent Nigeria's foreign relations that they began to make demands in 1952, eight years before independence, for the training of Nigerian Foreign Service personnel in anticipation of national autonomy. The British colonial administration at first refused the demands, describing them as unheard of. The demands were repeated in 1953,[3] when members of Nigeria's House of Representatives called upon the Council of Ministers "to initiate a special scholarship programme for the training of personnel, code experts, intelligence officers, language experts, interpreters and press officers, to man the Nigerian Foreign Service in the future."[4] The uncooperative attitude of the British colonial administration toward the move persisted. Not until 1956 were Nigeria's political leaders able to effect the publication of a white paper announcing the start of training of nationals for the conduct of independent Nigeria's foreign relations.[5]

In a policy statement to this end the governor-general of the federation said:

> [B]ecause a high standard of character, training and ability to carry out very responsible duties will be required of any Nigerian who is to represent his country abroad and because such standards cannot be attained in a moment, the training of Nigerians should not be put off until the time when Nigeria assumes responsibility for the conduct of its external relations and thus becomes entitled to exchange diplomatic representatives with other countries.[6]

Accordingly, plans were made for training a Foreign Service corps and for the conduct of foreign relations in general. It was projected that upon independence Nigeria would maintain only the following Foreign Service establishments: a Ministry of External Affairs in Lagos; offices of the high commissioners of the federation in London and in Accra (Ghana); a diplomatic mission in Washington, D.C.; a diplomatic mission in Khartoum (Sudan); a delegation to the United Nations in New York City; and consular offices in Jedda (Saudi Arabia), Fernando Po (Equatorial Guinea), and Libreville (Gabon).[7]

This planning for the establishment of a limited number of Foreign Service offices upon the attainment of independence was based upon considerations of Nigeria's national interest as defined by the ruling authorities: the expense of training and maintaining additional staff; the danger of engaging and training potential Foreign Service officers for whom employment might not become available for some time; and the danger that by setting the number too high the standards for recruitment would fall in the quest to meet the quota.[8]

In regard to the last of the three tangible considerations for establishing Foreign Service offices, the government stated that an independent Nigeria would be judged overseas by the quality of those who represented it and by the efficient administration of its overseas missions. The government emphasized that it was, accordingly, greatly concerned that Nigeria's future Foreign Service personnel should be composed of men and women of the highest quality who had undergone thorough training.[9]

The government, not unconcerned with the future, proposed to meet estimated needs by expanding existing offices overseas and by progressive selection and training of potential Foreign Service officers. The plan was conservatively sound, but it had one significant shortcoming. The government had sown for itself or its successor, if the plan was implemented to the letter (as indeed it later was), a seed of controversy by failing to establish at least one diplomatic mission in an East European or Eastern (that is, Communist bloc) capital. Members of the House of Representatives pointed to this omission in 1959.[10] One month following independence, critics of the government's foreign policy did indeed charge it with discriminating against the Eastern bloc and of preserving a colonial mentality.[11]

The government's conservative plan also explains why Nigeria had only four diplomatic and consular offices in all of Africa when the Congo crisis erupted and the United Nations mission to the Republic of the Congo began, and points to Nigeria's apparently inadequate preparation for understanding and dealing with African affairs in the manner to which its leaders, who believed it had a leadership mission in Africa, were aspiring. The plan would imply a reliance on British sources for gathering information and intelligence about the major issues of the period, including the crisis that precipitated the UN mission to the Congo.

Recruitment of trainees for Nigeria's diplomatic service, which began in November 1956, aimed at producing three main classes of staff: diplomatic representatives, consular and trade representatives, and the staff of a Ministry of Foreign Affairs within the federal government. Selection of candidates was based on three considerations: they should possess high academic standing and have a rounded education; they should be, or should be trained to be, civil servants divorced from politics; and they should have, or acquire, proficiency in languages.

The federal Public Service Commission selected the first twelve recruits for the diplomatic service of the federation in November 1956. Ten were drawn from among the public service employees of the three original regions, one directly from Oxford University, and the other from the Southern Cameroons. (Then part of the United Nations Trusteeship to Britain, the Southern Cameroons was being administered as part of the Eastern Region of Nigeria. See map 1.1.)

Four of those who had been educated entirely within Africa were

sent to spend a year at Oxford University in a course especially designed to provide them with a wider background before they embarked
upon any practical work. The same group later took a short course at
the Foreign Office in London designed for young diplomats. From
there they went, one each, to the British embassies at the Hague, Bonn,
and Rio de Janeiro, and to the British High Commissioner's Office in
Canada, to gain practical experience in the conduct of foreign affairs.

Seven of the recruits had already had considerable experience in
administration in Nigeria. Two of these were sent to the Nigeria Office
in London and one to the Nigeria Liaison Office in the British Embassy
in Washington, D.C. (This last trainee was later to proceed to France
for language study.) Four were sent directly to a French university to
study French. The twelfth recruit, the graduate of Oxford University,
was posted to the External Affairs branch of the prime minister's office
in Lagos, where he spent one year before proceeding overseas.[12]

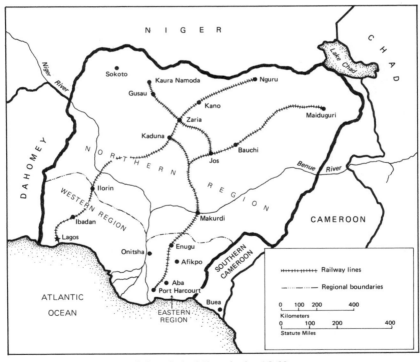

Map 1.1. Nigeria in 1960

Sixteen other trainees were selected in 1958; and it was hoped that by 1959 the federal Public Service Commission (which was then completing a series of recruitment interviews in the United Kingdom) would select fifteen additional trainees, bringing the total to slightly more than the forty planned by the date of independence.[13] The government hoped that there would be fifty-five career civil servants either trained or in training for overseas duty by the end of 1960.

A total of £500,000 was allocated to be spent by March 1960 in training Nigerians for the Foreign Service, and another £500,000 had been earmarked for the purchase of buildings to house Nigerian embassies.[14]

A Nigeria Office, established in New York City in September 1959, was expected to become, in time, the headquarters of Nigeria's delegation to the United Nations and would deal with questions of trade, economics, and the dissemination of information about Nigeria. In addition, the Nigeria Office opened in Accra, Ghana, in October 1959.

Such preparation not only made it possible for Nigeria to dispatch Foreign Service personnel to the United Nations on the eve of its national independence and to the Republic of the Congo barely a month after Nigeria gained independence on 1 October 1960; it also ensured that Nigeria's decision makers were kept informed of deliberations at the United Nations relating to the Congo crisis, that they would be in day-to-day contact with Nigerian diplomats regarding developments in the Congo, and that they would have relatively adequate information on which to base the nation's subsequent policies. In short, the preparations ensured that Nigeria's views and interests in the developments in the Congo crisis would be satisfactorily represented.

Another aspect of the preparations for the independent conduct of Nigeria's foreign relations concerned defense, a vital arm of the country's foreign relations. Responsibility for defense and for police had been handed over to the prime minister and the Council of Ministers by the governor-general of the federation, Sir James Robertson, about nine months before independence. But up to independence day, control of external affairs remained under the Colonial Office in London. Around January 1956, however, the governor-general put the office that dealt with Nigeria's foreign relations administratively under the then chief minister, Sir Abubakar, who thus received many of the documents on foreign relations that had previously gone to the governor-general. Thus when Sir Abubakar became prime minister the next year, he was already intimately associated with the formulation of foreign policy.[15]

Furthermore, the British Commonwealth Relations Office sent a representative to Lagos in 1958 to advise the federal government on external affairs.[16] By August 1959 the External Affairs Division in the Office of the Prime Minister became established as a self-contained unit, which, it was hoped, would be transformed without further reorganization into a Ministry of Foreign Affairs in October 1960. By the end of 1959 Sir Abubakar had established a national and international reputation, as his gradually maturing views on foreign policy became established, more clearly defined, and more objective.[17]

These various aspects of the preparations for Nigeria's independent foreign relations—Sir Abubakar's assumption of the responsibility for defense, his association with the machinery of foreign policy, the advice on external affairs by a representative of the Commonwealth Relations Office—had salutary effects on Nigeria's Congo policy. Sir Abubakar was able to respond with dispatch to the request by the United Nations to send military and police contingents to the Congo. His previous intimate association with the making of foreign policy facilitated his formulation of a realistic and comprehensive policy toward the Congo crisis.

Emergence of public awareness of foreign policy issues

The year 1959 is significant in Nigeria's diplomatic history. It marked the emergence of real public awareness of foreign policy issues and the beginning of full-scale discussions of the policy objectives to be pursued in the country's foreign relations. Prior to 1959 only a few of Nigeria's foremost political leaders had given adequate thought to foreign policy of a future independent Nigeria.[18] The bulk of the Nigerian intelligentsia had been too preoccupied with their country's domestic problems—the independence struggle, the type of constitution that would best suit Nigeria, the question of allaying the fears of minorities, etc.—to concern themselves in particular with the details of the external relations of independent Nigeria. Furthermore, since Nigeria's foreign relations had been almost wholly controlled by Great Britain before 1959, the Nigerian House of Representatives had very seldom, if ever, been called upon to express any opinion on the country's external relations; hence the Nigerian press appeared equally silent.

But 1959 saw a significant change in this situation. It was the year of Nigeria's preindependence federal elections. The elections were momentous in that they were to give Nigeria a government that would take over from Great Britain its sovereign national and international responsibilities. It was necessary, therefore, for all the political parties that were to contest the elections to present to the electorate not only comprehensive statements on their domestic policies but also their foreign policy platforms. Thus it came to be that, as Nigeria was on the threshold of independence, foreign policy issues and the international situation in general received steadily increasing attention not only among the various political parties vying for power but also among the Nigerian elite and the press.

Such political leaders as Dr. Nnamdi Azikiwe, Chief Obafemi Awolowo, and Sir Abubakar Tafawa Balewa spoke persuasively of the role their country was "destined" to play in world politics. The role of sovereign Nigeria in world politics, said Dr. Azikiwe, was "destined" to be important because of the country's size and its social and economic position. Nigeria, he said, would play a decisive part in the complete rejection both of racial bigotry and of any attempt to fasten upon Africans or peoples of African descent the badge of inferiority. Nigeria would work to emancipate from the bonds of colonialism not only the peoples of Africa but all peoples of African descent. It would dedicate itself to the maintenance of peace "everywhere in the world, and the extermination of man's inhumanity to man everywhere in the world." [19]

Nigerian Prime Minister Sir Abubakar himself expressed a strong belief in a flexible foreign policy based on domestic strength. He said that the greatest single contribution Nigeria would make to Africa, and to world peace generally, would be to show how such a diverse country can find peaceful solutions to its internal difficulties. [20] It was his earnest hope "that the visible strength of Nigeria will have a stabilising effect in this part of the world," and that its example would induce conditions favorable to orderly progress and development in Africa. [21] Sir Abubakar emphasized, fundamentally and realistically, that domestic strength and internal stability would make Nigeria's role and voice in world politics effective and respected.

Nigeria's major political parties included foreign policy statements in their election manifestos in August and September of 1959. During their campaigns and lectures, candidates had to explain to numerous audiences the lines of foreign policy they would pursue if their party were voted into power. [22]

What emerged from the campaigns and the foreign policy statements of the leading Nigerian political parties—the Action Group of
Nigeria, the Northern Peoples' Congress, and the National Council of
Nigeria and the Cameroons—was that the parties substantially agreed
on the basic tenets of the foreign policy an independent Nigeria should
pursue. They essentially concurred on Nigeria's membership in the
Commonwealth and the United Nations, its continued friendship with
the Western democracies, and its freedom to make new friends. Their
major differences centered around alignment with the Western powers
as advocated by the Northern Peoples' Congress and the Action Group,
as opposed to the National Council of Nigeria and the Cameroons' ad-
vocacy of pragmatic nonalignment with any particular geopolitical
axis; the acceptance in principle by the National Council of Nigeria
and the Cameroons of a West African Federation in opposition to the
other parties' rejection of it; and the emphasis by the National Council
of Nigeria and the Cameroons on strengthening the Nigerian armed
forces, which was deemphasized by the other two parties.

The parties' broad agreement on the nation's foreign policy was a
good omen for Nigeria's politics when one recalls the explosive domestic issues of preindependence and immediately postindependence
Nigeria and the particularist sectional interests that plagued postindependence Nigeria's social, economic, and political life. But it remained to be seen how faithfully the leaders who had championed the
positions on Nigeria's foreign policy advocated by their respective parties—and had supported the substantial accord among the parties—
would adhere to their preindependence election declarations.

One thing was certain: for the first time the broad outlines of foreign policy had received nationwide discussion and public debate in
Nigeria. Leading politicians had forthrightly criticized each other's
views on foreign policy for a free Nigeria. The various media supporting the politicians as well as their party publications had done likewise.
A precedent was thus set for Nigeria's policy on the Congo crisis to
receive nationwide public discussion and criticism.

Declaration of broad outlines of sovereign Nigeria's foreign policy

In the aftermath of the preindependence federal elections, a coalition
government by the Northern Peoples' Congress and the National Council of Nigeria and the Cameroons was formed, with the Action Group

as the loyal opposition. With the establishment of the new government and legislature, Nigeria was ready to claim for itself a position of significance in international politics.

Foreign policy continued to receive the attention of both the government and the legislature, which met in January 1960.[23] Prime Minister Sir Abubakar reiterated his belief in a flexible foreign policy and in a closer association with Britain and the Commonwealth.[24]

By April 1960 some members of the House of Representatives were already demanding the establishment of an all-parties parliamentary committee to formulate a common policy for defense and foreign affairs. The demands persisted even after independence, but they were rejected by the government.

A majority of the members of the legislature repeatedly urged that the foreign policy of the federal government should be placed before the House of Representatives for debate prior to independence.[25] Their leaders argued that because specific foreign policy measures had been promised by the parties during the federal elections of 1959, but no single party had won enough parliamentary seats to form the government alone, it was necessary for differing policy objectives, all enjoying broad popular support, to be reconciled in advance of Nigeria's assuming sole responsibility for its foreign relations and international obligations.[26]

In view of the fact that the government was a coalition of two parties espousing different ideologies, the demand seems not to have been unreasonable. Observers of Nigerian politics, noticing the ideological differences among the parties, had felt that foreign policy was likely to present the new federal government with some problems. The coordination of policy, however, was essentially the business of the coalition partners, and on this rationale, the government's rejection of the demand for an all-parties parliamentary committee was appropriate. What was sorely needed in its place was the introduction—by the prime minister and his relevant cabinet members—of a spirit of bipartisanship in foreign affairs to remove the issue of foreign policy from partisan politics. Such a system usually works by producing a measure of agreement on the basic orientation of the state's foreign policy between the governing party and the leaders of the loyal opposition, seeking legislative support from a substantial segment of the opposition party for key items in the governing party's foreign policy programs, and withdrawal of fundamental foreign policy issues from debates in political campaigns. Such a system necessarily implies consultation with leaders of the opposition party on policy issues, seeking their active participation in the execution of the decided policy, informing them of the policy's operation, and sharing credit (or blame) with them for the policy's success (or failure).

Recognizing the utility of a system of this nature, the prime minister attempted to meet the demands of the legislators on 20 August 1960 when he declared in the House of Representatives the major principles of his government's foreign policy.[27] The primary duty of his government in the conduct of Nigeria's foreign relations would be to "safeguard and promote the interests of the Federation and of its citizens." His government would secure Nigeria's membership in both the Commonwealth and the United Nations but would have a free hand to select the policies it considered to be most advantageous to Nigeria, subject always to its belief in the principles of the United Nations. His government would not "associate itself as a matter of routine with any power bloc." It would devote particular attention to adopting clear and practicable policies regarding Africa. But it would not allow preoccupation with African affairs to blind it "to the grave and vital issues which darken the wider international scene." On the contrary, his government would, through the United Nations and any other possible avenues, direct its "energies and influence to helping to reach solutions which will contribute to the peace of nations and the well-being of mankind."

The statement was succinct, but the principles enunciated by the prime minister held nothing particularly new. The statement did reveal that the federal government coalition parties had modified, if not harmonized, the stands they had taken on foreign policy during the 1959 elections. It also emphasized the fact that Sir Abubakar had adopted a policy of pragmatic nonalignment, a policy that underlined the fact that Nigeria would have "enduring interests" but no "permanent allies" to hamper the attainment of such interests. By the statement, too, Sir Abubakar provided his countrymen and the outside world with both an indication of the line of policy to expect when Nigeria became independent and a basis for an investigation of departures from the stated or expected course of policy should any occur.

The conduct of Nigeria's policy toward the Congo crisis, which indeed represented independent Nigeria's maiden international involvement (as subsequent sections of this study will show), was based on the principles embodied in the broad outlines of the foreign policy statement made by Sir Abubakar on 20 August 1960. Those principles, in turn, were based on the harmonized foreign policy platforms of the

Northern Peoples' Congress and the National Council of Nigeria and the Cameroons, the parties forming the federal government coalition. The Action Group, the loyal opposition, criticized only the peripheral elements of that Congo policy, indicating that it was in substantial agreement with the tenets and objectives of that policy and also attesting to the substantial agreement on the foreign policy goals that the three major political parties had presented to the Nigerian electorate during the federal elections of 1959. The lively interest Nigerian parliamentarians showed in foreign policy at this period was an indication that Nigeria's Congo policy would also receive extensive public discussion and debate,[28] as indeed happened. The UN mediating mission to the Republic of the Congo was to be a test of Nigeria's realistic foreign policy against the demands of international conflict resolution. To that conflict we must next direct our attention.

The Congo Crisis: A Summary of Its Causes
and the Course of Its Resolution

"MONSIEUR, THIS Independence the politicians told us was
coming, would it come by air, by sea, or by land?"
— A Congolese to his Belgian employer

LITTLE DID the Congolese who asked or the Belgian employer who
laughed at the ridiculous question know that there was to be some truth
in it. For no sooner did independence come than United Nations civil
and military assistance descended on the Democratic Republic of the
Congo by air, by sea, and by land in order to establish peace.[1]

In the recent history of the entire African continent, the independence of the Democratic Republic of the Congo stands out conspicuously. Only there, following a violent crisis of major proportions, has
complex, multilateral intervention been undertaken (a few days after
the proclamation of independence) by UN member states to ensure law
and order and to prevent the newly independent state from immediately becoming a satellite of Belgium or of Western European economic interests or of one of the ideological power blocs.

We do not attempt to review all aspects of the Congo crisis, about
which much has been written already.[2] Rather, the stage is set here for
examining Nigeria's first major involvement in world politics by iden-
tifying the Congo crisis and its causes, the major contending forces,
and significant highlights in the course of its resolution.

On 5 July 1960, five days after the proclamation of the birth of the
Democratic Republic of the Congo, Congolese soldiers in Thysville
and Léopoldville mutinied against their Belgian officers. The soldiers
believed they had been denied the fruits of independence—the material and psychological rewards that their civilian counterparts were enjoying. Within a few days the mutiny spread to other areas: Matadi
(Léopoldville province), Kindu (Lower Congo), Kongolo (Katanga),

and Luluabourg (Kasai). (See map 2.1 and table 2.1.) In the resulting disorder property was destroyed, Europeans and Congolese were injured or killed, several women were raped, and many panic-stricken Europeans, mostly Belgians, fled the Congo to Brazzaville and to Europe. Civilian life, together with political administration, was disrupted.

Five days after the mutiny of the Force publique began, Belgian authorities unilaterally deployed Belgian troops in Léopoldville, Elizabethville, Jadotville, Kamina, and elsewhere in the Congo in order, they said, to protect Belgian citizens and to restore order. This Belgian intervention was interpreted by Léopoldville authorities as an act of aggression against the Republic of the Congo.[3]

Ominously, on 11 July Moise Tshombe, president of Katanga province, proclaimed the independence of Katanga and immediately appealed for and received Belgian military aid to uphold his regime. The Léopoldville authorities interpreted the declared secession of Katanga as a Belgian "preparation" aimed at securing a perpetual Belgian hold on the Congo.[4]

Faced with these grave events, Congolese central government authorities, namely, President Joseph Kasavubu and Prime Minister Patrice Lumumba, cabled appeals to the United Nations (12 and 13 July) for an "urgent dispatch" of military assistance "to protect the national territory of the Congo against the present external aggression which is a threat to international peace."[5] The two Congolese leaders later (14 July) cabled Soviet Premier Nikita S. Khrushchev to the effect that their lives were threatened by Belgian troops aggressively occupying their country. They urged him to keep a close watch over the situation. An appeal by the Congolese cabinet for direct American assistance had earlier been made to U.S. President Dwight D. Eisenhower.[6]

On 5 September another episode culminated in a series of constitutional crises: President Kasavubu and Premier Lumumba mutually dismissed each other from office. Congolese Army Chief of Staff Joseph Mobutu thereupon announced the arrest of Lumumba (12 September), and the army took over the Congolese central government on 14 September 1960 to "neutralize" the governments of Lumumba and Joseph Ileo, whom Kasavubu had appointed to replace Lumumba as premier.

All these events—the mutiny of the Force publique, Belgian unilateral intervention, Katanga's secession, and the constitutional crises—comprised the original components of the Congo crisis. From them it became clear that the Congo was without stable political in-

Map 2.1. The Republic of the Congo and its neighbors, 1960

Table 2.1. The Congo's provinces: economic and geographic analysis

---

Equator Province. —

Low, hot; probably poorest province of Congo. 1.8 million people. Vast jungles. Little industry or livestock. Exports: palm oil, coffee, sugar, rubber. Stood with central government throughout the crisis.

Eastern Province. —

Produced 7,400 kgs. of gold in 1959 (70% of Congo's total output). 2.5 million people. Sizable cattle and goat herds; big hardwood forests. Province was in revolt under Lumumba, then Gizenga; reconciled under the central government.

Kivu Province. —

Has most of Congo's tin and some gold. Also exports coffee, tea, pyrethrum for insecticides. Great forest of tropical hardwoods. 2.3 million people. Rebelled in 1961 under Kashamura; reconciled under central government.

Katanga Province. —

Secessionist province under Tshombe. Richest area in readily mined minerals: copper, uranium, manganese, zinc, coal. 1.7 million people. Brought under central government by the last and most decisive phase of the Congo operations, which ended with the peaceful entry of UN troops into Kolwezi, 21 January 1963.

Kasai Province. —

Congo's diamonds found here: 14.9 million carats in 1959. 2.2 million people. Seceded under Kalonji but reconciled under the central government.

Léopoldville Province. —

Seat of the central government. Most heavily populated province: 3.3 million people. Tropical climate. Exports: palm oil, nuts, and cacao.

---

stitutions; lacked a secure government; was in total confusion; in short, had an almost absolute vacuum of political and constitutional authority. For the Congo, resolution of the crisis demanded concrete and effective plans and measures to restore law and order, to remake the republic, to provide or refurbish it with the institutional structures that it either lacked or had been deprived of by the chaos, and above all to reunite its peoples and maintain its territorial and political integrity.

At the international level, however, the crisis involved more issues, the implications of which were grave indeed. From the African point of view, the crisis constituted, among other things, a major threat to successful decolonization and to the movement to rid Africa of every vestige of racism and the stigma of presumed racial inferiority.

On the global scale, the crisis constituted a potential threat to international peace and a germ of possible confrontation of the nuclear powers over central Africa. Furthermore, the wealth of the Congo, the size and strategic location of the republic, made the crisis a major foreign policy concern not only for virtually all independent African states but also for Belgium, for the United States and the Soviet Union, and for Great Britain, France, and other nations. The global significance of the crisis was underlined by Dag Hammarskjöld, then secretary-general of the United Nations, in his address to the UN Security Council (22 July 1960):

> There should not be any hesitation (in responding to the appeal of the Congolese authorities) because we are at a turn of the road where our attitude will be of decisive significance, I believe, not only for the future of the United Nations Organization but for the future of Africa. And Africa may well in the present circumstances mean the world.[7]

Causes of the crisis

Essentially nations want to be independent because they want to govern themselves. But to be self-governing it is not sufficient merely to declare independence. It is also vitally necessary to have representative institutions through which the mass of the people can participate in the government and so be *truly* self-governing. In the Congo this important requisite was either nonexistent or defective as a consequence of the colonial policy of the erstwhile suzerain, Belgium.

Belgian colonial policy in the Congo. — Part of the root causes of the Congo crisis lay in the fact that Congolese independence had been proclaimed before provisions were made for the requisite institutions to sustain it. The failure was plainly Belgium's, whose policy was "benevolent paternalism" rather than political education.[8] Political development was subordinated to economic and social advances. Belgian colonial administration in the Congo had completely ignored the political education of the Congolese people because Belgian colonial policy did not envisage independence for them until almost the very hour that independence was promised. It had been assumed, rather, that the Congo would remain a province of metropolitan Belgium.[9] As such, by gradual assimilation of the Congolese people, the colony's developed middle classes would transform the Congo into a Belgian Eurafrican state.[10] This philosophy, also referred to as one of "controlled acculturation," was espoused by the Centre d'Études des Problèmes Sociaux Indigènes in Elizabethville:

> The colonial experience of European nations must incite us to avoid creating hastily a class of highly privileged natives from whom would spring probably the elements seeking to win over the ignorant mass to accede to power and deprive it of the still indispensable assistance of the coloniser. It is, on the contrary, appropriate to favour above all and by all means the creation of middle classes. The middle class will be finally composed of blacks and whites and will constitute the foundation upon which future elites can solidly base themselves.[11]

Belgian and other European settlers in the Congo wholeheartedly supported such a policy. In their letter to Belgian Colonial Minister Buisseret in 1959, Belgian settlers in the Congo wrote:

> We must organize a class of évolué [developed] natives, who will declare their acceptance of the ideals and principles of our Western civilization, and who will be, if on equal standing, our equals in rights and duties, less numerous than the native mass, but powerful and influential. They will be the allies it is indispensable for us to find in the native communities. These middle classes will be the black bourgeoisie which is beginning to develop everywhere, which we must help to enrich itself and or-

ganize itself and which, like all the bourgeois of the world, will be opposed to any disruption, internal or external.[12]

Belgian colonial policy used other measures to stifle the political education of the Congolese people. The colonial administration isolated the Congolese from the progressive forces and political movements in Africa and the outside world. It suppressed domestic political movements among the people and imposed severe restraints on free expression of political opinion. The administration's policy, in effect, isolated the Congolese elite from each other and encouraged the provincial capitals (usually the seedbed of national movements in other African countries) to develop their own elites, each to be preoccupied with their own issues. Another consequence of this administrative measure was that no political elections took place in the Congo until 1957. Hence, the Congolese were to have only three years of crude political experience before their independence in 1960.

In addition to the foregoing aspects of Belgian colonial policy, the preindependent Congo was controlled, even ruled, by a "colonial trinity" comprising the Belgian colonial administration, big business, and the Roman Catholic Church.[13] The civil administration, like the political, was concentrated in Belgian colonial hands. The system, as it operated, was such that the Congolese people had no experience whatsoever in the higher levels of their country's civil administration. At the time of the Congo's independence, only one Congolese national, Jean Bolikango, had been moved to the higher echelons of the emerging nation's civil service.[14]

Big business, owned in Belgium and other Western European countries, controlled every aspect of Congolese economic life. The Congolese provided the labor but were bound to their employers by a *contrat de travail* rather than the *contrat d'emploi*.[15] The best jobs belonged to the whites, and between the blacks and the *petit blancs,* who belonged on the lower rungs of the economic ladder, the difference in wages was enormously in favor of the latter.[16] Just as in the realm of political and civil administration the Congolese were denied the opportunity to acquire administrative experience, so in the economic sphere they were denied the opportunity to acquire managerial experience and skills, which are essential to political and economic stability.

In basic agreement on the quantity and type of education suitable for Congolese nationals, the colonial trinity entrusted the education of the Congolese to the Roman Catholic Church (plus some Protestant denominations), which thus exerted a predominant influence in the educational and social life of the Congo.[17] The education dispensed by the Church was tailored to Belgian colonial needs and not to the all-round development of the students.[18] It concentrated on primary school education, belatedly recognizing the importance of secondary education and vocational training. Higher education had been ruled out until 1954 and 1956, when the first two universities were established in the colony.[19] Pursuit of further studies overseas by Congolese students was proscribed so as to limit the peoples' horizon and to keep them "where they belonged."

"Benevolent paternalism" was another aspect of Belgium's colonial policy that had a significant bearing on the outbreak of the Congo crisis. Belgian paternalism emphasized, and provided for, the material and physical needs of the Congolese while neglecting their other needs, assuming that "what the [Congolese] needed was work, money in his pocket, food in his belly, [managed] education, religion, and technical training."[20] Professor Thomas Hodgkin's description of this paternalism and its objectives is superlative:

> Platonism is implicit in the sharp distinction, social and legal, between Belgian philosopher kings and the mass of African producers; in the conception of education as primarily concerned with the transmission of certain unquestioned and unquestionable moral values, and intimately related to status and function; in the belief that the thought and behaviour of the mass is plastic, and can be refashioned by a benevolent, wise, and highly trained elite; that the prime interest of the mass is in welfare and consumer goods—football and bicycles—not liberty; and in the conviction that it is possible, by expert administration, to arrest social and political change.[21]

Belgian paternalism, therefore, concludes Professor Hodgkin, "attempted to control the lives of the mass of the Congolese at every point, from cradle to grave—through the churches, the schools, the social centres, the scouts, the football teams, the savings banks—through educative labour and the curfew."[22]

The bane of Belgian paternalism in the Congo lay not in any absence of good will nor in the predominance of the material objectives of the policy, but in both its lack of a solid political foundation on which to rest and its "failure to involve the beneficiaries in any way other than as passive recipients of the largesse." [23] Thus it sapped the Congolese of their initiative, denied them the vital experience that comes from practice, and bequeathed them intractable dilemmas the instant the "benevolent father" departed.

When the anticolonial revolution in Africa and the United Nations compelled Belgium to accept the principle of decolonization and to de-emphasize its policy of benevolent paternalism, Belgian authorities at first assumed that the process of decolonization would remain under full Belgian control and required no urgent action. Decolonization was to be attained through a process of controlled gradualism. This resolve was best expressed in both King Baudouin's Royal Message and the Government Declaration of 13 January 1959:

> We are today resolved to lead without fatal delays, but also without precipitate haste, the Congolese populations to inde-pendence in prosperity and peace. [24]

Belgium's assumption ignored the trends and realities in Africa and the contemporary world. It was indeed unrealistic, a false hope, to believe that Belgium would effect decolonization in the Congo by its own timetable. Perhaps what encouraged this illusion and thereby made Belgian colonial policy detrimental to Congolese political emancipa-tion was that neither the policy nor the colonial establishment, until 1959, had experienced any serious indigenous Congolese challenge, no constant pressure, which was the case elsewhere in West and East Africa, and by then it was almost too late. Before 1959 there had been no Congolese "tactical action," no Congolese "Mau Mau" movement, no Congolese "national liberation movement." Instead, the Congolese had accepted the colonial status quo and the idea of a Belgian Eurafri-can state in the heart of Africa.

But when challenge and constant pressure came in a flood with the riots of 1959, Belgian authorities were compelled to realize that their assumptions about decolonization had been outrun by events. It be-came clear to them

> that time was not going to be limitless, that the "empire of si-lence" would dissolve under the gradual coagulation of latent nationalist forces, that African society was ceasing to be mal-leable clay in the hands of the colonizer, that a handful of Af-

rican barkeepers could not be a black bourgeoisie vigilant to defend the colonial order. The tides of nationalism would not be reversed simply by building more schools and hospitals, issuing a few immatriculation cards to the prominent members of the modern elite, or admitting a few well-groomed Congolese to European restaurants.[25]

Hence the Belgian authorities decided on a Round Table Conference in Brussels (January 1960), which eventually fixed a date for the end of Belgian colonial rule in the Congo without any insurance of political institutions and experience to replace it. Belgian colonial policy in the Congo had swung from a refusal to acknowledge the right of independence for the Congolese, to an espousal of controlled gradualism in decolonization, and finally to a precipitate haste to terminate Belgian rule in the Congo.[26]

The great error in this shift of Belgian colonial policies was not merely Belgium's initial refusal to acknowledge the Congolese right to independence but its failure, upon belated acknowledgment of that right, to provide, in cooperation with the Congolese political leadership, a longer period of political apprenticeship for the Congolese people.[27] Hence one cannot help but conclude, as the *Rand Daily Mail* put it, that

> It is useless to expect people to be responsible when they have never been given an opportunity to develop responsibility. For years the Congolese have been shielded from "politics" and protected from the dangers inherent in learning the rudiments of self-government. They were given no chance to fail on a minor scale and profit by their mistakes, with the result that when the test came, they failed on a major scale.[28]

Mutiny of the Force publique. — The mutiny of Congolese soldiers in the Force publique against their Belgian officers was the immediate event that touched off the chain of other events that comprised the Congo crisis. The mutiny had its roots in several years of discontent among the soldiers and can be traced also to Belgian colonial policy in the Congo. It marked the climax of the reaction of the Congolese soldiers to the accumulated oppressions and injustices they believed they had received for years from their European officers. It was also, initially, a terroristic reaction directed against the new Congolese rulers, who, in the view of the soldiers, were fraternizing with the "oppressors" whom the soldiers wanted to replace.

Revolt in the Force publique was not new. The army had mutinied in 1895, in 1897, and again in 1944.[29] And before Congolese independence, unrest had long been brewing in the Force publique. What made the 1960 mutiny unique was its extent and its repercussions. The discontent and frustrations of the soldiers arose from poor pay and the fact that the officers were all Europeans, mainly Belgians. (The few Congolese noncommissioned officers were officers in name only.) The European officers maintained a rigid policy of color bar and looked upon the Congolese as inferiors. In addition, the soldiers were largely illiterate; they had no opportunity for advancement; and their several plans to Africanize the army were ignored by the colonial regime. Their demands received no sympathy from the Congolese politicians, who initially regarded the army as an instrument of colonial repression. Patrice Lumumba is credited with having said (in a Brussels speech in 1960) that "it is not because the Congo is independent that we can turn every private into a general."[30] Ironically, that was very close to what he did barely one week after the proclamation of Congolese independence, when he promoted every member of the Force publique by one rank.

An "open letter" from the noncommissioned officers and soldiers, published after the Congolese political leaders had returned from the Round Table Conference, articulated the grievances and intentions of men of the Force publique very clearly. Among other things the letter said:

> We, the soldiers of the Force publique, are following with close attention the present course of politics, and we note with great astonishment that the present colonial government and our good representatives aren't considering anything to better our fate. . . . We vehemently condemn the attitude of our representatives and publicly charge as self-centered our present political leaders who ignore our multiple difficulties. . . .
>
> There is no human contact between us and our officers. . . . We are veritable slaves. We are thought of as belonging to an inferior race. So far as Africanization of the staff is concerned, there is total immobility. All of the higher grades are held only by whites even though there are Congolese soldiers capable of

assuming the duties of officers. At this time, the unanimous desire of all Congolese soldiers is to occupy posts of command, to earn a decent salary, to put an end to all traces of discrimination in the midst of the Force publique.

We take the liberty of declaring publicly and without equivocation that if by June 30 [1960] you have not put into operation adequate means to dignify our standard of living and have not moved toward an extensive appointment of black officers, we assure you that the independence of June 30 will be unsteady.[31]

It seems that their pleas and warning were ignored, for on the eve of independence the soldiers again complained:

It astonishes us to see our African brothers forget us. . . . There will be two branches of Congolese independence. First there will be . . . the class of the great Congolese leaders and their white counsellors. These will benefit from all the advantages of the new independent state. . . .

A second dishonored wing, which will include the inferiors, the criers of "Vive Independence" on June 30, 1960, will be and remain the servants of the first branch.

M. Lumumba judges us incapable of taking the place of the officers.

Dear Lumumba, friend of the Europeans, . . . we guarantee you the infernal ruin of your powers as long as you insult us as ignorant and incapable of taking the places of your white brothers.[32]

After the airing of these grievances, a token concession was made, at the eleventh hour, to the soldiers' demands for Africanizing the army's officer corps. (Their other demands were ignored.) A number of Congolese young men were selected for training as potential officers in the army. The soldiers, however, still had their qualms. Their fears and suspicions increased when, a few days after independence, the Force commander, Lt. Gen. Emile Janssens, made a number of pronouncements maintaining that the European officers of the Force publique would keep their places in the independent Congo as they had in the Belgian Congo. According to him, there was no independence for the army.[33]

The policy of the new rulers, who appointed Belgians to Congolese national defense posts, gave credence to the Force commander's pronouncements and aroused the ire of and an even deeper resentment in the soldiers, who had been on almost continuous and exasperating duty from April through the May elections to independence. Their civilian brothers—politicians—were moving up the economic ladder. But to the soldiers independence had brought no bonus, nor time off to celebrate, nor any concrete signs that either the rigid racial demarcation between them and their Belgian officers would be relaxed or that they would replace, in time, those officers. Their hopes and aspirations frustrated, the soldiers turned against their officers and unleashed a series of events unforeseen by either the new Congolese rulers or those they had replaced.

Belgian intervention. — Belgium's sending of troops, without the request or consent of the Congolese central government, to stem the tide of the army mutiny in the Congo and to contain the unrest the mutiny had unleashed, enlarged the dimensions of the Congo crisis. It was seen as an act of external aggression and a threat to fluid international peace. It presaged the dangers of intervention by third powers should the United Nations, to which the Congolese authorities immediately appealed, fail to cope adequately with the crisis.[34] Thenceforth, the crisis was no longer a domestic one. It had become internationalized.

The intervention began with the arrival of metropolitan Belgian troops in Elizabethville, Luluabourg, Kamina, and Jadotville on 10 July 1960. There were already Belgian metropolitan troops confined to two large Belgian bases at Kitona on the Atlantic coast and at Kamina in Katanga province. By 18 July the intervention had encompassed twenty-eight Congolese localities. President Kasavubu and Prime Minister Lumumba originally acquiesced to the presence of Belgian troops in the areas where they had first landed, on the proviso that the troops' mission was to be restricted to the protection of life and property. This proviso was violated on the following day, 11 July, when Belgian warships and planes attacked the port city of Matadi, from which all Europeans had already been evacuated.[35]

The radio network of the Force publique exaggerated the extent of the attack and emphasized the African casualties in its appeal for an onslaught against Belgian residents in the Congo. The appeal was not unheeded. Mutineers in widely separate areas engaged in unrestrained violence against Europeans to avenge the attack on Matadi.

Another unfortunate and ominous aspect of the Belgian attack on Matadi was the fact that it occurred on the same day Moise Tshombe proclaimed the "independence" of Katanga province and used Belgian troops to disarm and expel those Congolese members of the Force publique who were from areas unsympathetic to his political party, the Confédération des Associations du Katanga. Moreover, members of the military and technical mission, set up by Belgian authorities to support Tshombe's new regime in Katanga, prevented the landing of President Kasavubu and Prime Minister Lumumba at Elizabethville Airport on their visit of reconciliation with Tshombe (12 July). The highest authorities of the Republic of the Congo had been slighted and humiliated in their own domain. Belgian intervention had once again gone beyond the goal of protecting Belgian citizens and property; this was, in fact, a formal violation of the Treaty of Friendship signed by the two countries the day before the Congo's independence.[36]

Congolese interpretation of this Belgian act and of Belgium's motives is best understood in the context of the fears and suspicions of "neocolonialism" in contemporary Africa. Lumumba was quick to charge the Belgians with "neocolonialist machinations" aimed at maintaining a hold on the Congo. His break with Belgium was now complete, and the Congolese fatherland was to be rid of Belgium's effort at "reconquest." Hence appeals for military assistance were cabled to the United Nations, and the Soviet Union was urged to watch the Congo situation closely in the event of any Western plot against the republic's sovereignty.

Seen in this light, Belgian intervention in the Congo, regardless of interpretations of its humanitarian motives, was an essential ingredient of the Congo crisis.

Secession of Katanga. — Moise Tshombe's declaration of the secession of Katanga, another chapter in the Congo crisis which came *pari passu* with full-scale Belgian military intervention in Congolese domestic affairs, was the climactic event that brought the Republic of the Congo to its knees.[37] Tshombe, a former schoolteacher and successful businessman, had developed an active interest in politics by 1958. He soon became president of the Confédération des Associations Tribales du Katanga, and in 1960 he was elected deputy to the Katanga provincial government. A conservative, Tshombe frequently consulted white advisers whose tutelage he accepted. He was definitely pro-West, in the parlance of the times, in his political ideology and conservative bent. He was actively assisted by white residents in Katanga and by the Belgian government because he served the interests of Belgium and the West in the Congo and the whole of Central Africa.

Katanga, at the time Tshombe declared its secession from the republic, contained about 12 percent of the population. It produced more than 60 percent of the new republic's wealth[38] and was the "economic heart" of the Congo. The Katanga mines form the core of the complex of industrial and financial interests upon which was based the economic and social development of the country. Without Katanga, the Congo would be, despite its plantations and small industries, a comparatively poor country. But the province had become an invaluable asset "because of the contributions made by the Congo as a whole over generations of slow growth and development." [39] Its wealth and economy comprised an integral part of the wealth and economy of the whole country. (See table 2.1.) Therefore, to rob the republic of this vital asset was, to African nationalists, a deliberate crime against the Congolese nation.

To create for Katanga a special relationship with the rest of the Congo was an idea that had long before taken deep root in Tshombe's thinking. He had pleaded in vain for decentralization at the Round Table Conference and had thereafter persisted in spearheading secessionist attempts. The Belgian administration had opposed such attempts and every idea of a separate Katanga state;[40] Belgium had ruled the Congo as a unitary state. Article 6 of the Loi fondamentale, the constitution that the Belgians had forged for the Congo, provided that the republic "constitutes, within its present boundaries, an indivisible and democratic state." But the turn of events had created for Tshombe the opportune moment to make a final bid to realize his long-time ambition. And on this occasion, for reasons not far to seek, he was fully supported by Belgium.

In explaining his reasons for proclaiming the secession of Katanga Province, Tshombe held that Katanga is geographically, ethnically, and economically a region completely separate from the rest of the Congo. Only the Belgian colonialists, in their own interests, he explained, had treated it as a part of the Congo. He maintained that after independence he had endeavored to cooperate with the central government in Léopoldville within the framework of the Loi fondamentale but had found its provisions unworkable. Tshombe emphasized that while a provincial government possessed the various powers enumerated in Article 220 of the constitution, it had no adequate financial resources to function autonomously. These matters, he said, he had sought to discuss with Lumumba during the first few days of July 1960, but the prime minister, who, Tshombe charged, was following a communist line, had refused to meet him. When the army later mutinied, plunging the country into disorder and chaos, Tshombe said he had no alternative but to secede so as to save Katanga.[41]

Tshombe further stated that there was no Congolese capable of ruling the Congo as a unitary state. The best that could be done was for each leader to devote his attention to developing his own province.[42]

These reasons do not sufficiently explain Tshombe's personal declaration of independence for Katanga. Tshombe's own economic and political interests were important factors behind his secessionist adventures. He found secession advantageous in terms of his own position in Congolese domestic politics. While he belonged to the richest province of the Congo, his political position within both Katanga and the central government was weak. He complained that his party, the Confédération des Associations du Katanga, had not been given enough places in the central government coalition cabinet.[43] According to the accounts by Professors Herbert F. Weiss and King Gordon, the legality of the process by which Tshombe had become president of the provincial government of Katanga was widely disputed.[44] He lacked supporters at the national level, and, being apprehensive that the central government might, in support of his provincial opponent Jason Sendwe, intervene either in favor of holding new elections or by reshuffling the provincial government in a manner most likely to be unfavorable to himself, Tshombe decided to withdraw his province from the rest of the country.[45] There was in his actions also some element of personal revenge against Lumumba and Kasavubu. They had commanded the greater respect in the Round Table Conference, and Tshombe had waited a long time but in vain to meet with them in Léopoldville shortly after independence.

There were other forces that supported, if they did not encourage, Tshombe's secessionist moves. Belgium, whose investments in Katanga were enormous, was foremost among these. "It is easy to see," as Colin Legum has written, "how in that dark hour with all their hopes and plans crumbling, their people fleeing in all directions, and their large investments threatened, the Belgians were tempted to grasp at the last straw offered by Tshombe" (*Congo Disaster*, p. 118). It was a temptation they failed to resist. Ousted Belgian army officers also found it in their interests to support Tshombe.

Union Minière du Haut-Katanga found it equally advantageous to support the secession of Katanga. In fact, many within and outside the Congo believed that it was this mining company that, in its own interests, heavily financed Tshombe's Confédération des Associations du Katanga from its very inception.

"Katanga's copper, cobalt, uranium, and other minerals . . . ," wrote the *New York Herald Tribune*, "are exploited by Belgian interests, chiefly the Minière du Haut-Katanga. It is becoming more and more obvious that these interests would prefer an independent Katanga which would guarantee them in the mines without saddling them with any responsibility in the rest of the Congo." [46] U Thant, as the acting secretary-general of the United Nations, in retrospect agreed with this opinion. "The core of the Congo problem," he said, "is that of the secession of Katanga; the problem of the Katanga secession is primarily a problem of finance; the problem of finance, in turn, is the problem of the major mining companies [in Katanga]." [47]

Tshombe also found support in the colonial and settler states south of the Congo River, namely, Portuguese Angola and Mozambique, the Federation of Rhodesia and Nyasaland (now defunct), and the Union of South Africa (now a republic). It was in the interest of these states to support Tshombe's ambitions. Portugal's support for Tshombe stemmed from obvious reasons. An independent and united Congo was generally believed to constitute a grave threat to Portugal's colonial empire in Angola and Mozambique, since it was seen as a particularly crucial and inspiring event for the Angolan nationalist movement. Following the independence of the Congo, the Bakongo nationalists of Angola began a revolution that successfully used the border between Angola and the new Republic of the Congo to evacuate civilian refugees from Portuguese repression and to refurbish military contingents. An extension of the Angolan revolution along the entire Angolan-Congolese border, which a reconciliation between the central government and Katanga would inevitably encourage, would prove too difficult for Portugal to contain. [48] (See map 2.1 and table 2.1.)

The white settlers in the Rhodesias faced similar threats of radical nationalism, which would be encouraged by a united independent Congo. Hence, they too felt it was in their interest to thwart every effort at reconciliation between Tshombe and the Congolese central government. [49]

South Africa was, perhaps, the most important settler state south of the Congo River that supported Tshombe's secessionist intransigence. The secession of Katanga met South Africa's interests, too, for it would ensure (but only for a season, whether South Africa realized it or not) that the advance of African nationalism and the movement for the end of racial bigotry in Africa were kept farther away from South African borders. South Africa was also interested in preventing the collapse of the Portuguese hold on Angola in order to safeguard its own hold on South West Africa (Namibia). These goals a divided Congo could make easier to accomplish.

It must also be added that Tshombe had other foreign sympathizers: the American Committee for Aid to Katanga Freedom Fighters,[50] and some former French army officers who later served as Tshombe's mercenaries and who had fought in Algeria under the banner of the Organisation de l'armée secrète. These disappointed "Algeria-is-French" fanatics rallied to Tshombe's banner for their own ideological interest, which was to defend Katanga as a bulwark against the surging tide of African nationalism, thereby maintaining white political and economic hegemony south of the Congo.

It may thus be reasonably concluded that the proclaimed but ill-fated secession of Katanga was a political stratagem designed to advance the economic and political interests of Tshombe and his supporters—the Belgian government, Belgian residents in Katanga, and foreign investors in Union Minière and other economic enterprises in the province. These interests marched with those of the powers who desired perpetuation of Portuguese and settler states' domination south of the Congo.

While Tshombe's declaration of the secession of Katanga was supported by foreign interests, it received no popular support in the province. His authority, which seems to have been confined to the southern part of Katanga, even there did not rest on a large measure of popular support. His Confédération des Associations du Katanga had no mandate for such an action, for in the provincial elections held in February 1960, it had won only twenty-five of the total of sixty seats in Katanga's Provincial Assembly (legislature). In northern Katanga, where Baluba elements predominated, the population was violently hostile to Tshombe.[51] Despite this hostility, Tshombe's obduracy persisted and made the secession of Katanga the most intractable aspect of the Congo crisis.

On 8 August 1960 Albert Kalonji of South Kasai, the leader of the breakaway Movement Nationale Congolais and a former lieutenant of Lumumba, followed Tshombe's precedent. He proclaimed the birth of a "diamond state" in the Baluba area of Kasai Province. Thus a second region of the Congo—the region that produced more than 90 percent of the republic's diamond wealth—had also become "independent."

Foreign interests. — Far more was at stake in the Congo crisis than either political squabbles between the Congolese central government and Tshombe's Katanga regime or Belgian intervention in Congolese affairs. The Congo's mineral wealth and strategic location provoked the interests and rivalries of the world's great powers,[52] notably those belonging to the North Atlantic Treaty Organization (NATO) and the Warsaw Pact. The leading NATO powers already had substantial investments in the Congo's mining companies—Union Minière (copper and uranium), Forminière (diamonds)—and in companies in the new republic's neighbors such as Unilever, Tanganyika Concessions, Ltd., and the Diamond Company of Angola. These investments the NATO powers considered vital to their economic health. In addition, Britain and France, as colonial powers in Africa, believed they had to preserve their freedom of action and to control the pace of change in Africa if they were to maximize their economic and political objectives in the continent.

United States interests in the crisis were ideological, political, and economic. As the leading NATO power, the United States was primarily concerned in the Congo and in Africa in general with the sensibilities of its colonialist allies. In the Congo crisis it was therefore an understanding and cooperating supporter of Belgium and its other allies, recognizing as legitimate the desire of its NATO allies and economic partners to protect their interests in the Congo. The United States also had an interest in the potential markets and mineral resources—cobalt, copper, industrial diamonds, and tantalum—of Katanga and South Kasai. The United States especially needed to secure its source of cobalt and tantalum, the uses of which in aerospace and jet engine production were strategically important. In addition to economic interests and its obligations under the NATO alliance, the United States had ideological interests in the Congo. Viewing the Congo through a prism of cold war ideology, American policy-makers sought to preserve Western Europe's political and economic advantages there and elsewhere in Africa. Early in the Congo crisis, having convinced themselves that Lumumba was flirting with the idea of a drastic political realignment in Southern Africa and was likely to consolidate political power in the Congo, they became actively interested in intervention in Congolese affairs through the United Nations. The

United States supported the ouster of Lumumba by Kasavubu in September 1960 and took the lead in the UN General Assembly for a credentials vote that ultimately favored Kasavubu over Lumumba. The consistent political and ideological strategy of the United States was to install in Léopoldville conservative political leaders favorable to a close political and economic cooperation with the United States and the West.

The other superpower, the Soviet Union, had already embarked, for ideological and other reasons, on a program of securing a substantial hold on Africa. It sought to win the Congo, its peoples, and its resources, for the Soviet bloc. Even so it was the concerns and activities of the Western powers, more than any opportunistic moves by the Soviet Union, that aggravated the Congo crisis.

In addition to Western and Soviet interests, India had designs on the Congo inspired by its search for raw materials and outlets for its surplus population.[53] Nearer home, independent African states themselves had various goals in the Congo, including its successful decolonization, and the furtherance of Pan-Africanist ideals, leadership and influence, and ideological expansionism.

These foreign interests—economic, political, ideological, Pan-Africanist—caused the major world powers to ignore the basic needs of the Congolese themselves and to vie instead for their own parochial interests, interests that dictated their interpretation of the crisis and their contribution both to the UN General Assembly's debates on the crisis and to the UN operations in the Congo.[54]

Political ambitions and Congolese ethnic antipathies. — Another cause of the Congo crisis derived from the personal ambitions and "ethnic nationalism" of Congolese political leaders besides Tshombe. With little or no experience in the politics of a multinational state, the majority of the Congolese political leaders approached politics from the perspectives of their own personal interests and their particular ethnic groups. The mushrooming political parties (some fifty-two of them, none of which claimed a sizable national following)[55] that sprang up with the 1959 charter granting freedom of speech, press, and association to the Congolese, reflected ethnic and provincial divisions, interests, and antipathies. Only Lumumba and members of his Movement Nationale Congolais, founded in 1958, eschewed ethnicity in favor of an all-embracing Congolese nationalism. Even that movement split into two factions. Whereas Lumumba and his associates advocated a strong unitary government for the Congo, their opponents, mainly the Alliance des Bakongo, led by Kasavubu, and Tshombe's Confédération des Associations du Katanga, opted for a federal system of largely autonomous provincial governments based on primary ethnic group alliances. Tshombe accurately expressed this propensity for essentially ethnic politics succinctly: "Let us face the truth. . . . Democracy does not exist here. We have a tribal structure. The last election showed everybody voted according to his own tribe." [56]

These differences and ethnic antipathies presaged another dimension of the crisis—the issue of constitutional authority in the Congo. They intensified the conflict, sharpening the divisions between the competing, provincially based, foreign-interest-supported political factions, none of which was capable of imposing its will on the whole country.

The constitutional crisis. — The constitutional crisis stemmed in part from the inadequacies of the Loi fondamentale, but it was precipitated by the mutual dismissal of each other from office by President Kasavubu and Prime Minister Lumumba on 5 September 1960. Kasavubu initiated the action, and his dismissal of Lumumba from the premiership was precipitated by a number of factors. First, Kasavubu was apprehensive about a Soviet intervention, which would upset the delicate balance of power between himself and Lumumba. Second, external influences from the West (Belgian advisers and U.S. Central Intelligence Agency officials) encouraged Kasavubu's action. They provided him not only with legal arguments and counsel, assuring him that it was within his authority to dismiss Lumumba, but also with rewards for the ministers who countersigned the dismissal. [57] The local climate of suspicion, personal rivalries, and ethnic antipathies had encouraged the external political powers to pursue their own interests. In addition to the external factor and the background of envy and political conflicts, however, Kasavubu and the more moderate elements in the Congolese central government had come to distrust Lumumba because of his increased leaning toward Moscow. [58] Lumumba's connections with persons considered to have "extremist reputation" such as Serge Michel (a Russian émigré purported to be an Algerian citizen) and Felix Moumie (an exile and former leader of an extremist political faction in Cameroon) added to the distrust. Finally, Lumumba's clash with UN Secretary-General Dag Hammarskjöld, and his behavior, which seemed to many of his critics to be erratic and irrational, further alienated him from his political rivals and top officials of the UN Secretariat.

The actions of President Kasavubu and Prime Minister Lumumba in dismissing each other were annulled by a vote of sixty to nineteen in the Chamber of Deputies. The Senate, too, by a vote of forty-one to two, rejected Kasavubu's decision to replace Lumumba with Joseph Ileo.[59] Kasavubu remained intransigent and immediately decreed the formation of a new government. To counter this the Senate and the Chamber of Deputies met jointly on 14 September 1960 and conferred full powers on Lumumba. Kasavubu's reply was to suspend Parliament on the same day. This uncompromising struggle for power led the army, under its chief of staff, Col. Joseph Mobutu, to take over in a purported "peaceful revolution."[60]

One of the primary causes of the constitutional crisis was the Loi fondamentale itself. While Article 22 of the constitution authorized the president to appoint and dismiss the prime minister, other articles (16, 17, 19, 21, 42, 51) suggested that supremacy in such matters lay with the Parliament, whose confidence the prime minister had to enjoy to remain in office. Thus the constitution seemed to create a nonresponsible chief of state for the republic and to invest Parliament with exclusive competence to interpret the constitution.[61]

In addition to failing to identify clearly the focus of power in the Congolese central government, the Loi fondamentale was inadequate and ill-adapted to the political conditions in the Congo in other ways. President Kasavubu spoke of this inadequacy when he addressed the delegates to the preparatory Round Table Conference of Congolese leaders on 25 January 1961:

> If we wish to create a stable and durable society which will be secure from the overweening ambitions of certain people, we must go to the root of the trouble. We inherited a system of institutions which turned out in practice to be ineffective and inappropriate to the situations to which it was intended to be applied. We must give fresh thought to the *Loi Fondamentale* and the institutions derived from it, with a view to adapting them to our ideas and the requirements of a country which is so large in the geographical sense and whose peoples are so diverse.[62]

Even Tshombe denounced the Loi fondamentale as a Belgian imposition since it had not been ratified by the Congolese people. The Belgians, he said, had drafted it to suit their own purposes and interests.[63]

The political conflicts and personal antagonisms among Congolese political leaders were another source of the constitutional crisis, but much more deeply rooted than the inadequacies of the constitution. Lumumba believed a strong unitary government was necessary to ensure the future of the young republic. He believed any compromise with semiautonomous regional units based on ethnic loyalties would be disastrous to the future of the country. Effective national planning would be thwarted, and the predominance of the authorities of ethnic groups would constitute a hindrance to the republic's economic and social progress. The only remedy, therefore, was to create a functioning, strong, central administration.

In the light of the new republic's colonial experience Lumumba had a strong case. But his point of view also became for him a blind spot. His political opponents, the secessionist factions in Katanga and South Kasai and Kasavubu and his political associates, were diametrically opposed to Lumumba's policy of centralized administration. They called for a federal government on the grounds that the immensity of the country demanded increased provincial autonomy in the interest of efficiency. Provincial autonomy was also necessary to forestall the inevitable resentment a powerful but distant central government would arouse. The inability of the Congolese authorities to resolve this conflict partially explains the constitutional crisis.

The interests and policies of the great powers further complicated the constitutional crisis. The Soviet Union supported Lumumba's position, a position it believed would frustrate "NATO's imperialist plots" in the Congo. The Western powers, on the other hand, with their economic interests in Katanga, supported Kasavubu and his federalist philosophy. Lumumba, in their view, had become a Soviet puppet who, in return for Soviet aid for limited objectives, would serve Soviet aims and interests in the very heart of Africa.

Conflict and rancor between the United Nations and Lumumba. — One cannot discuss the myriad causes of the Congo crisis without mentioning the relationship between the Congolese central government and the United Nations which it invited into the Congo. During the early phase of the crisis the relationship between the two became the major bone of contention among the member states of the United Nations and between the secretary-general and Congolese Premier Patrice Lumumba. The essential question was twofold: whether the UN operation in the Congo was to act as an arm of the Congolese central government, aiding it to realize its objectives, or whether, detached, the

United Nations could tell the Congolese how to rule themselves; in other words, would the Congo be converted into a kind of UN trusteeship?

Lumumba felt the UN mission should operate as a branch of his government in dealing with the crisis; he could not subscribe to the idea of the United Nations meddling in Congolese internal affairs without the express consent of his government or converting his country into any kind of UN trusteeship. Essentially, Lumumba held that the UN operation should be involved in the withdrawal of Belgian troops from the Congo, the protection of lives and property, and the maintenance of Congolese territorial integrity—including the reintegration of Katanga—and the establishment of the central government's authority over the entire country.[64]

United Nations members were divided on the question. Secretary-General Dag Hammarskjöld held that the UN operation in the Congo could not be an adjunct of Lumumba's government, nor could the United Nations tell the Congolese how to rule themselves. He insisted that the primary goals of the operation were to bring about the withdrawal of Belgian troops, to prevent the crisis from degenerating into a larger world conflict, and to protect lives and property by helping to maintain law and order.[65] The secretary-general's interpretation of the objectives of the UN operation in the Congo was thus more restrictive than Lumumba's, and his definition of the means of achieving the objectives rejected the hierarchy of the Congolese central government as conceived by Lumumba. Hammarskjöld's views prevailed and caused considerable conflict and rancor between him and the Soviet Union and some Afro-Asian member states of the United Nations, and between him and the field officials of the UN operation on the one hand and Lumumba's government on the other. In this sense, this clash of views contributed fundamentally to the prolongation of the Congo crisis.

Highlights in the course of the resolution of the crisis

A very brief survey of the major events in the course of the resolution of the Congo crisis will place Nigeria's role in proper perspective.

United Nations intervention upon invitation. — The first significant step was the appeal by the Congolese central government to the United Nations for help "to rescue [the] young nation's independence and to nurture it to a freedom it had never known,"[66] and the response to that appeal—namely, UN intervention in the Congo crisis. The appeal itself clearly showed that the Congolese central government was incapable of coping with the crisis alone: it was an inviting challenge, promptly accepted, to the United Nations not only to rescue the independence of the young republic but also to offset a threat to international peace. Acceptance of the challenge was expressed in the resolution drafted by the African states within the UN organization, submitted by Mongi Slim of Tunisia, and adopted by the Security Council on 14 July 1960. That resolution said:

> The Security Council,
> Considering the report of the Secretary-General [15th Year, 873rd meeting, pars. 18–29] on a request for United Nations action in relation to the Republic of the Congo, Considering the request for military assistance addressed to the Secretary General by the President and the Prime Minister of the Republic of the Congo [S/4382],
> 1. Calls upon the Government of Belgium to withdraw its troops from the territory of the Republic of the Congo;
> 2. Decides to authorize the Secretary-General to take the necessary steps, in consultation with the Government of the Republic of the Congo, to provide the Government with such military assistance as may be necessary until, through the efforts of the Congolese Government with the technical assistance of the United Nations, the national security forces may be able, in the opinion of the Government, to meet fully their tasks;
> 3. Requests the Secretary-General to report to the Security Council as appropriate.[67]

The resolution makes clear the objectives of UN intervention: evacuation of Belgian troops from the Congo and restoration and maintenance of law and order. In his report, required by the Security Council resolution, the secretary-general announced the creation of a United Nations Force to implement the resolution.[68] The force was to be placed "under the exclusive command of the United Nations, vested in the Secretary-General under the control of the Security Council," and was to have "freedom of movement" and access to all facilities necessary for the accomplishment of its mission. It could not take orders from the host government and could not operate with it "either in competition or in cooperation." The force was not to be authorized to initiate any coercive action except in self-defense. It could not become a party to internal conflicts in the country, for by doing so it "would seriously endanger the impartiality of the UN and of the operation," nor could it "be used to enforce any specific political solution of pending problems or to influence the political balance decisive to such solution." Thus the UN operations were to "be separate and distinct from activities by [Congolese] national authorities."

Regarding the composition of the force, the secretary-general appealed first to independent African states for contribution of troops "as an act of African solidarity," and then to other states that met the general requirements for the composition of a UN force, so as to emphasize the "element of universality" in UN operations. Troops from the states who were permanent members of the Security Council were not accepted. The personnel of the operation were enjoined to act in strict conformity to the basic UN rules for international civil service. They were to give full loyalty, throughout the operation's duration, to the UN command and not to their country of origin inasmuch as dual loyalty could otherwise deprive the operation of its international and impartial character.

In keeping with these principles, about 3,500 troops, initially contributed by independent African states, were flown to the Congo on 15 July 1960. (See map 2.2.) Dr. Ralph Bunche, who was then the secretary-general's special representative in the Congo, was appointed commander ad interim of the force. On 18 July Maj. Gen. Carl Van Horn of Sweden took over the command. The troops, deployed in strategic areas in the Congo with the exception of Katanga, initially established some degree of order. With later additions the force succeeded in overseeing the evacuation of Belgian troops in most parts of the Congo, but not in Katanga, where over two hundred Belgian officers and men had remained to serve in Tshombe's gendarmerie in violation of the Security Council's resolution. By the end of the operation, in June 1964, about 20,000 men, officers, and specialized personnel from thirty-five states had served with the UN force in the Congo.

At the beginning of the operation the secretary-general created a Congo Advisory Committee consisting of the permanent representatives of the countries that had contributed troops to the UN force in the Congo. The secretary-general also organized an informal but powerful "Congo Club," which acted as his "cabinet" for the Congo operation.[69]

In addition there was an extensive civilian aspect to the UN operation. The acute shortage of trained Congolese personnel in almost

Map 2.2. Deployment of UN forces in the Congo, 31 July 1960

every field of civilian administration and profession was exacerbated by the mass exodus of Belgian and other European professional workers, technicians, and administrators from the Congo following the army mutinies. It was vital to replace these foreigners, upon whom the efficient functioning of Congolese civilian life had depended, to prevent a complete breakdown of all public services and a collapse of the economy. The secretary-general appealed to all UN member states for technical assistance, food, and medical supplies under the aegis of the organization.

Although initially they were agreed on UN intervention in the Congo, the member states came to be divided on the mission. Most took positions that reflected their particular interests and not those of the Congolese. Hence several ambiguous resolutions were adopted, and protracted debates on the conflict engaged the entire membership, another reason the crisis lasted much longer than many had hoped.

The seating of the Kasavubu delegation. — Kasavubu's and Lumumba's dismissal of each other from office led to the sending of rival Congo delegations to the United Nations in New York, forcing the United Nations to decide which delegation to seat. Eventually it seated the Kasavubu delegation,[70] a decision influenced by intense lobbying by the United States and the pressuring of various UN member states by other NATO powers.

The UN Conciliation Commission for the Congo. — Another highlight of the Congo operations was the establishment on 5 November 1960 of a Conciliation Commission by the UN Congo Advisory Committee in consultation with the secretary-general. Consisting of fifteen member states with troops in the Congo, the commission was required to visit the entire territory of the Congo to make a comprehensive study of the situation; it was to direct its efforts "without interference in the internal affairs of the Congo, towards the attainment by the Congolese of solutions of present difficulties in the Congo."[71] The commission was to help ensure that such solutions would be conducive to maintaining and strengthening the unity, territorial integrity, and political independence of the Republic of the Congo within the framework of the constitutional and legal structure of the new state.

The commission was explicitly enjoined to "assist in decisions being reached [in the Congo] with a view to the speedy restoration of parliamentary institutions in the Republic of the Congo . . . ." The commission, accordingly, undertook its assignments, starting on 19 December 1960. By 20 March 1961 it submitted its report and recommendations to the Congo Advisory Committee, which in turn transmitted the report to the General Assembly.[72] A majority of the members, including the Congolese central government, endorsed the report.

The death of Lumumba. — One week after his dismissal from office, Lumumba was arrested by Colonel Mobutu and later (January 1961) transferred from Léopoldville to Thysville and then to Katanga. His supporters in the United Nations were very critical of the failure of the UN force to prevent his arrest or to arrange his release. Both the Security Council and the General Assembly were split into factions over his arrest and demands for his release. While debates continued on the issue, Godefroid Munongo, minister of the interior in the provincial government of Katanga, announced on 13 February that Lumumba and his two political-prisoner companions, Maurice Mpolo and Joseph Okito, had been killed while attempting to escape from prison on 12 February.[73]

Many years later, during the hearings of the U.S. Senate Select Committee on Governmental Operations, chaired by Sen. Frank Church of Idaho, it was disclosed that the U.S. Central Intelligence Agency was definitely implicated in the murder of Lumumba. Lumumba had been viewed with alarm by U.S. policy-makers because of what they perceived as his charisma and his leanings toward the Soviet Union. Accordingly, covert CIA operations to have Lumumba killed were set in motion early in the Congo crisis and involved the highest levels of the U.S. government, including the State Department. Resolved to permanently dispose of Lumumba to suit American and Western interests, CIA officers in the Congo advised and aided Congolese contacts who intended to assassinate the leader. They developed several stratagems to accomplish this objective. Lumumba's murder was the triumph of their plots.[74]

The Afro-Asian world was shocked at the murders. Violent demonstrations took place in several cities, including Lagos and Enugu, Nigeria. The Soviet Union was furious. It demanded the termination of UN operations in the Congo and the dismissal of Hammarskjöld, whom it accused of direct responsibility for the death of Lumumba. The United Nations reacted to the announcement of the murder by appointing a thirteen-member commission, chaired by M. U. Aung Khine, a judge of the Burmese Supreme Court, to inquire into the circumstances of Lumumba's death.

While Lumumba had been held prisoner, Antoine Gizenga, formerly vice premier in the dismissed government, established a regime in Stanleyville, which he asserted was the legitimate Congolese central government. His government was recognized by the Soviet Union, the People's Republic of China, and five African states—Ghana, Guinea, Mali, the United Arab Republic, and Morocco.

The summit conferences of Congolese leaders in Tananarive and Coquilhatville

Three weeks after the announcement of Lumumba's death, Congolese leaders (except for Gizenga and Jason Sendwe) held a summit conference (6–12 March 1961) in Tananarive, Malagasy Republic. Convened at the suggestion of the UN Conciliation Commission for the Congo, the conference was a triumph of secessionist views.[75] Dominated by Tshombe's views, the conference agreed on the formation of a confederation of Congo states, an agreement later nullified by a second summit conference, held at Coquilhatville 23–28 May 1961. The Coquilhatville conference, whose convening had also been strongly encouraged by the United Nations, was dominated by Kasavubu and the moderates from Léopoldville. It agreed to convert the Congo into a "Federal Republic" of states having a single diplomatic service, a unified military force, and a common currency. It decided that the Congolese Parliament should be reconvened without delay under the protection of the United Nations; and it was determined to see the reintegration of Katanga into the political structure of the Republic of the Congo. During this conference Tshombe was arrested by the Léopoldville authorities (26 April, after he had walked out of the meeting on the day before). He was placed under house arrest but was subsequently released (22 June 1961) on the promise that he would participate in the proposed meeting of Parliament in July.

Reconvening of Parliament. — Following the 21 February 1961 Security Council resolution, which called for the withdrawal of foreign military, paramilitary, and political advisers from the Congo and the reconvening of the Congolese Parliament, there was continued UN diplomatic pressure on the Congolese leaders to find a solution to their constitutional crisis. The summit conferences at Tananarive and Coquilhatville were steps in that direction. After the Coquilhatville meeting, Kasavubu announced that Parliament would be reconvened—in Léopoldville. The UN operation played a key role in overcoming the opposition of the Gizenga regime in Stanleyville to the reconvening of Parliament in Léopoldville. Parliament was reconvened on 19 July

1961 at Lovanium University outside Léopoldville with full UN protection provided for the entire body.[76] Tshombe and his Confédération
des Associations du Katanga deputies refused to attend; however, after
two weeks of continuous efforts to reconcile the parties, Kasavubu
named Cyrille Adoula prime minister.

Cyrille Adoula had been a trade unionist. Prior to the Congo's independence he served as the secretary-general of the Congolese section of the Belgian Socialist trade union movement, the Fédération
Générale du Travail de Belgique. He was associated with the International Confederation of Free Trade Unions, which was dominated by
the American Federation of Labor and Congress of Industrial Organi-
zations. Adoula became vice-president of Mouvement National Congolais but broke with Lumumba in 1959. Elected to the Senate from
Equator province in May 1960, he joined Joseph Ileo in opposing
Lumumba's leadership. He frequently consulted white advisers; represented Kasavubu in the United Nations in October 1960; and became,
successfully, the American candidate for Congolese premier in 1961.[77]

On 2 August Adoula and his cabinet were unanimously endorsed
by both houses of Parliament, thus ending the eleven-month constitutional crisis. But Tshombe's Katanga remained a major problem for
both the new central government and the UN operation in the Congo.

The search for a constitution. — Of the other tasks that remained —
reducing the number of dissidents in Stanleyville, restoring normalcy
to the economic and social life of the republic, and the search for more
suitable institutional structures to replace the interim Loi fondamentale—the last was given top priority. In June 1961 the Congolese Foreign Minister Justin Bomboko asked the United Nations for legal experts to help the central government prepare a draft federal constitution
on the basis of the Coquilhatville summit meeting recommendations.
The United Nations accordingly designated three legal experts, from
Nigeria, Italy, and Switzerland, to undertake the task. The documents
produced by these experts helped Adoula's government to develop its
position on negotiations with Tshombe.

The Adoula-Tshombe negotiations broke down several times. In
July 1962, at the request of Adoula's government, the United Nations
designated a second group of legal specialists, from Nigeria, Canada,
India, and Switzerland, to prepare another draft constitution for the
Congo. This document formed part of the arsenal of the U Thant plan
for national reconciliation for the Congo.

The Katanga problem—end of secession. — The ending of Katanga's secession marked the climax of the resolution of the Congo crisis. But it was achieved only after several dramatic frustrations. Adoula's government of national reconciliation facilitated concerted efforts to end Tshombe's intrigues and Katanga's secession. With the cooperation of Adoula's government, the UN operation was able, though not without difficulties and protracted negotiations and military actions, to implement the 21 February 1961 Security Council resolution: namely, the expulsion from Katanga of foreign military and paramilitary personnel not connected with the UN operation, the prevention of civil war by a last resort to force, and the protection of the territorial integrity of the Congo. Of these objectives, the first to be achieved—the expulsion of foreign military personnel and mercenaries serving in the Katanga forces (as requested by the Adoula government's Ordinance No. 70)—was undertaken as "Operation Rumpunch" on 28 August 1961.[78] About 338 mercenaries and 443 political advisers were rounded up and expelled from Katanga.[79] This operation was followed by two military clashes between Tshombe's forces and the UN force in September and December 1961—"Morthor" and "Round Two."[80]

"Morthor" failed to achieve its objectives, which had been apprehension of Tshombe's remaining mercenaries; arrest of Tshombe and Munongo (Tshombe fled to Northern Rhodesia); occupation of public buildings; and, in short, the end of Katanga's secession. Shortly after "Morthor," Secretary-General Hammarskjöld died (17 September 1961) in an air crash en route to Ndola for a conference with Tshombe. This military intervention in Katanga, followed closely by the death of the secretary-general, made the Congo situation even more unstable. After a protracted search for a successor to Hammarskjöld, U Thant of Burma was elected acting secretary-general of the United Nations.

Meanwhile a cease-fire had been arranged. It lasted until 5 December 1961, when hostilities were resumed. "Round Two," which lasted from 5 to 18 December 1961, was a military success for the UN force and the Congolese central government. After significant installations in Elizabethville were seized, Tshombe expressed his willingness to negotiate with Adoula on the condition that his safety was guaranteed. The two held discussions at Kitona (20 December 1961) in front of Dr. Ralph Bunche representing the secretary-general. In an eight-point agreement issued by the two leaders, Tshombe recognized the Loi fondamentale, the "indissoluble unity" of the Congo, the supremacy of the central government over every province of the republic, and President Kasavubu as Congolese chief of state. Tshombe also agreed to the return of Katanga's representatives to the Parliament and to Katanga's participation in preparing a draft constitution, and to respect UN resolutions on the Congo.

But Tshombe and the Katanga Assembly nullified the Kitona agreement by eight reservations. Encouraged by the United Nations, Adoula and Tshombe held further negotiations in Léopoldville between 18 March and 19 April 1962 and between 19 May and 26 June. These meetings also produced no positive substantial results. When the negotiations thus failed, U Thant appealed (1 August 1962) to all member states to use their influence to exert pressure on Katanga, including, if necessary, economic pressure, "to achieve a reasonable and peaceful settlement in the Congo." On 20 August he promulgated a Plan of National Reconciliation for the Congo.[81]

Both Adoula and Tshombe accepted the U Thant plan, but the application of its provisions was stalled by Tshombe's usual Fabian tactics. To overcome this impasse U Thant informed Tshombe that economic sanctions would be applied against Katanga because he had failed to implement the provisions of the plan. Tshombe countered by announcing on 19 December 1962 that he would resort to a "scorched earth" policy rather than acquiesce in any forcible integration of Katanga into the Congo republic. Subsequently his gendarmes began firing on UN troops (24–28 December 1962), signalling that the end of Katanga secession was to be achieved only by force. The UN force undertook that task as "Operation Grandslam" from late December 1962 to early January 1963. On 14 January 1963 Tshombe succumbed and announced to the world the termination of the secession of Katanga.

The Congolese central government took immediate steps with the assistance of the UN Operations in the Congo to reintegrate Katanga. Mobutu, who had become an army general, supervised the integration of the Katanga gendarmerie into the Congolese National Army. The Katanga problem could now be said to have been solved. The UN force nevertheless remained in the Congo until 30 June 1964, when the last troops, under the command of Maj. Gen. J. T. U. Aguiyi-Ironsi of Nigeria, left Léopoldville for their homelands.

This admittedly simplified account of the UN mission in the Republic of the Congo presents the stage on which Nigeria acted her first major role in the complex drama of international politics.

Nigeria's Policy on the Congo Crisis

AT THE OUTBREAK of the Congo crisis, Nigeria, still a British dependency, was not legally responsible for the conduct of its external relations; those remained basically a British responsibility, including any official views on the crisis. Although the major world powers would have taken note of any views on the crisis expressed by Nigeria's political leaders, Nigeria's federal government, under Sir Abubakar, had no internationally recognized articulate means of expressing its opinion and intentions on world issues. Characteristically, Sir Abubakar was not the man to rock the boat. Officially, therefore, his government remained essentially silent but by implication acquiescent to British policy toward the crisis. Such an attitude of silent affirmation was not, however, tantamount to indifference to the Congolese situation. On the contrary, Sir Abubakar, in his characteristic manner, quietly devoted himself to a study of the crisis and the acquisition of a thorough understanding in order that the eventual proclamation of his nation's policy would be more influential and compel more attention.

Note that Sir Abubakar had parried demands for a declaration of foreign policy by members of Nigeria's federal House of Representatives very early in 1960. He stated that such a declaration could not be made until independence was at hand.[1] His government's first statement on foreign policy was issued on 20 August 1960, less than a month and a half before Nigeria became a sovereign nation. Hence it is not difficult to understand his approach to and apparent silence on the Congo crisis while Nigeria remained a British dependency.

It could be argued that Sir Abubakar was too preoccupied with the preparations for Nigeria's independence to devote his time to extraneous events beyond his country's borders. The burden of such preparations on Sir Abubakar and his cabinet is not sufficient to explain the prime minister's silence, however. In fact, ceremonial preparations for Nigerian self-rule had begun almost a year earlier, while constitutional and other preparations for the transfer of sovereign power had begun fourteen years before the attainment of independence. Furthermore, no event in any African country, particularly events of such magnitude as those in the new Democratic Republic of the Congo, could be regarded by the political leadership as extraneous to Nigeria's interests. To the contemporary Nigerian political elite, the problems of Nigeria and of other African countries were similar and their fates were intertwined.[2] These leaders also believed Nigeria had other reasons to be concerned with the Congo problem.[3] In addition to the anxiety that the Congo situation bred among Nigerians as fellow inhabitants of the African continent, the inevitably disastrous consequences for all humanity would be shared by Nigerians if the Congo situation adversely affected world peace.

Any notion, therefore, that Sir Abubakar was initially silent on the Congo crisis because of his preoccupation with independence preparations and because the events in the Democratic Republic of the Congo were extraneous to Nigeria cannot be supported. Aside from the fact that Great Britain was in charge of Nigeria's foreign relations, a better explanation of Sir Abubakar's initial silence lies in the character of the man himself. A man of caution, perhaps to a fault, the prime minister sought, at the threshold of Nigeria's independence, more appropriate means of demonstrating his country's concern for a sister African country than by the mere issuance of press releases or flamboyant declarations. Sir Abubakar's government vindicated this view by seconding Francis Nwokedi, of its ministry of Labour, through the United Nations to the Congo to help the Congolese government solve labor problems even before Nigeria's attainment of independence.

Nevertheless, while their government remained silent on the developments in the Congo, articulate Nigerians and organs of the leading Nigerian political parties did not hesitate to make their views on the crisis known.[4] Their interpretations of the situation, which did not in some respects differ markedly from those of radical Pan-Africanists elsewhere in Africa, reflected the impact of the forces at work on the continent and in the world generally. Among these forces were Pan-Africanism, i.e., the search for the political solidarity, total liberation, and advancement of the welfare of the peoples of Africa; the question of residual colonialism and the dignity of the African; the fear of continued economic exploitation of Africans by forces based outside Africa; and the politics and policies of the great powers directed at Africa and the developing nations, particularly their ideological politics.[5]

These forces and the unofficial Nigerian views on the Congo that they animated were among Sir Abubakar's considerations in formulating his policy on the crisis.

Official Nigerian views on the crisis. — Interpretations of the crisis by Nigerian authorities can be gleaned from various sources: official pronouncements and lectures by the prime minister within and outside Nigeria; parliamentary debates; and speeches by Nigeria's representatives to the various meetings and committees of the United Nations, at international conferences, and to Pan-African groups. Initially, Sir Abubakar and his advisers were uncertain about the actual machinery of transfer of power to the Congolese people and about whether Lumumba's Léopoldville government represented the majority of the Congolese people. The Nigerian government officials believed that events in the Congo and statements by Congolese political leaders demonstrated that the people were dangerously divided. It followed, in Sir Abubakar's view, that a stable central government in the Congo had been threatened and destroyed (his exact words were that "as a result of the many waters that have flowed into the River Congo the *de jure* Government established [in the Congo] immediately on independence was no longer functioning")[6] and that the Léopoldville government had become unable to maintain domestic law and order.

Sir Abubakar and his advisers reasoned further that the filling of the political vacuum created by the crisis, along with the restoration of political and economic stability and hence of peace and order in the Congo, could be achieved if the Congolese people were reunited.[7] The crux of the matter, according to this analysis, was how to bring about political understanding and the political will to cooperate among Congolese political leaders. Thus viewed, Belgian intervention in the Congo was recognized as a vital part of the crisis, but it was not seen as the central factor.[8] The primary cause was the political conflict among the Congolese leaders, which made it difficult to expel the Belgians from the Congo as Lumumba had asked the United Nations to do. If the Congolese leaders could agree on the best course for their country and on the basic tasks necessary to follow it, the Belgian factor would not constitute a significant problem. Therefore, the crisis was essentially domestic, in the Nigerian analysis. Disinterested aid, specifically from the United Nations, was needed to help the Congolese leaders resolve their political differences.

Sir Abubakar's definition of the crisis had an inherent weakness: it underrated the extent and tenacity of the hold the Belgians and their

Western allies had on Congolese leaders—Tshombe, Kasavubu, and Mobutu—and on mineral-rich Katanga. It did not recognize that the crisis involved a struggle for mastery in the Congo at the level of the great powers. His view did not appreciate the subtlety and decisiveness with which these outside forces use native surrogates to advance their interests, particularly in a new state with inexperienced leadership. It did not consider that the Congo was a fragile creation of Belgium and that its disputing leaders represented only their own political ambitions and the parochial interests of their particular nationality groups. The assumption of disinterested aid from the United Nations put too much faith on an international organization whose actions are dictated by the often conflicting interests of its members.

Having defined the Congo crisis, Sir Abubakar's government delineated its implications for Africa and the world. The crisis was considered a serious challenge to the African states in part because it was being used by the detractors of black people and defenders of colonialism to buttress their argument that Africans were unable to rule themselves. The London *Economist* defined this challenge to Africa in lucid language:

> If the Congo survives as a recognisable entity in the coming months, Black Africa will consider that it has justified beyond question its capacity for self-government elsewhere.
>
> If it disintegrates, as a good number of eyes covertly watching it from the south and east confidently expect it to do, the resistance to African emancipation in Africa's remaining colonial or semi-colonial territories could stiffen into horrified rigidity. . . .
>
> The worst outcome for the Congo, and for its neighbours, would be if the centrifugal forces there were to bring about its disintegration before the remainder of Central Africa has contrived to put its house in order.[9]

Sir Abubakar's government also believed that the Congo crisis constituted a serious threat to the stability of independent African states and would, if not contained, throw the Congo and its sister African states open to the depredations of neocolonialist forces seeking to keep Africans in perpetual thralldom. The Hon. Jaja Wachuku emphasized this threat when he addressed the UN General Assembly. He reminded the delegates that it was the same Congo they were discussing that, as a consequence of Western European interests, had brought about the Berlin Conference of 1884–85. That conference, he said, had created the dismemberment of Africa and a host of attendant problems. "Let us hope," he warned, "that now the independence of the Congo will not also lead to the disintegration of Africa that is becoming independent." [10]

This threat of disintegration, Sir Abubakar reasoned,[11] was particularly ominous because the Republic of the Congo had a common boundary with nine other African countries—Congo (Brazzaville), Angola, Zambia, Tanzania, Burundi, Rwanda, Uganda, Sudan, and Central African Republic—with the line of demarcation between free Africa and colonial Africa passing through its frontiers. (See map. 2.1.) Also the Republic of the Congo formed a pivot for the French- and English-speaking countries and a sort of bulwark against the migration northward of the apartheid policy of the South African government. A strong and stable Democratic Republic of the Congo, while advancing African strategy for complete eradication of colonialism and racial bigotry from Africa, could concomitantly open Angola and the white-ruled neighboring countries to nationalist subversive activities and uprisings. Indeed, Sir Roy Welensky, prime minister of the Rhodesian Federation at the time, was frightened by this possibility, and had supported Tshombe's secessionist activities, stating that the Rhodesian Federation "has 2,000 miles of open frontier with Katanga, and the tangled web of tribal affinities across that frontier is such that peace and stability in Katanga are matters of the most vital interest to the Federation." [12]

The opponents of African freedom had reason for concern: to perceptive political observers it was clear that a Lumumba government securely in power in the Congo would give extensive support to an emergent Angolan national liberation movement. The potential of such support to Angola would have been analogous to that which Tanzania later gave to the Mozambique Liberation Front. But with more resources than Tanzania's, the support would have come much earlier, when the Portuguese were far less prepared for it and the Western world less certain of its immediate stance; thus it

> could have made a considerable difference to the whole history of liberation movements in Southern Africa. Portugal might have crumbled, Rhodesia might never have been able to proclaim a unilateral declaration of independence (UDI), and

South Africa might have found itself without buffers. The Congo crisis gave the white forces of Southern Africa crucial time in which to consolidate their defensive structure.[13]

The Nigerian government believed that, in addition to playing a political role in the complete decolonization of Africa, a united, strong, and prosperous Congo could contribute immensely to functional cooperation and political stability on the continent.[14] But given its prevailing circumstances the Congo could not fulfill these hopes; instead, the African continent appeared to be in grave danger as the opposing power blocs seemed poised to disturb world peace and security in the pursuit of their interests in the Congo. The inability of the former metropole, Belgium, to maintain stable and cordial relations with the new republic made the likelihood of big power intervention and the ominous implication for world peace very real.[15]

Responsibility for the crisis

In apportioning responsibility, Sir Abubakar's government recognized that the causes of the crisis were complex. Believing that the United Nations had not at first appreciated the immensity of the task it was called upon to assume in the Congo, the Nigerian leaders asserted that the organization had made inadequate plans to deal with the crucial stages of the crisis; that it had haphazardly deployed the troops contributed for its use, and thus that it had advanced the interests of the major world powers and contributed to the complex causes of the crisis.[16] While this position has some merit, and while the great powers, seeking to advance their interests, were indeed responsible for whatever shortcomings the United Nations may have displayed in the initial response to the crisis, it was foreseeable that once the Congolese took their conflict to the United Nations the self-interests of the practitioners of power politics were bound to complicate the crisis.

Sir Abubakar based his apportionment of responsibility for the crisis, just as his interpretation of it, on legalistic principles. According to him the "nature and type of constitution" under which the Congo became independent was one primary cause of the crisis. In his opinion it was highly centralized and unsuitable for the Congo's heterogeneous society. No one, he believed, could say with certainty how the constitution had come about, particularly whether there had been any discussion with the Congolese leaders, and at what levels. He did not believe that there had been any serious and countrywide consultations with the people of the Congo before the drafting of the constitution that gave them independence. The document was, instead, imposed from above as a provisional measure to lead the Congolese people to independence, after which "they could sit down by themselves and draw up a new Constitution to their own liking." Sir Abubakar added that the Belgian government, which had governed the Congo on a unitary basis, made no attempts during its colonial rule to truly unite the provinces of its erstwhile colony.[17] Rather, the colonial experience had served to strengthen ethnic loyalties of the provinces and to weaken their Congolese national identification.

The prime minister believed further that the crisis was "the ghastly and tragic result of the mistaken policy" of the Belgian government, which had "concentrated on providing material benefit for the Africans but denied them political development."[18] A corollary was the contention by Dr. T. O. Elias, then Nigeria's attorney general and minister of justice, that the crisis was partly due to the fact that the Belgian administration had provided only a small, shaky foundation for the rule of law in the Congo before the transfer of power.[19]

Sir Abubakar equally condemned the attitude of Congolese political leaders whose ethnic jealousies, he said, had aggravated the situation they inherited from the Belgian administration. It was unfortunate, he reasoned, that the legally appointed president dismissed the legally appointed prime minister, who in turn dismissed the president. "One man," he went on, "broke away and said his province was a separate state. Another man within that same province said his own portion had become a State, and another man set up himself somewhere else and said he had created a new province, and he has a separate state."[20] In the view of Sir Abubakar the Congolese National Army imitated this dangerous precedent set by the political leadership. That is, it splintered. Although each of the army's splinter groups claimed to follow one or another of the claimants to the rightful leadership of the Congo, those fragments, uncontrolled by either the political leaders or their officers, simply roamed about stealing and looting.[21]

Sir Abubakar believed interference from both within and outside Africa had been crucial in precipitating the Congo crisis. He told Nigeria's federal Parliament that even from the time Belgium granted the Congolese a constitution "to start them off" to independence, "some countries within Africa and outside Africa suddenly became interested in the affairs of the Congo Republic." It was unfortunate, he went on, that these forces, instead of allowing the Congolese people "to be by themselves, to have time to think and to understand themselves and to know their country . . . started to dictate to the Congolese leaders what they should and should not do." [22] "It might be,"

> that the former colonial power [i.e., Belgium] have their hands in this matter. It might be that some of the great powers have their hands in it, and it might be that some of the independent African countries have their hands in this confusion. It might be possible, and I think that from the reports which the Reconciliation Committee published . . . especially on documents submitted to the Committee by President Kasavubu, one could see that there are indications that some countries in Africa and outside Africa have really interfered in the affairs of the Congo. [23]

Despite this convincing mass of evidence attesting to his outrage at outside interference in Congolese affairs, Sir Abubakar talked in equivocal language and thereby offended his more dynamic countrymen, who desired him to denounce the "neocolonialists" in no uncertain terms. He had said that there were countries, both in the Western and the Eastern power blocs, who were prepared to cause trouble anywhere. He had cited how European officers were leading the splinter army units in the Congo; how European mercenaries were joining these units; and how many foreign countries were supplying arms to the splinter groups and so-called governments of the Congo. [24] But to his countrymen he appeared "too soft" on the NATO powers, the "arch supporters of Belgium's atrocities and manoeuvres in the Congo." Such a stance was contrary to the "destiny" of Nigeria in African affairs and to all they had fought for during their own struggles for independence. [25]

Such critics were consoled by the fact that Sir Abubakar's softness on this particular Congo issue was compensated for by the flamboyance of his minister of economic development, the leader of Nigeria's delegation to the United Nations, Jaja Wachuku. Whereas Sir Abubakar had described the Congo crisis as a result of the mistaken policy of Belgian administration, Jaja Wachuku said:

> The *criminal negligence* of Belgium in deliberately refusing to allow the Congolese people to develop themselves as fully as

was humanly possible was, broadly and generally speaking, a fundamental cause of the trouble in the Congo. If the Congolese people had been able to have the basic training that would have equipped them sufficiently to be able to withstand and to live in accordance with 20th-century standards we should not have had this chaos in the Congo.[26]

Sir Abubakar had spoken in generalities and in equivocal terms that "it might be that the great powers had contributed to the Congo situation"; Jaja Wachuku charged that vested interests, tacitly and by implication, effectively undermined the Congolese authorities and the Congolese economy and eventually weakened the state. The prime minister had talked merely of foreign interference in the affairs of the Congo; Jaja Wachuku spoke of a conspiracy to dismember the Congolese state by withdrawing the one portion that was most developed and perhaps richest at the time.[27] This move, Wachuku said, was the political stratagem of people who were more interested in the copper, cobalt, uranium, diamonds, and gold with which Katanga was richly endowed, than in the welfare of the peoples of the Congo and Africa.[28] The mineral mongers and plotters in Katanga knew themselves, he said. He did not have to mention them by name to make his point.

Nigeria's officialdom thus allocated responsibility for the Congo crisis as summarized in the following paragraphs.[29]

Belgium was one of the major culprits, having refused to prepare the Congolese people for the responsibilities of self-rule. Its "vicious" colonial policy had not only kept the Congolese away from the stream of political developments in Africa and the outside world, but had also helped them to exploit ethnic differences for their own ambitions. In that policy lay the seeds of discord that culminated in the Congo crisis. The Belgian administration failed to establish a solid foundation for the rule of law in the Congo. Under its tutelage an unsuitable highly centralized constitution was forged. The conflicts initiated by the Belgian administration contributed to the collapse of that constitution, and Belgium was quick to exploit the situation to reestablish and perpetuate its hold in its former colony.

Congolese leaders comprised another major cause of the crisis. In blind pursuit of their personal ambitions they unwittingly played into the hands of Belgian and other foreign interests: Tshombe and the Belgians; Lumumba and the Soviets; Kasavubu-Mobutu and the Americans; the Force publique and the UN operations.

Outside interference by some African states also contributed to the protracted crisis. Some African states gave poor advice to their Congolese proteges as they sought to entrench themselves in central Africa.

Finally, the United Nations was allotted its share of the blame. It initially underrated the immensity of its task as the great powers vied for dominance in central Africa, and Dag Hammarskjöld, under whom the mission began, immobilized the UN mission by his rigid interpretation of its mandate.

The Nigerian policy: objectives, principles, and major tenets

Objectives. — Nigeria's policy on the Congo crisis embraced five main objectives: to restore peace and stability in the Congo so the legitimate aspirations of its people could be achieved and the republic could play an effective role within its own borders, in Africa, and in the world; to help the Congolese resolve their constitutional problems so they could prove to cynics that Africans are capable of self-rule and that given the proper political and constitutional setting the black man is capable of fulfilling the obligations of self-rule in a modern world; to safeguard international peace and security, since only peaceful conditions were most conducive to the development of the Nigerian federation and the welfare of its peoples; to ensure a bond of friendship with the Congolese people and so create the kind of atmosphere necessary for Nigeria to fulfill its role as Africa's most populous nation; and to keep the ideological struggle between the power blocs out of Africa. Africans could then address their unique problems from their own vantage points and in manners they considered appropriate.

Principles. — Having decided on these objectives, the prime minister selected seven principles, adherence to which would best ensure the achievement of the goals. Most important was the recognition of the Republic of the Congo as a sovereign and independent state, which meant that neither Nigeria nor any other state could dictate the interests of the Congolese people, recognizing that the Congolese were the best judges of their interests. The second principle was a corollary of the first: noninterference in the domestic affairs of the Congo. This meant, among other things, that Nigeria would remain strictly impartial in its attitude toward Congolese domestic problems. It would support no faction, only the legitimate government of the republic. Standing on the principle, Nigeria insisted that she would not uphold any attempts inspired by forces outside the Congo and aimed at the dismemberment of the republic.

The third principle was that the solution to the crisis was not military but political. A military solution would have grave consequences and would only be ephemeral, but a political solution achieved through resolute diplomatic negotiation would tend to be more lasting. The fourth principle stated the necessity of rendering a disinterested service to the new republic to minimize the adverse impact of the crisis on Africa as a whole. Again, such service would leave a lasting imprint on Nigeria's bilateral relations with the Congo and would enhance the stature of both nations in and outside Africa. The fifth principle called for dealing with the situation through cooperation rather than competition with all other nonaligned states supporting the UN mission to the Congo. This principle was related to the sixth, that is, steadfast and wholehearted support for the United Nations as the only suitable organization to seek a just resolution of the conflict.

The rationale was that officials involved in the UN military and civilian operations in the Congo could not be drawn from only one state or a parochial group of states with designs on making the Congo a colony of such a state or group. Again, Nigeria was a new and relatively weak state. Given the circumstances of the crisis, it could achieve the objectives of its policy in the Congo only through the United Nations. It could not successfully compete with the great powers, whose particular interests in the Congo were apparent if not a matter of record. Another factor to be considered was the power available for achieving Nigeria's policy objectives. (The course it chose is amplified in chapter 5.)

The seventh principle was that the solution of the Congo problem was primarily a concern of the African states working through the United Nations.

Major tenets. — On the occasion of Nigeria's admission to the United Nations (7 October 1960), Sir Abubakar declared to the world his nation's policy on the Congo crisis. His government had hitherto remained silent on the crucial issue perplexing the heart of Africa.

Before stating Nigeria's policy on "the recent tragic events in the Republic of the Congo . . . uppermost in all our minds," the prime minister engaged in an elaborate exposé of a number of points that required clarification before any solutions to the crisis could be suggested.[30] He acknowledged that many features of the "intractable"

Congolese problem remained obscure to him. He was in "some doubt as to the actual manner in which the Constitution granting independence" to the former Belgian Congo "was drawn up" by the Belgians. He had misgivings as to "the degree of consultation" that had taken place among the Congolese peoples themselves regarding the machinery of transfer of power and at what level such consultation, if any, had been carried out. He was particularly concerned about whether the Loi fondamentale was "imposed from above," that is, by the Belgians, or whether it was freely accepted by the Congolese. He equally had misgivings as to "how widely the provisions of the new Constitution were known" in the whole country. He doubted whether there had been provided "any pattern of administration going up from the village to the provincial and to the national level" in the whole country before independence was granted. These doubts stemmed from Sir Abubakar's experience with the development of Nigeria's constitution.

In Sir Abubakar's opinion two other issues regarding the granting of self-government remained to be clarified: the quality and strength of the human resources in the country necessary for its fulfillment of the responsibilities of self-rule; and the kind of governmental machinery that was available to implement whatever policies the Congolese government decided upon. In his opinion the resolution of these issues remained obscure and constituted a major part of the background of the Congo crisis.[31]

After outlining these misgivings, Sir Abubakar proposed three "important" factors to be considered in dealing with the Congo. Foremost was that "Africa must not be allowed to become a battleground in the ideological struggle" between the Western and the Eastern power blocs. To forestall this dangerous situation, he suggested that the Congo crisis be dealt with at the political level primarily by the African states that were members of the United Nations.[32] Second, his government believed that to create a real political life in the new Republic of the Congo it would be necessary "to start at the bottom, by seeing that local and provincial authorities" were established "while maintaining the essential unity of the country." Third, his government believed the Congolese people were right in appealing solely to the United Nations for aid in rebuilding their country.

The suggestion that Africa must not be allowed to become a battleground in the ideological struggle was a diplomatic gesture toward keeping the cold war out of Africa. However, when Sir Abubakar made his pronouncement in 1960, had not Africa already become a battleground in the ideological struggle? Is it true, as some, particularly among the prime minister's colleagues, contended, that the Congo crisis introduced the cold war into Africa?

No; the cold war had been in Africa before the independence of the Congo. Largely responsible for this situation were Africa's struggle for political emancipation from the colonial powers of the Western world, the sympathy that struggle received from the Communist world, and the reaction that sympathy provoked in the Western world, particularly in the United States. Consider the manner in which the French pulled out of Sekou Toure's Guinea, the repercussions of the Anglo-French-Israeli attack on Nasser's Egypt in 1956, the nationalist struggles in Algeria—the Franco-Algerian war—and the Sharpeville massacres in South Africa. Furthermore, it is well known that the Communist-dominated World Federation of Trade Unions and the Western-dominated International Confederation of Free Trade Unions had been competing for influence over the politically significant trade unions in the emerging states of Africa before the independence of the Congo. Consider the propaganda beamed from radios of both power blocs toward the peoples of Africa.

The Congo crisis did not introduce the cold war into Africa; nor was it responsible for Africa's becoming a battleground in the struggle. Rather, it accentuated the struggle and gave perceptive African leaders good reason for concern. The demand then that Africa not be allowed to become a battleground betrayed some degree of naïveté regarding the political realities in contemporary Africa. Africa was already involved in the cold war; Sir Abubakar himself had initialed a defense pact with Britain, and although no section of the pact was specifically directed against any of the Eastern powers it could easily be deduced that the Eastern bloc was its major target. Britain was already a member of NATO, the Southeast Asia Treaty Organization, and the Central Treaty Organization. Against whom else could the pact possibly be directed, since Nigeria herself did not initiate the agreement or envisage any confrontations with sister African states or distant Asiatic states? Furthermore, is Belgium not a NATO power, and had not the Republic of the Congo concluded a similar agreement with her? The voting record of former French African colonies at the United Nations before and during the period the demand was made speaks for itself. It was influenced by the stand of Paris, and France too belonged to NATO.

To demand then that the Congo situation be entrusted to African states to deal with at the political level in order to prevent Africa from becoming a battleground in the ideological struggle was not the point, for some African states were already committed to sympathy toward cold war ideology. Handling the situation alone would not have kept Africa out of the cold war. The cold war was a peripheral issue which accentuated the crisis. The primary issue, which Sir Abubakar ignored, was foreign economic interests. Under such circumstances, the Congo and Africa should have appealed for a quarantine of detrimental foreign economic interests; this action would have been more appropriate and would have served as a better basis for the suggestion that the Congo situation should be handled primarily by African states at the political level.

The second important factor outlined by Sir Abubaker, that of creating a real political life in the Congo by starting from the bottom and ensuring the establishment of local and provincial authorities, was, under the circumstances, a long-term objective. Anyone who believed that it could be achieved immediately was unrealistic. Such a political life was not the solution the new republic needed at the time, although the desire for such a government does indicate the impact of Nigerian domestic politics on Sir Abubakar's thinking. In fact, he was advocating for the Congo the type of government that was operating in Nigeria, one which concentrated power in the component regions and eventually paralyzed the weakened central government.

The third factor, approving the Congolese appeal to the United Nations only, is not out of order. But the prime minister failed to call upon member states of the United Nations to submerge cold war politics and considerations of foreign economic interests so that they could tackle the Congo problem mainly in the interest of the Congolese people and generally in the interest of world peace and security.

Continuing his policy statement before the UN General Assembly, Sir Abubakar made several proposals to help solve the Congo problem. He called for a fact-finding commission of African states to investigate thoroughly the sources of the troubles that had afflicted the new republic. He maintained that without such a proper and thorough analysis of the causes, it would be "idle to pretend that an effective remedy" could be prescribed. He suggested that the "great powers" should be excluded from the fact-finding commission, because, he reasoned, "however honest their intentions, it would be inevitable that they would be regarded as having particular interest in the problem." [33] Jaja Wachuku, then Sir Abubakar's minister of economic development and leader of Nigeria's delegation to the United Nations, was later appointed chairman of the UN Congo Conciliation Commission, an indication that Sir Abubakar effectively made his point before the General Assembly and was, in fact, prepared to take active steps toward its implementation.

The prime minister also proposed holding new elections in the republic in the hopes of establishing an administration capable of governing the country. As an additional salutary effect the new elections would provide properly constituted and authorized leaders with whom the United Nations could cooperate in its Congo operation. Emphasizing this, Sir Abubakar said it was important that the United Nations would work only with those whom

> I have termed the authorized leaders. They may seem to some of us to be far from perfect, and to some even objectionable; but if they are duly chosen by a majority then they must be supported. It would be the height of folly to attempt to impose a Government which was not founded on popular support, and the result would only be even greater confusion.[34]

He dismissed any suggestion of the Republic of the Congo becoming a UN trust territory as impracticable and a negation of the principle of the sovereignty of an independent nation. The United Nations, he maintained, should arrange for assistance and advice for the republic on an agency basis without infringing on its sovereignty. Pending the new elections, which could not be held overnight, Sir Abubakar urged that the United Nations act more firmly than it had in the past to support the Congolese government in maintaining law and order and in keeping the machinery of day-to-day government moving. Such action would necessitate granting additional powers to the UN force and to other UN agencies in the Congo but only for a limited period, until the new elections had taken place.

Sir Abubakar called for new elections in the Congo, but he did not describe how these were to be carried out under the prevailing circumstances or who was to conduct them. Probably he intended for them to be held under the auspices or supervision of the United Nations. Furthermore, the proposal to hold fresh elections implied that Sir Abubakar believed the central government of the Congo at the time was either a fraud or incapable of governing. This position would earn him criticism from his own countrymen and the possible ill will of the Congolese politicians, who would drain their resources to contest such called-for elections.

Sir Abubakar urged the United Nations to help organize discussion by the Congo's chosen representatives to determine the form of government most suitable and generally acceptable to the people of the republic. Here he demonstrated once again the impact of Nigeria's political development on his reasoning. Nigeria's independence constitution, it will be recalled, had been formulated in a series of conferences among representatives of all shades of political opinion in the country, and the details of the constitution, no matter the weaknesses later discovered therein, had been determined by Nigerians themselves in cooperation with the British Colonial Office. The delegates to the Nigerian constitutional conferences, as Chief Dennis C. Osadebay later put it in "Next? Nigeria Needs a One Party System," did not divide.[35] Their constitution was not the result of the government versus the opposition. When a delegation did not agree to a point, the matter was discussed, adjustments were made, and, through compromise, unanimous decisions were recorded. Sir Abubakar believed that the strength and uniqueness of Nigeria's independence constitution depended largely on this method. The constitution was not imposed on the people by Britain or by Nigerian lawyers.[36] This kind of constitution was what he wanted for the Congo.

Sir Abubakar also proposed that, since revenue allocation would be a root problem if the Congolese people decided on a confederal or federal constitution, the United Nations should provide the republic with "the most able and experienced experts" who would inquire, advise, and help the authorities to reach agreements on such and similar matters. Here too he spoke from his experience of the domestic problems of Nigeria where revenue allocation negotiations had been held in 1958. Then a Fiscal Commission, appointed for the purpose, allocated sources of revenue to the various governments of the federation in a manner that worked fairly satisfactorily until it was improved by the Binns Commission in 1965.[37]

Finally, Sir Abubakar called for a training program for the Congolese people. Such a program was necessary to fill the higher positions of the central government and "to ensure that the ordinary day-to-day government was kept working, because if that was allowed to collapse, the difficulties would be increased a thousandfold." He called upon those African states with similar views to join with Nigeria in providing places in secondary and technical schools for hundreds of Congolese students. He was sure that if many Congolese people saw how other African countries managed their own affairs the effect would be beneficial; it would help the Congolese people to broaden their views and to realize fully the importance of preventing a breakdown of the constitution.

Sir Abubakar concluded with a special appeal to African states. "We African states," he urged,

> should come together to assist the Congolese to solve their problems. I feel sure that we can do so, but it must be done collectively and not merely as so many individual States.
>
> We must do it together and we must be entrusted with this responsibility by the United Nations and be given full backing. Nor would I limit advice and assistance to African countries, but would welcome the participation of other States, though I would repeat, I think it would be advisable to exclude the Great Powers.[38]

Despite what the critics in the Nigerian federal government coalition and members of the opposition considered the major shortcomings of Sir Abubakar's Congo policy—mostly its tone of moderation—that policy was generally comprehensive and imaginative. Only its periphery, not its substance, was criticized. Its coherence and broad outlook comprised the touchstone of the difference between it and the UN quibblings on the crisis. In its deliberately consistent pursuit of the policy, Nigeria clearly dissociated itself from the inconsistency of certain nations which, though supporting the UN mission in the Congo, carried on clandestine activities calculated to negate the organization's objectives there.[39]

Nigeria's policy in relation to those of the power blocs and the other African states

Nigeria's Congo policy was formulated independent of overt pressures by the major power blocs, although the government was aware of their views and actions on the crisis. In broad outline its policy diluted that of those Western powers which supported the UN efforts in the Congo, albeit for their own national interests, at the same time that the Soviets lost out.[40]

There is no positive evidence that Nigeria "toed" the British line on the Congo conflict. There were significant differences between the policies pursued by the two Commonwealth members. Although Nigeria believed that the solution to the Congo problem was essentially political and not military, it raised no objection to the use of force by the United Nations when necessary. Britain, on the other hand, rejected *in toto* the use of force by the United Nations. Then, too, Nigeria as a new and relatively weak nation passionately believed in the UN Congo mission and wholeheartedly supported the organization in its operations there. But Britain was cautious, almost distrustful, of the UN mission. Her support was half-hearted where it was not actually negative and hostile.

Furthermore, Britain's attitude toward the crisis, unlike that of Nigeria, was dictated by its own economic interests in Central Africa. The British had substantial shares in Union Minière du Haut-Katanga. British investments in Northern and Southern Rhodesia (now Zambia and Zimbabwe, respectively) and Nyasaland (now Malawi) were also considerable. Naturally, Britain sought to protect such interests. Its policy was also influenced by political interests in Central Africa. It is difficult to separate British interests in Central Africa from those of the cold war strategists and particularly from those of the white minority settlers in the Rhodesias as represented by the maneuvers of Sir Roy Welensky and later of Ian Smith. Britain, too, as a member of NATO, naturally owed allegiance to its allies in the Congo issues. Nigeria was not encumbered by any of these considerations.

In relation to the policies of other African states regarding the Congo crisis, Nigeria's policy placed it summarily among the moderates, comprising Ethiopia, Liberia, Libya, Togo, Tunisia, Somalia, and the Sudan. These states recognized the complexity of the crisis and allocated responsibility for it to Belgium, irresponsible Congolese leaders, and interventionists from within and outside Africa. Their approach was legalistic, and they sought to uphold the rule of law and Congolese political institutions. But when there occurred a vacuum of constitutional authority in the Congo, they sought expanded role and authority for the United Nations Operations in the Congo to enable that group to establish both the peaceful conditions and the legal institutions essential to the return of orderly government.

But Nigeria's policy differed from those of the other remaining African states, which Robert C. Good described as "radicals" (Ghana, Guinea, Morocco, and the United Arab Republic [now Arab Republic of Egypt]) and "conservatives" (Cameroon, Chad, Congo-Brazza-ville, Dahomey, Gabon, the Ivory Coast, Malagasy, Mauritania, Niger, Senegal, and Upper Volta).[41] The radicals attributed the crisis solely to the "maneuvers" of Western "neocolonialists" and their African col-laborators. They supported both Lumumba's strong centralized gov-ernment philosophy as conforming to Pan-Africanist ideals and his insistence that the UN operations should be an arm of his central gov-ernment in dealing with the crisis. While they supported UN efforts in the Congo, they were willing to lend Lumumba direct aid to crush "imperialist plots" and to ensure a unified Congo under his regime. Some withdrew their military contingents from the Congo following Lumumba's assassination.

The conservatives, on the other hand, blamed "communist imperi-alists and their African puppets" for the outbreak of the crisis. They supported Lumumba's opponents who called for a decentralized gov-ernment. Also they wanted the United Nations to limit its role in the Congo strictly to the maintenance of law and order and to the preven-tion of interference in Congolese domestic affairs.

4

Formulation of Nigeria's Congo Policy: Factors and Determinants

THE FORMULATION of foreign policy is essentially a decision-making process. As such, it is influenced by a multitude of variable factors, chief of which include the value orientations of a nation's decision makers, their past objectives, their aspirations for the future, the institutions and personalities involved in the process, and the interaction of these forces within the nation with those of other nations.[1]

These factors affected the formulation of Nigeria's policy on the crisis in the Democratic Republic of the Congo. Because of Nigeria's experience as a British colony, the political and international orientations of her decision makers were permeated by Western concepts and sympathies. Those political concepts and sympathies in conjunction with Nigeria's economic and cultural links and other legacies of the imperial era gave Nigeria's policy on the Congo a pro-Western orientation.

Nigeria's decision makers were also influenced by their cultural heritage and this militated against adopting any policies on the Congo crisis based wholly on foreign norms and influences. Also, the country's political leaders believed that Nigeria's position as Africa's most populous independent state required it to foster the political and economic emancipation of Africa and to spearhead the impact of the "African personality" in world affairs.[2] Thus the indigenous and the acquired idiosyncrasies[3] of Nigeria's decision makers influenced most of the decisions they made during the Congo crisis and also helped to characterize the tone and orientation of Nigeria's Congo policy.

The process of policy formulation

The role of the prime minister and his cabinet. — According to the provisions of Nigeria's independence constitution the formulation and conduct of Nigeria's policy on the Congo crisis was the exclusive preserve of the federal government. This responsibility was executed by the prime minister and minister of external affairs, Sir Abubakar, and members of his cabinet. Careful to avoid exacerbating an already confused situation, Sir Abubaker cautiously weighed every piece of evidence before making any pertinent statements. He had ample time to study the crisis, appreciate the reactions of Nigeria's intelligentsia, and analyze the policies of the major world powers toward it. He was in a much better position than many of his counterparts in the older states to view the early stages of the crisis with hindsight and to benefit from the mistakes of those states that had already declared their policies. Above all, Sir Abubakar had already formulated the general outlines of his policy toward all sister African states and their problems. The Congo crisis was an integral part of Africa's problems. His government's response to it was an elaboration of that policy.

The general policy outline toward African states was based on five principles: involvement or no neutrality in any issue affecting the destiny of Africa; recognition of the equal status of African states; noninterference in the domestic affairs of sister African states except insofar as their actions are incompatible with African solidarity and the well-being of African peoples; respect for the territorial integrity of all African states; and discouragement of subversion and/or any acts of detachment against any African state. The Katanga secession from the Democratic Republic of the Congo was viewed as just such an act of detachment.

Elaborating on this position, Sir Abubakar announced that it was the aim of his government to assist any African state to find solutions to its problems and to foster the growth of a common understanding among all the new states of the continent. "We rejoice," he added,

to see so many countries becoming independent, but . . . we are troubled by the signs which we see of the ideological war between the Great Powers of the world creeping into Africa. We shall therefore take steps to persuade the African leaders to take serious note of this particular trend and we shall make every effort to bring them together, so that having made them aware of the danger we may all find a way to unite our efforts in preventing Africa from becoming an area of crisis and world tension.[4]

The Congo crisis thus became a laboratory in which Sir Abubakar experimented with the difficulties of implementing these aspirations of his government and people in Africa. His government's response to the crisis conformed to the principles he enunciated in August 1960.

The Congo policy was formulated by Sir Abubakar in consultation with Hon. Jaja Wachuku. A National Council of Nigeria and the Cameroons member of Parliament, Hon. Wachuku had been promised the portfolio of the External Affairs Ministry not only because he was qualified to hold the office but also as part of the Northern Peoples' Congress coalition requirements and agreements with his party.[5] There was not much consultation between the two and Sir Abubakar's other cabinet ministers before a definite stand was taken on the Congo crisis. The other ministers, however, were routinely briefed on the details of the policy.[6]

Information sources. — There are important questions pertinent to this topic. How did Sir Abubakar collect the information, that is, carry out the intelligence-gathering operation, on which the formulation of his government's Congo policy was based? What impact did the information source have on the decisions he made? These questions are relevant because an information source may withhold and/or color facts to suit particular or vested interests. The second question is especially relevant because it points to a test of the ability of the decision makers to accurately evaluate collected information as a basis for a pragmatic policy.

News reports, the report of the Nigerian delegation to Congolese independence celebrations, and his study of the Loi fondamentale (the Congolese constitution) were among Sir Abubakar's original sources. But we have concluded, based on interviews with officials of Nigeria's External Affairs Ministry in July 1966, that British intelligence-gathering facilities were the initial source. This fact is important as the British had obvious interests in the Congo conflict.

Sir Abubakar's initial use of a British source is understandable in light of the fact that the crisis erupted three months before Nigeria attained independence. Nigeria had established no diplomatic relations with the Congo; thus there were no Nigerian Embassy officials or intelligence officers to report the developments in the Congo. The British governor-general was still legally in charge of Nigeria's foreign relations, which he conducted by means of directives from the Colonial Office in London. Since he had earlier started to introduce the prime minister to the workings and machinery of the country's foreign rela-

tions and since the United Kingdom had interests in the Congo conflict
and was aware of the place and potential role Nigeria could play in
African affairs, Sir Abubakar probably collected the larger part of
the information on which he based his policy from UK government
sources. While speaking on the white paper regarding the training of
Nigerians for the diplomatic service, the prime minister had stated that
Nigeria would rely on the British government to represent its interests
in those countries where, for financial reasons, it did not open diplomatic missions. Furthermore, the chief secretary to his cabinet, Peter
Stallard, a British expatriate officer, was a carry-over from the colonial
regime.[7]

The absence of any clause condemning foreign economic maneuvers in the Congo in Sir Abubakar's Congo policy statement, when he
was fully aware of Britain's economic interests in the Congo and its
lukewarm attitude toward efforts in that troubled land, points to his use
of British information sources. But, above all, the absence of any such
clause points to the compromise Sir Abubakar had to make to accommodate Nigeria's competing cluster of interests. Obviously his policy
benefited from any interchange of ideas and consultations he might
have had with British officers or from his use of British information
sources. His hand was not forced in selecting his government's course
of action.

The role of the Ministry of External Affairs in policy formulation.
— The External Affairs Ministry (its officials remain anonymous) is

> usually the policy-making agency where the impressions from
> the outside world are gathered and evaluated, where foreign
> policy is formulated and where the impulses emanate for the
> diplomatists abroad to incorporate into reality. It is in this re-
> gard that the foreign ministry of a country constitutes itself as
> the brain of foreign policy. Its diplomatic representatives are
> its eyes, its ears, its mouths, its fingerprints and indeed its itin-
> erant incarnation.[8]

This may be essentially true of foreign ministries in long-estab-
lished parliamentary democracies. But Nigeria's External Affairs Ministry was at the time of the crisis very young and could not be expected
to match the performance of longer-established ones. In fact, it is not
quite clear what specific role its officials played in the formulation of
Nigeria's Congo policy. Officials of the ministry in Lagos were ex-

tremely reluctant to grant interviews for the study. Those who did talked in generalities because their role in the initial policy formulation was nil or at best minimal. The diplomats and secretaries in the field and in the headquarters in New York were definitely better informed and had more input into the process of policy implementation than formulation.

As already indicated, Nigeria had no diplomatic representation in the Congo at the time the policy was formulated. Diplomatic relations were established later, in October–November 1960, when a chargé d'affaires, O. Ogunsulire, was sent to Léopoldville. The first Nigerian ambassador to the Congo, Albert Osakwe, assumed office in Léopold-ville in October 1962. However, as soon as diplomatic relations were established with Léopoldville, Sir Abubakar was able to maintain daily contact with the foreign ministry officials there, who transmitted to him, through the ministry, details of the events in the Congo and the wishes and needs of the Congolese government. He maintained similar communication with Nigeria's delegation to the United Nations in New York. These contacts ensured that the prime minister had ample information on which to base his government's subsequent policies on the crisis.

Impact of Nigeria's national interest on the policy formulation. — "National interest," a concept on whose precise nature scholars are not completely agreed, is considered the "yardstick of choice" in foreign policy formulation. Hans J. Morgenthau, one of the leading exponents of international power politics, states in his *Politics Among Nations: The Struggle for Power and Peace* that the national interest of a nation can only be defined in terms of national security, where national se-curity is defined as the integrity of the national territory and of its fundamental institutions. National security as such, he maintains, is the "irreducible minimum that diplomacy must defend with adequate power without compromise."

But the moralist school of thought in international politics believes that national interest coincides substantially with the moral principles and virtues a nation holds dear. Hence governments, as national agents, the moralists affirm, are morally bound not to compromise the national interest of the state. Rather, they are required to apply the totality of the values and purposes of the state and the means available for their realization to every set of circumstances. Yet to a number of other scholars, national interest comprises the preservation of a nation's independence, the nation's self-sufficiency in the conduct of foreign relations, its national prestige and aggrandizement.

Considering the intangibles connoted by these various perceptions, the concept of national interest is elusive and can have various definitions to meet the interests of a nation as conceived by its political leadership in particular sets of circumstances. It can thus be described as comprising all the concepts a nation's policy makers may apply in trying to influence the world environment to the particular nation's advantage. It follows that the fundamental element in the foreign policy decision-making process is the identification of the national interest in specific circumstances. In a democracy this identification must be such that should win public support; otherwise the implementation of a course of action chosen for the realization of the interests would be very difficult indeed.

Considerations of Nigeria's national interest played a key role in Sir Abubakar's formulation of his government's Congo policy. What is more significant, however, is the prime minister's conception of Nigeria's national interest in the Congo crisis. At the outbreak of the crisis Sir Abubakar's government had a number of major concerns that it viewed as an integral part of Nigeria's national interest. The first was preserving the political and territorial integrity of independent African states, which would prevent what Hon. Jaja Wachuku referred to as "imperialistic escapades" or wars of irredentism by any African or non-African state. Such a policy was necessary not only because the states had become real but also because if African states and their foreign collaborators set about restoring ethnic and geographical unity by force, they would set in motion a chain reaction that might result in interminable interstate wars. The states involved would devote all their energies and resources to maintaining armies and police forces at the expense of constructive effort in the all-important sphere of economic and social development.[9] Another objective was to prevent the ideological war between the major world powers from taking a firm hold on Africa and thus to safeguard the vital interests of Africa. The third national interest consideration was the eradication of all remnants of colonialism in Africa. Fourth was to bring African leaders together to make concerted efforts to unite through cultural and functional cooperation.[10] Restoring confidence in the African, and, as Hon. Jaja Wachuku elaborated, the elimination of "the humiliations that have been his lot in the past" was the fifth consideration.[11] Nigerian political leaders were notably distressed by the "gibes" thrown at the Congolese by the non-African world. Numerous references to "another Congo" in response to proddings by African states that the colonial powers should grant independence to the remaining dependent African countries amounted, in the view of Sir Abubakar's government, to a diminution of the integrity of all Africans. Accordingly, the government believed that to arrest situations that mauled the identity and self-confidence of Africans was part of Nigeria's national interest.[12]

These basic concerns, uppermost in the minds of Nigeria's political leaders at the outbreak of the Congo crisis, formed part of what they believed to be Nigeria's "cluster" of national interest. It was these considerations that Sir Abubakar's policy on the Congo crisis sought to safeguard.[13]

Economic considerations. — Economic development is a vital part of Nigeria's national interest. It was natural for its policy makers to consider every aspect of foreign policy in order to eliminate those factors that might adversely affect the country's economic and social development. Such factors would include actions that might drive away potential foreign investors or alienate those governments—the Anglo-American bloc—from which necessary aid came and would come. In fact, a statement by Sir Abubakar in London in 1958 is very instructive. The prime minister told the press on that occasion:

> However tempting it may be to adopt a neutralist position in world affairs, I myself very much doubt whether Nigeria will be wise even to contemplate such a course. She will depend to such an extent for her successful development on the goodwill of the people and Government of Great Britain, of the British Commonwealth and the Western world, that I don't myself see any future Government of the Federation being in much doubt about the main principles on which to base its foreign policy.[14]

Certainly economic considerations explain to a large extent the manner in which the African-associated members of the European economic community voted on the debates on the Congo crisis and on a number of other international issues.[15] In the case of Nigeria the prime minister's reticence on the crisis and his major emphasis on the ideological war between the East and West rather than on foreign economic interests tend to add some weight to the supposition that considerations of attracting foreign investment and aid had some impact on Nigeria's policy on the crisis. This is especially so in light of the fact that several African states, from the evidence of events supported by certified data, had charged Belgium and its Western supporters with neocolonialist maneuvers in the Congo. But Sir Abubakar, in his major policy statement on the crisis, made only passing reference to neocolonialist forces. Nevertheless, he did show he appreciated the difficulties and implications of Nigeria's economic weakness and underdevelopment. For example, it was because of such difficulties that he advocated before Nigeria's House of Representatives the wisdom of Nigeria seeking membership in the Commonwealth upon its independence.[16] Sir Abubakar later told the General Assembly (7 October 1960) that economic weakness exposes a new country to every kind of pressure and results in other countries depriving its peoples of the freedom to choose a suitable form of government. Insidious infiltration through technical assistance, he added, tends to rob an underdeveloped country of its freedom to pursue policies suited to its national interests.[17]

These facts notwithstanding, Nigeria's policy makers did not formulate Congo policy on purely economic considerations; concern with driving away foreign aid and investment was not a primary determinant. The major criticism of the government by the leader of the opposition in the federal legislature, Chief Awolowo, was that it lacked correct ideological orientation on the Congo crisis.[18] Concerning economic considerations Chief Awolowo said only that the government was allowing the fear of driving away foreign investment to "detour it from the path of true socialism."[19] Thus, Nigeria's Congo policy was not criticized because it was in any way essentially based on considerations of attracting foreign aid.

Although a country that sympathizes with the economic systems and ideological stance of the major foreign aid donors and "toes" their line on cold war issues could assure itself of more economic aid, there are measures essential to attracting foreign aid and investment. Of particular importance is the creation of an economic and political climate conducive to attracting both public and private foreign investment. A government following such a policy usually embarks on measures such as the following: it gives assurance to potential foreign investors and donors that it would pursue no detrimental radical policies within and outside the nation; it guarantees against nationalization or offers guarantees for adequate compensation in the event of nationalization; it undertakes an arrangement whereby either the government or the nationals as private enterprisers or both go into partnership with the foreign investors; it offers to grant new enterprises tax-free holidays; and it takes measures to ensure that its domestic market is or remains wide and promising.

These measures, which Nigeria was utilizing to attract foreign investment at the time its Congo policy was formulated, had been the concern of the country's political leaders on the eve of independence. After that period they were still the object of nationwide debates and detailed discussions. All the governments of the federation had by 1957 declared:

> Our governments have no plans for nationalising industry beyond the extent to which utilities are already nationalised, nor do they foresee any such proposals arising. Nevertheless, they are anxious that there should be no doubt in the minds of overseas entrepreneurs that Nigeria will provide adequate safeguards for the interests of investors in the event of any industry being nationalised in the future. Should this occur, then fair compensation assessed by independent arbitration would be paid.[20]

In fact, in praise of foreign investors, Chief Awolowo had said, while he was premier of Western Nigeria:

> This implicit trust and confidence on the part of foreign interests to supply both capital and technical know-how to our economic and industrial development of necessity places certain responsibility on Nigerian political leaders. We are morally obliged to reciprocate this trust and confidence and to acknowledge, by our conduct towards them in future years, the valuable contributions which they have made to our economic advancement and prosperity. I take this opportunity to assure our foreign partners in this project, and other foreigners who have brought money and modern industrial techniques into this country, that their capital investments are indefensibly guaranteed against any form of exploitation, sequestration or confiscation.[21]

It was unequivocal assurances of this nature that foreign investors needed. Chief Awolowo, it is true, gradually but significantly departed from the policy to advocate one of nationalization, but his colleagues on the national scene and in government continued to advocate against nationalization.[22] They maintained that Nigeria's needs for outside development capital were so great that it would be acting to its own detriment were it foolishly to embark on a policy of nationalization which would cut off at once the help it so much required.

Thus we may conclude that Nigeria's Congo policy was formulated independently of overt foreign economic pressures.[23] Its own economic and political potential in Africa, at once attractive to the major Western powers from whom most of its aid came, were assets which tended to shield it from undue politico-economic pressures. However, considerations of trade with a stable and prosperous Congo were part of the determinants of the Nigerian policy on the crisis.[24] Accordingly, commercial agreements were concluded by the Lagos and Léopoldville governments before the UN operations in the Congo terminated.

Impact of domestic conditions and experience. — Nigeria's political experience as a federation of heterogeneous nationalities and disparate economic resources provided a useful background for the formulation of its Congo policy. Hon. Jaja Wachuku's explanation to this effect is apropos:

> We examined the [Congo] situation as we saw it, and in the light of our experience in Nigeria, because we had our own Katanga problem in 1953. One of our . . . three original regions wanted to secede, and this was encouraged from the outside too. At that time that state was the wealthiest . . . in Nigeria, because it was the most developed. It was exactly the same thing as Katanga . . .
>
> Other resources, later discovered by geological surveys, had not then come to the surface. They even wanted the [revenue allocation] returned 100 percent. We agreed and, just like the Congo, where you had a military Government, we found that in order to keep our country together we had to create a federal institution. Then later, in 1954, in 1957 and in 1958, the other regions found their own resources. Geological surveys showed more resources in other . . . regions, and there was development all around. Today that same region is one of the strongest advocates of the unity of the country.
>
> Now, in the light of that experience . . . we believe in our

own country that the Congo, organized as a federal state, can
be unified with strong powers for the central legislature and the
Central Government.[25]

Thus it came to be that the constitution that Dr. T. O. Elias helped
to draft for the Congo republic reflected a federal structure just as the
Congo Conciliation Commission, chaired by Hon. Jaja Wachuku, had
recommended. Also, Nigeria's political integration and economic and
social development required conditions of peace and security and the
financial wherewithal to bring these about. Given the aspirations of Nigeria's political elite regarding her "mission" in Africa, a protracted
conflict in the Congo would tend to deflect political attention from
these domestic priorities, interfering with the use of scarce domestic
and external capital needed for development. These are among the reasons Nigeria supported a multilateral peacekeeping mission to the
Congo. It was hoped that such a mission would bring about an immediate return to peace and security and hence an orderly process of development to the troubled republic and the entire African region.

The role of Parliament and public opinion. — Nigeria's Congo
policy was formulated at a time when Nigeria's federal legislature was
somewhat far removed from the machinery responsible for foreign relations. Initially, therefore, its role was not as significant as perhaps it
would have been had that relationship been closer.[26] However, through
criticism of the policy already announced and the process of its implementation, legislators offered views that the federal government either
accepted or rejected in its subsequent actions on the conflict.

As was the case with the federal legislature the role of public opinion in the formulation of Nigeria's policy on the Congo crisis was nonexistent, or, at best, minimal. This political situation was not unique.
In the older democracies it was not until after World War I that foreign
policy came under the scrutiny and impact of public opinion.[27] However, the Nigerian press and the intelligentsia did express views on the
Congo crisis that the prime minister and Jaja Wachuku considered to
be either ill-formed or in keeping with the views of radical Pan-Africanists.[28] In general, Nigerian public opinion was content to accept the
basic tenets of Sir Abubakar's Congo policy but as reflected by radical
politicians, labor unions, university students, and youth groups, it demanded a more dynamic government voice on the Congo. The public
wished the government to denounce the activities of Kasavubu,
Tshombe, and Mobutu and give its full support to Lumumba and

Gizenga.[29] Following the murder of Lumumba, Sir Abubakar was under many pressures regarding Nigeria's attitude toward the Congo situation.[30] His resultant explanations of his government's Congo policy and his criticism of the UN measures as well as those of certain African countries in the Congo indicate his sensitivity to those pressures.

The Nigerian news media performed a valuable service in educating the Nigerian public and stimulating public discussion on the Congo policy.[31] The dailies published editorial comments and a series of articles on the crisis and its developments.[32] *The West African Pilot* serialized a copy of the Loi fondamentale made available to the editor by Jaja Wachuku.

Considerations of forces operating within Africa. — As Nigeria is an integral part of Africa, its policy makers could ill afford to ignore the issues and forces operating within the continent. It was no secret that there was a leadership complex among the political leadership of African states. That competition was keenest between Ghana and Nigeria in the years immediately following the latter's independence. It was part of the reason that Nigeria, before her independence, had enthusiastically welcomed the UN mission to the Congo republic. Definitely, Sir Abubakar did not want such a rivalry to be any feature of the Congo crisis because it would compound the difficulty of arriving at a solution. This was one reason he demanded that African states work collectively and not as individuals in their efforts to help the Congolese resolve their problems.

Sir Abubakar also considered the differences of opinion among African states regarding African unity, economic development, relationships between the new states and the former colonial powers, and residual colonialism. African states, he believed, were capable of exploiting the situation in the Congo to support factions there which appeared amenable to their own political and economic views.[33] To him differences in political and economic views in Africa were secondary to the immediate needs of the Congolese people. How to prevent African states from taking advantage of the Congo conflict to entrench their ideologies in the Congo and thus worsening the conflict was, therefore, one of the issues he addressed in formulating his policy.[34]

Summary

Nigeria, in formulating its first major foreign policy on a crisis that was more that three months older than its independence, followed the path of political realism in the choices it made in pursuit of its national interest. Sir Abubakar had a fairly accurate estimate of Nigeria's influence and how that influence could be wielded. There was neither misapprehension of his own influence nor exaggeration of Nigeria's status in world politics. Nigeria was a new and relatively weak nation, unwilling to forget its old friends. Its interests in the Congo conflict could be realized, in collaboration with other African states, through the United Nations. In making the choices, Sir Abubakar's government made effective use of its association with Britain. Although his government's policy had a pro-Western orientation, its stance was not in any appreciable fashion detrimental to Nigerian, Congolese, or larger African interests.

There is evidence that undue emphasis on moral and legal principles was placed on Nigeria's Congo decisions. There was an inherent danger in doing so. While such principles have their place in international affairs, morality and diplomacy seldom travel well together. In anarchic situations, law is itself frequently a function of power. Undue emphasis on moral and legal principles tends to constrain political action required by the imperatives of national interest. The saving grace in this instance for Nigeria was that it was a new and relatively weak nation. Accordingly, it selected a pragmatic policy. The support the policy received from the Nigerian legislature, which had not participated in its formulation, conferred on it a measure of legitimacy and widespread national acceptance.

The caution that characterized Nigeria's policy was tinged with irony. The Nigerian political elite spoke loudly of their country's position of leadership in Africa—an assumption other African states had not yet conceded. But, when that leadership was first put to the test the Nigerian prime minister chose a cautious rather than a bold approach. Why? Perhaps to accommodate Nigeria's competing cluster of interests; to ensure that its leadership was built on a firm foundation; and to avoid intimidation, to win thereby for Nigeria the confidence of its nervous smaller neighbors. But perhaps also because of the character and idiosyncrasies of the man, Sir Abubakar, the prime minister, who was unwilling to embark on an adventurous undertaking of uncertain outcome.

From these perspectives, and in view of the overall situation, Sir Abubakar's approach to the Congo crisis was both realistic and appropriate.

5

Avenues of Policy Implementation:
The United Nations

WHEN THE CONGO crisis erupted in 1960 there was no effective African regional organization to which the disputing parties could turn. Therefore, despite constant big-power rivalries in the United Nations, it was from the world organization that the government of the Democratic Republic of the Congo sought help. By the time sovereign Nigeria's Congo policy was formulated the United Nations was already in the Congo.

Developing nations have great faith in the United Nations.[1] It affords them opportunity to play their role in the international scene unhampered by "big stick diplomacy." It offers them, especially the new states of Africa, a meeting place for coordination of policies and diplomatic strategies on basic international issues. They prefer its multilateral aid, whether financial or technical, because it minimizes the danger of political strings that are often attached to aid from the major world powers individually. In the case of the Democratic Republic of the Congo, the United Nations was in the best position to meet the expenses involved and to provide the technical knowledge that would enable the Congolese to rebuild their country; this it could do without the republic's becoming a satellite of a major power, thereby losing its status, in practice, of a sovereign state.

Thus, the United Nations was the primary avenue Nigeria used to implement its policy on the Congo crisis. It declared this policy to the General Assembly on 7 October 1960. Following Nigeria's admission into the United Nations its representatives began to play an increasingly constructive role in every part of the organization that dealt with the crisis. In addition to the usual delegation that each member state accredits to the United Nations, Nigeria seconded some Nigerian officials specifically for service in the Congo. Consequently, Nigeria participated very effectively in the United Nations Advisory Committee on the Congo,[2] the secretary-general's "Congo Club,"[3] the General

Assembly debates on the Congo, the Congo Conciliation Commission, and the Fifth Committee dealing with the organization's administrative and budgetary questions. Nigeria also played an active role in the UN military and civilian operations as well as in discussions of the Security Council on the Congo situation, although its representatives did not vote in such discussions inasmuch as Nigeria was not then a member of the council. Discussion of Nigeria's specific role in each of the relevant branches of the UN operations in the Congo follows.

General Assembly debates on the Congo situation

The UN decision to accede to the request of the Congolese government to intervene in the crisis had already been made before Nigeria was admitted into the organization. But debates on the organization's intervention and its proper role in the crisis continued until 1963, and Nigeria's delegation effectively participated in all of them. One aspect of the Congo crisis before the General Assembly at the time of Nigeria's admission in October 1960 was the seating of the Congo delegation. The constitutional crisis had led to the dispatch of two delegations— the Kasavubu faction and the Lumumba faction—to the United Nations. Because of the obscurity of the new republic's constitutional and political position, the General Assembly referred the question of the representation of the Congo to the Credentials Committee. Meanwhile, some Afro-Asian states—notably Guinea, Ghana, the United Arab Republic, India, Ceylon (now Sri Lanka), Indonesia, and Mali— urged the seating of the Lumumba representatives pending the General Assembly's decision on the report of the Credentials Committee. There was much wrangling in the General Assembly on this issue.[4]

Ghana's representative moved an adjournment of the debate until the Conciliation Commission, which had been set up on 5 November 1960 and scheduled to proceed to the Congo, had returned and submitted its report. Nigeria's delegation supported the motion on the grounds that adjournment would prevent a hasty decision as well as obviate possible complications of the work of the Conciliation Commission. Nigeria's delegates insisted that the seating of either delegation would not resolve the Congo problem. The motion of Ghana's representative was adopted.

Later, however, Kasavubu visited the UN headquarters in New York to advocate recognition of his delegation. The adopted Ghana resolution was shelved as pro-Kasavubu forces within the United Nations succeeded in convincing the Credentials Committee to submit its report on the issue of which delegation to seat. When the committee recommended the seating of the Kasavubu delegation, the African member states and the entire UN membership were divided on the issue. One faction accepted the recommendation to seat the Kasavubu delegation, but another vehemently opposed it and advocated the seating of the Lumumba delegation.[5] Jaja Wachuku, leader of Nigeria's delegation, abstained from taking part in the debates and from voting on the recommendation on the grounds that his participation would prejudice his work as chairman of the Congo Conciliation Commission. He could not vote for one side without earning the suspicion, if not the ire, of the other. His country would not make the mistake of other African delegations by apportioning blame. He and the other delegates from Nigeria wisely did not take sides when such a great responsibility had been entrusted to their country's representative.[6]

The recommendation to seat the Kasavubu delegation was approved by fifty-three votes to thirty-two with fourteen abstentions. Wachuku himself avoided condemnation of the Kasavubu delegation, but its seating was condemned at home by Nigerian parliamentarians and in the publications of the major political parties, although they generally upheld the role of the Nigerian delegation.[7]

The seating of the Kasavubu delegation did not resolve the constitutional crisis in the Congo. The United Nations continued its efforts toward that objective and toward the reintegration into the Congo republic of Katanga and the other seceded fragments. Nigeria's delegation called for such efforts and urged that they should aim primarily at the needs of the Congolese people rather than at those of foreign economic forces. It supported all the Security Council resolutions on the crisis. When the General Assembly was called upon, because of cold war politics which were eroding the effectiveness of the Security Council, to assume an increasing role in the peacekeeping operations of the United Nations, the Nigerian delegation figured prominently in General Assembly resolutions to end the conflict.[8] It relentlessly urged the implementation of proposals it believed would achieve that objective. A number of these proposals reinforced those made by the Nigerian prime minister in his speech to the General Assembly. Others were offered in response to later developments in the Congo and to the attitudes of the UN membership to such developments.[9] Special emphasis was placed on restoring Congolese order and stability, reconvening the Parliament, and ending intervention by member states in Congolese domestic affairs. Member states were urged to channel all their aid and advice to the Congo through the United Nations and to eschew the practice of helping to liquidate certain persons who had genuine contributions to make toward reconstruction.

Nigeria's delegation incessantly appealed to the superpowers to submerge their ideological differences and to approach the Congo problem in a mature manner, in terms of Congolese interests not their own, and with an eye to the need of the new states of Africa for peace and security.[10] It deplored the African states' "dangerous split" into three factions, none of which was capable of playing an effective role in the Congo, and it urged them to recognize that "the Congo was a challenge." African members had a special responsibility to assist the United Nations in finding a solution to the problem of the Congo. To do so effectively, it was necessary, the delegation emphasized, that African states mobilize to avoid allowing themselves "to become robots or puppets pulled here and there by remote control."[11] Africans, Nigeria's delegates pleaded, could not afford to think in terms of the East or the West, because Africa is neither East nor West; rather, Africa is "in the middle." Because Africa is in the middle and because the Congo crisis was essentially an African problem, it was the responsibility of the African states to "find a middle way of solving the Congolese problem."[12]

The protracted crisis in the Congo had become a question of the survival of the United Nations itself. Infuriated by Secretary-General Hammarskjöld's rigid interpretation of the Security Council mandate on the Congo, the Soviet premier, Nikita Khrushchev, in a speech in the General Assembly on 23 September 1960, called upon him to resign and proposed a *troika* (three-man directorate) arrangement for administering the Secretariat. (These directors would, in effect, represent respectively the interests of the Western power bloc, the Eastern power bloc, and the developing nations.) This demand precipitated a constitutional crisis in the United Nations that occupied the attention of the General Assembly for a considerable length of time.

Nigeria opposed Khrushchev's demand. In clarifying his country's stand on the issue, Jaja Wachuku said:

> Since we support the United Nations in its entirety, we feel that the office of the Secretary-General is one of the major institutions of the United Nations. We find that any discussion about the resignation or nonresignation of the Secretary-General, at

this juncture in connexion with the operation in the Congo, is irrelevant.

Therefore, my delegation cannot support any suggestion that the Secretary-General should resign his post now. His resignation or non-resignation will not add to or subtract from any attempt to solve the Congolese problem. If there is any desire for a change, it should be achieved either by amendment of the Charter or by some other means that may be devised by the General Assembly. I would certainly like this particular subject to be withdrawn from any discussion involving the Congolese problem, so that we may be able to think objectively and view the problem in its proper perspective.[13]

Although his delegation did not believe the position of the secretary-general was any part of the Congo problem, Jaja Wachuku continued, it believed and demanded that the adviser to the secretary-general on African affairs should be an African.

Wachuku used the occasion to offer an additional suggestion. In the light of his own Conciliation Commission experience in the Congo, Wachuku implored the secretary-general to ensure that the person who represented him in an African situation would be one who could appreciate the difficulties and yearnings of the people. Only a representative sensitive to the circumstances of the people could effectively assist them in addressing their needs.[14] This suggestion was a subtle attack on Ambassador Dayal of India and his predecessors, who had been severely criticized by the Congolese people.

In addition to these proposals the Nigerian delegation sponsored a seventeen-power draft resolution. Among its six major proposals the resolution called upon the General Assembly "to appoint a Commission of Conciliation of seven members to be designated by the President of the General Assembly to assist the Congolese leaders to achieve reconciliation and to end the political crisis."[15] The Nigerian delegation explained that the proposed commission would increase UN effectiveness in the Congo since it would be composed of a select group who would dedicate themselves to assisting and not bullying the Congolese people. The delegation believed that representatives of African states should predominate in the commission not only because the Congo crisis was essentially an African problem but also because Africans had a better grasp of the circumstances than had non-Africans.[16] The draft resolution was adopted, but no second Conciliation Commission for the Congo was appointed. The rationale for the proposed commission was faulty; the crisis was now more than an African problem. Because of their colonial experience, Africans were still, in large measure, strangers to one another.

In other General Assembly proceedings the Nigerian delegation took a strong stand against the secession of Katanga, arguing that the end of the secession was one of the sine qua non conditions for a viable and stable Congo republic. It rejected the argument that it was appropriate to apply the principle of self-determination to Katanga. On this issue Jaja Wachuku repeated before the General Assembly his reply to an American group that had asked him about self-determination in regard to Katanga:

> How would you as an American like it if the state of New York or the state of California were to be cut off from the U.S. because the people wanted self-determination? You want the most economically developed area of the State to be dismembered . . . and then you expect the Congo to survive economically. If you will not agree that the state of New York should be taken out and created as an independent entity, and if you will not allow the state of California to be taken out of the U.S., then you should understand how the Congolese feel. You may call it a province, you may call it a state, but it is [the] same thing.[17]

Jaja Wachuku further claimed that because of economic investment some members of the United Nations favored the dismemberment of the Congo and had armed the provincial government of Katanga to achieve this objective.[18] To meet the legitimate needs of all Congolese people, which he asserted were paramount, his country believed that the Congo could be organized as a federal state with strong powers for the central legislature and central government. This, he affirmed, was possible since the Congolese constitution had already provided a quasi-federal structure.[19] On this basis the Nigerian delegation deplored the decision of Congolese leaders at the Tananarive summit conference to establish a confederation of Congolese states. It gave wholehearted support to Prime Minister Cyrille Adoula's Congolese central government of national reconciliation, which advocated federalism.

Regarding the activities of the United Nations in the Congo, the Nigerian delegation lost no time in expressing its dissatisfaction before the General Assembly. It criticized the Secretariat for its narrow and rigid interpretation of the Security Council mandate on the Congo. That interpretation, it asserted, had confused and prolonged the crisis. It deplored the manner in which the secretary-general had met and reached agreement with Tshombe, a provincial president, concerning the manner of the entry of UN troops into Katanga, without consulting the Congolese central government.[20] It condemned the way in which the United Nations had been "the eyewitness of an unceasing succession of disasters plunging the Congo and Africa into greater and greater misery."[21] This, said the delegation, was the result of the machinations of the permanent members of the Security Council, who had pursued their selfish interests and were detrimental to UN efforts to resolve the Congo conflict. It believed that history would judge those members for doing so.[22]

Obviously Nigeria's arguments before the General Assembly were expressed in idealistic and moralistic terms; they betrayed innocence and a certain degree of naïveté on the part of the delegation. Perhaps this tone was inevitable since Nigeria could not exercise enough power to exert sufficient influence for the realization of its objectives in the Congo conflict. Again, the appeals of the Nigerian delegation to the major powers to approach the problem solely in terms of Congolese interests and the needs of Africa definitely ignored the basic determinant of any foreign policy: national interest. It was unrealistic to expect the powers to overlook their own national interests in the conflict. However, despite the error in judgment, the outspoken manner in which the delegation conducted itself in various UN activities relative to the Congo crisis was consistent with Nigeria's objectives in the conflict.

The UN Conciliation Commission for the Congo

The Congo Advisory Committee, in consultation with the secretary-general, created a Congo Conciliation Commission comprising fifteen Afro-Asian states on 5 November 1960. The establishment of the commission was in accordance with the provisions of paragraph 3 of an earlier (20 September 1960) General Assembly resolution, 1474 (ES-IV). But the proposal on 7 October 1960 by Nigeria's prime minister, Sir Abubakar, that the United Nations should send a fact-finding commission to the Congo provided the immediate impetus for its creation. The commission was mandated to conduct a comprehensive study of the Congo situation to help the Congolese people solve the problems that had hampered their unity and territorial and political independence.[23]

The commission held its first meeting on 17 November 1960 in New York and elected Jaja Wachuku chairman. The next meeting, scheduled to be held in Léopoldville in November, was postponed because of complaints concerning the establishment of the commission and its proposed dispatch by President Kasavubu. Kasavubu stated (just as Nigeria's delegation had reasoned during the General Assembly debates on the seating of the rival Congolese delegations) that the Congolese people would not believe that the commission, drawn from representatives of governments that had publicly taken a stand on the domestic problems of the Congo republic, could play any effective conciliatory role in the situation. Moreover, he insisted that the dispatch of the commission with such a mandate would constitute a dangerous precedent. Kasavubu's fears were allayed after Ambassador Dayal, special representative of the secretary-general in Léopoldville, had assured him that the commission would "undertake its task in close collaboration with the lawful institutions of the Congo without any derogation of their authority and without attempting to impose any solution."[24] So the stage was set and the commission began its work early in January 1961 under the chairmanship of Nigeria's Jaja Wachuku.

Nigerians were elated that within two months of their independence their country was associated so conspicuously with the work of the Conciliation Commission as part of UN efforts to restore stability, law, and order to the Congo.[25] Political observers in New York and elsewhere predicted that by the appointment of Jaja Wachuku as chairman of the commission, Nigeria's influence and role as peacemaker in the Congo would assume greater proportions. Wachuku's experience as a parliamentarian of some ten years' standing, as a man of letters, and as a distinguished barrister were important assets in his work in the Congo. Commenting on his fitness for the chairmanship, the *London Times* said that Wachuku's interest in and understanding of international affairs was vast; that he was neither a moderate nor an extremist but a reasoned assessor of facts having a way of collecting relevant information unobtrusively. The paper held that the rich understanding of human nature, the transparent honesty of purpose, and the impartiality and good sense he had displayed when he served as the first Nigerian Speaker of the Nigerian federal House of Representatives were qualities that would help ensure the success of his Congo assignment.[26]

Since Nigeria had a federal form of government, Jaja Wachuku's conspicuous connection with the Conciliation Commission was very apropos. He had contributed to the formulation of his government's constructive policy on the Congo. When Speaker of the Nigerian federal House of Representatives, he had consulted with the prime minister regarding Nigeria's foreign affairs before Sir Abubakar's 20 August 1960 declaration of the broad aims and objectives of the federal government's conduct of Nigeria's external relations. Wachuku was among the Nigerian leaders who advocated a functional approach toward an eventual United States of Africa: a union in which every African state would contribute culturally and economically toward the dignity of the African and world peace. He had been present at the UN General Assembly when the Nigerian prime minister suggested a UN fact-finding commission for the Congo. Naturally, these experiences influenced his role and effectiveness on the Conciliation Commission.

In addition, there were other considerations that strengthened Wachuku's resolve to play a very effective role in the conciliation mission. He was appalled that the black race was not recognized as the equal of others. Developments in the Congo, he regretted, had cast aspersions on the grudging recognition that had been bestowed on the independence of African states by non-African states. Wachuku was above all distressed that Africa was divided on the Congo issues on purely foreign ideological grounds. He believed there was much to be learned from the superpowers; but for the continent to be divided, on an issue that touched the heart of Africa, solely on such outside-interest grounds was a disservice to Africa. Jaja Wachuku was therefore determined to do his best to bring about the reconciliation of the Congolese leaders and the establishment of a stable government. Doing so would, among other results, thwart foreign intervention, which he believed was copious and had worsened the Congo conflict.[27]

Before departing for the Congo on the conciliation mission Wachuku said to a press conference in Lagos:

> To us in Nigeria, a stable Congo is an absolute necessity, not only for strategic reasons but also in the interest of emerging Africa. The Congo Republic is greater in area than Nigeria, therefore the influence of a stable Congo added to that of Nigeria, Ghana, and other African States, is bound to produce a decisive pressure on affairs in South, East, Central and North Africa and to mould world opinion in general.[28]

Any solution prescribed for the confused situation in the Congo, Wachuku went on, should provide for the unity and stability of the republic. Anything contrary to that would also be contrary to the interests of both the Congo and all of Africa. The commission, he indicated, regarded its guiding principle to be to work toward the peace, unity, and stability of the Congo. If the Congolese people accepted a federation, the commission would recommend it, provided it would implement the achievement of peace, unity, and stability for their country.[29]

Upon its arrival in the Congo, the commission consulted with Ambassador Dayal, special representative of the secretary-general, and with the other principal officers of the UN operation. It studied the Loi fondamentale to aid in diagnosis of the constitutional crisis and to have a frame of reference for suggestions to the Congolese leaders regarding the solution of their constitutional crisis, among other problems. Thereafter, the commission met with the Congolese chief of state and the presidents of the central and provincial institutions established at Léopoldville. It then toured the provinces, meeting the largest possible number of Congolese political leaders and carefully recording their views. However, repeated efforts to see Patrice Lumumba and a number of other Congolese political prisoners proved futile.

The death of Lumumba was officially announced (13 February 1961) while the commission was still carrying out its inquiries. The commission strongly condemned his murder, which had compromised its mission, and called for an impartial trial and the punishment of all persons responsible for his death. A message from Jaja Wachuku to the UN Advisory Committee on the Congo on this occasion reads:

> The Conciliation Commission has been deeply shocked by the tragic and untimely death of Patrice Lumumba and his two colleagues. It strongly condemns the evil practice of resorting to violent means to eliminate political opponents as a denial of the most elementary human rights. The unfortunate event may well compromise the chance of a peaceful solution of the Congolese crisis. The Commission trusts that those responsible for this heinous crime will be impartially tried and punished.[30]

The commission held its last meeting in the Congo on 20 February 1961, then proceeded to Geneva where it drafted its report.[31]

In explaining his personal observations during this mission Jaja Wachuku cited Cyrille Adoula as the one Congolese leader he found to be sincerely interested in the Congolese people rather than in factions or in the ideological struggle between the power blocs. Most of the other self-proclaimed Congolese leaders, he said, merely gave lip service to their countrymen's interests and were more interested in themselves than in the welfare of the people. They had yielded to foreign counsels, an action which, he held, made the crisis more confusing. During the mission Wachuku had strongly advised Mobutu's young commissioners to return to the university to prepare themselves to better serve their homeland; he pointed out that there was no provision for them as commissioners under the Loi fondamentale. Jaja Wachuku also reiterated a suggestion he had earlier made to Kasavubu, in New York in 1960, that the Congolese government should be very wary in accepting foreign aid not channeled through the United Nations.

Meanwhile the completed and approved report of the commission was submitted to the Advisory Committee, which formally transmitted it to the General Assembly on 20 March 1961. The report related the views of the Congolese political leaders and their supporters and made general comments on the causes of the crisis and on the Loi fondamentale. Among others it made the following recommendations: broaden the base of Joseph Ileo's "provisional government" in order to make it a government of national unity;[32] reorganize the Congolese National Army and insulate it from politics; reconvene the Congolese Parliament under UN protection; release political prisoners; call an immediate halt to the military operations in Katanga (and to others which were likely to be launched elsewhere) in order to avert the dangers of civil war; amend or replace the Loi fondamentale, which the commission believed was incomplete and ill-adapted to the needs of the Congo, by a new constitution (but until that was done, all concerned in the Congo "should uphold the Loi fondamentale as the basic law of the Republic"); extend UN technical assistance in the form of a team of experts who could cooperate with the Congolese authorities in their endeavor to return to legality and constitutionality in the revision of the Loi fondamentale or in the drafting of a new constitution and in the administration of justice; adopt a federal form of government, which the commission believed was the only one that could preserve the national unity and territorial integrity of the Congo; withdraw foreign nationals not under UN command and strictly enforce Security Council and General Assembly resolutions regarding channeling of all aid to the Congo through the United Nations.[33] A text of the Congolese constitution and other documents from Congolese leaders were appended to the report to enable the General Assembly and all others concerned to understand and properly evaluate the Congo conflict.

Chairman Jaja Wachuku signed the report with some notes and reservations.[34] The notes dealt with the legality of President Kasavubu's dismissal of Lumumba from his premiership; the constitutionality of Kasavubu's lengthy suspension of Parliament; and the legality of Antoine Gizenga's claim to represent the legal government of the Congolese republic before and after the death of Lumumba. The notes explained that these issues involved constitutional and legal interpretations on which the commission, because of its mandated terms of reference, could express no opinion. His reservations referred to paragraphs 20, 30, 35, 44, 59, 62, 64, 65, 73, 108, and 126 of the commission's report.[35]

The work of the commission was neither a complete success nor a total failure. Because of the intransigent attitude of some of the Congolese leaders, the commission's attempts to reconcile the various opposing factions did not lead to any immediate positive results. Lumumba, one of the parties to the dispute and the man who had invited the United Nations into the Congo, was cruelly murdered while the commission was in the Congo. The commission's study of the views of most of the Congolese leaders led to important conclusions, however, which the United Nations used as the basis for subsequent Congo conciliation efforts. The summit conference of Congolese leaders at Tananarive, the reconvening of the Congolese Parliament under UN protection, the dispatch of UN legal experts to the Congo to help draft a new constitution, and the adoption of a federal constitution were eventual products of the commission's efforts.[36]

Nigerians seconded to the United Nations for service in the Congo

Three Nigerians, T. A. B. Oki, Francis Nwokedi, and Dr. T. O. Elias, in addition to Godfrey Amachree, Queen's Counsel and former solicitor-general of Nigeria who served as under-secretary in charge of UN civilian operations in the Congo, were seconded by the Nigerian government to the United Nations for service in the Congo. Oki, senior crown counsel in the Ministry of Justice, was assigned to the Congo, where he helped the Congolese deal with the problems of legislation in 1961–62.

Reference has already been made to Francis Nwokedi's participation in the secretary-general's Congo Club. Prior to this, in 1960, Nwokedi, then permanent secretary to the Federal Ministry of Labour, had been seconded to the UN administration staff in the Congo to help the country deal with its labor problems.[37] He had cooperated with other public administration experts, part of the UN Operations in the Congo team, in assisting Congolese authorities to establish a department responsible for the civil service and charged with defining the jurisdiction of other departments in accordance with constitutional requirements and the demands of efficient operation.[38] Nwokedi later served as executive assistant to the secretary-general's special representative in the Congo, Ambassador Rajeshwar Dayal of India. He had also been a member of the three-man commission that studied the situation in Kamina base before the United Nations took over the base from Belgium as recommended by the commission.

Throughout the UN peace efforts in the Congo, Secretary-General Hammarskjöld and his successor, U Thant, used envoys to implement Security Council and General Assembly resolutions and recommendations and in efforts to bring about rapport between the United Nations and Congolese authorities. Following the Security Council resolution of 21 February 1961, the relationship between the United Nations Operations in the Congo and Congolese central authorities became increasingly strained. The Congolese authorities claimed that the resolution (operative paragraphs 1 and 2 of part A and operative paragraph 2 of part B, in particular) constituted a flagrant infringement of the Congo's sovereignty.[39] The pertinent paragraphs had urged that the United Nations should "take immediately all appropriate measures to prevent the occurrence of civil war in the Congo, including arrangements for cease-fires, the halting of all military operations, the prevention of clashes, and the use of force, if necessary, in the last resort"; that "measures be taken for the immediate withdrawal and evacuation from the Congo of all Belgian and other military personnel and political advisers not under the United Nations Command and mercenaries"; and that "Congolese armed units and personnel should be re-organized and brought under discipline and control, and arrangements be made on impartial and equitable bases to that end and with a view to the elimination of any possibility of interference by such units and personnel in the political life of the Congo."[40]

The Léopoldville authorities resented these provisions and indignantly vowed that the Congolese people would never permit implementation of them. They called upon the Congolese people "in their

regional diversity and with their sense of common Congolese nationality to stand ready at all times to carry out any measures for the defense of Congolese sovereignty which may be decreed by the Government of the Republic of the Congo," against any attempts by the
United Nations to implement the hated provisions of the resolution.[41]
To calm their apprehensions the secretary-general dispatched Nigeria's
Francis Nwokedi and Robert A. Gardiner of Ghana to Léopoldville in
the third week of March 1961.[42] The two UN envoys assured Kasavubu
and his political associates that the sovereignty of the Congo would be
respected with regard to the reorganization of the Congolese National
Army and the elimination from the Congo of foreign military and paramilitary personnel and political advisers not under the UN command.
They proposed the creation of two joint UN-Congo commissions to undertake these tasks, but the Léopoldville authorities rejected the proposal. They wanted instead a plan whereby the reorganization of the
army would remain under the authority of the Congolese central government, with some UN cooperation, and whereby a national defense
council under the Congolese president would recruit military advisers
through the United Nations.[43]

Nwokedi and his colleague reached a compromise with Kasavubu
and Justin Bomboko on 17 April 1961. The Léopoldville authorities
agreed on the implementation of the 21 February Security Council resolution, in particular the provision for the removal of deleterious foreign influences from the Congo, with the proviso that the UN Operations in the Congo would not expel foreign military advisers that had
been recruited by the central government. It was also agreed to organize the army on the basis of Kasavubu's proposals.[44]

Nwokedi also participated in the UN conciliatory negotiations with
the various Congolese factions in efforts to restore a legal central Congolese government. Following the Coquilhatville summit conference
of Congolese leaders (April–May 1961), which had agreed on a feder-
ally organized state, President Kasavubu announced his intention to
reconvene the Congolese Parliament in Léopoldville. Antoine Gizenga, who still claimed to be the head of the legal government, countered by announcing that the Congolese government would meet at Kamina under UN protection. His threat was real not only because he
controlled enough Parliamentary seats to deny Kasavubu a quorum but
also because he was supported by a number of Afro-Asian states, the
Soviet Union, Albania, Czechoslovakia, and Poland. At this stage the
United Nations, committed to the establishment of a legal government

in the Congo, intervened to bring about a rapprochement between the principal factions. Nwokedi and Gardiner were again assigned to undertake this task. After strenuous efforts they succeeded in arranging a meeting of the delegations from Léopoldville and Stanleyville (the seat of Gizenga's government) on 13 June 1961 at the Léopoldville headquarters of the UN Operations in the Congo. The two delegations reached an agreement on 19 June: The Congolese Parliament would meet at the University of Lovanium, Léopoldville, and all members of Parliament and its administrative personnel would be housed in Lovanium during the session. They were to have no contact with the outside world. The two delegations requested, among other things, that the United Nations provide free passage for the members of Parliament and invite all other political factions to subscribe to the agreement.[45]

To effect the last aspect of the request the United Nations delegated Nwokedi and Dr. Conor Cruise O'Brien to meet with Tshombe in Katanga to urge him to take part, under UN safe conduct, in a summit conference of Congolese leaders at Léopoldville to prepare the way for a Parliament in which Léopoldville, Stanleyville, and Elizabethville would all be represented. Tshombe formally agreed to participate but insisted on a change of venue to Brazzaville or Tananarive. The two envoys took great pains to convince Tshombe of the difficulty they would encounter in seeking to persuade the Léopoldville and Stanleyville authorities to agree to a summit meeting outside the Congo. Tshombe then suggested Kamina, and the envoys agreed to recommend his choice to the other authorities. But before they could complete this task Tshombe reneged and insisted on the independence of Katanga.[46]

Tshombe's intransigence did not prevent the Parliament from convening, however. It met, as agreed upon by the Léopoldville and Stanleyville authorities, on 16 July 1961. From this meeting Adoula's government of national unity and political reconciliation emerged, on 2 August 1961. With Parliament's endorsement of this government the consitutional crisis was ended, thanks in large part to the efforts of the UN envoys, including Nwokedi of Nigeria.

Congo constitutional reviews

The drawing up of a new constitution acceptable to all factions of the Congo republic was one of the priorities of Adoula's government of national reconciliation. The Loi fondamentale, under which the Congo became indepedent, had been criticized as ill-adapted to the country's needs and had been regarded by many within and outside the Congo as responsible for the constitutional crisis in the republic. The UN Conciliation Commission for the Congo had recommended its amendment or replacement and had also suggested UN technical assistance in such a revision or in the drafting of a new constitution. Adoula's government, seeking to carry out these recommendations, reiterated an earlier request to the United Nations (made in June 1961) by the Congolese foreign minister, Justin Bomboko, for three legal experts to help the Léopoldville government draft a new constituion. Accordingly, such experts were selected from Nigeria, Italy, and Switzerland.

This request provided the occasion for Dr. T. O. Elias, then Nigeria's attorney general and minister of justice, to serve in the Congo. A scholar with considerable experience in constitutional law, Dr. Elias shared the belief of Nigeria's federal cabinet that a federal system of government would best suit the political and economic needs of the Congo republic. He believed that Nigeria's experience, particularly with regard to revenue allocation under a federal system of government, could be of great help to the Congolese leaders. Upon their arrival in the Congo, his colleagues—Professors Rowland Quadri of Italy and W. Geiger of Switzerland—elected Dr. Elias chairman of the group.

The constitutional draftsmen were from the very beginning of their work in the Congo faced with a problem. There was no Congolese with whom they could discuss in depth the constitutional problems of the country. Only the minister of justice in Mobutu's College of Commissioners, Marcel Lihau, who had some training in law, provided help. The experts thus found it difficult to fulfill their assignment. They held extensive consultations with Kasavubu, Adoula, and Mobutu to determine their views and the form of government they preferred. They also interviewed a number of other Congolese, particularly those who had earlier met at Coquilhatville and had agreed on the adoption of a federal constitution for the Congo. They made a close study of the Loi fondamentale, then produced a federal constitution based on it and on the wishes of the Congolese leaders as ascertained during the interviews and discussions. In formulating the constitution the experts also took into account the French culture (particularly the language and legal system), under which the Congo had been ruled by Belgium, and the country's heterogeneous population.[47]

The draft constitution, among its other provisions, recommended the retention of the six original Congolese provinces, two houses of Legislature—a Senate and a Chamber of Deputies—and the establishment of a constitutional court based on a continental European model. The court was to be composed mostly of politicians who would have sole responsibility for review of political problems. The experts completed their assignment in October 1961 and deposited copies of the draft constitution with the Congolese central government and at the headquarters of the UN Operations in the Congo for transmission to the secretary-general.

This 1961 draft constitution did not meet the approval of all sections of the Congolese republic. Some Congolese desired a unitary or quasi-unitary state; others talked of a federation comprising twenty-six provinces based on ethnic divisions. Tshombe and his Katanga associates who insisted on greater local autonomy still posed the greatest problem. This was the general situation when in July 1962 Adoula formally proposed a new federal constitution for the Congo which many hoped would meet the constitutional needs of the republic as well as Tshombe's demands.

The proposed constitution provided that each province would control its local administration, make its own economic arrangements, and maintain law and order within its boundaries. To the federal government was assigned the responsibility for external affairs, defense, customs and excise taxes, foreign trade, immigration, and communications. The proposed constitution also required that the lower House of Parliament would be elected according to population and that the states would be equally represented in the upper House.[48] Adoula's proposals met the approval of Tshombe, who welcomed them as "what we have always wanted."[49] However, Tshombe added that Adoula should demonstrate his sincerity by inviting the provincial governments and assemblies to offer their advisory opinions in the final drafting of the proposed constitution.

As it had done previously, Adoula's government requested the United Nations to send a team of constitutional experts to draw up the proposed constitution.[50] The secretary-general acceded to the request and offered the services of four jurists from Nigeria, India, Canada, and Switzerland. To this panel the United Nations had nominated Chief H. O. Davies of Nigeria without prior consultation with Nigeria's federal government, which regarded the nomination as a breach of protocol and as a slight to Nigeria's sovereignty.[51] It protested very

strongly to the UN Secretariat and asked the secretary-general to suspend the nomination until the United Nations had made formal application to the Nigerian federal government for the release of an internationally recognized Nigerian jurist. The secretary-general sent a
formal apology and then forwarded an official request as directed. The
federal government thereupon nominated its choice, Dr. T. O. Elias,
who had helped to prepare the 1961 draft constitution for the Congo.

This action caused some furor in Nigeria. Chief Davies protested,
arguing that the offer of Dr. Elias in his place meant not only that the
Nigerian federal government expected to be consulted in such matters
but also that it had assumed the right of choice. This stand, in his view,
was "rather objectionable" and suggested "undue control by the Government of individuals and infringement of their fundamental human
rights."[52] The Congo assignment, he said, was offered to him on his
personal merit. "It will be a sorry day for Nigeria," he charged, "when
the individual who has attained professional or technical eminence
cannot be invited outside Nigeria to render assistance without the interference of the Government."[53] Chief Davies's arguments notwithstanding, the federal government preferred Dr. Elias to serve on the
panel for a number of reasons. The Congolese government had been so
satisfied with his previous work for them that it had written a glowing
letter of thanks to the Nigerian federal government. Since the federal
government attached particular importance to the issue of stability in
the Congo, Dr. Elias's familiarity with this policy and his previous experience in the Congo were considered desirable elements. Dr. Elias
had also assisted at the Nigerian constitutional conferences and had
helped to draft the constitution that he was then helping to implement
as attorney general and minister of justice. It was proper, the Nigerian
federal government believed, that he should be the one to undertake
the assignment.[54] But above all the federal government considered
Chief Davies a radical. Not unmindful of opinions expressed by Davies's Nigerian associates in preference for a unitary government for
the Congo,[55] Nigerian authorities believed that Nigeria's own objectives in the Congo would not be achieved by persons with such views.
Dr. Elias's nomination was approved by both the UN Secretariat and
the Adoula government.

On 20 August 1962, shortly after Adoula's request for constitutional experts had been approved and fulfilled, Acting Secretary-General U Thant announced a Plan of National Reconciliation for the
Congo, which included the following major provisions.

First, the national government, after consultations with the provincial governments and interested political groups, would present a draft federal constitution to the Parliament in September 1962. The United Nations would provide legal experts to assist in drafting the document. Under the proposed federal constitution certain powers were to be reserved exclusively to the national government. Such powers were to include control of foreign affairs, national defense (other than local police functions), customs, fiscal policy, interstate and foreign commerce, taxes, nationality and immigration, and postal and telecommunications. All diplomatic or consular representatives or missions abroad that were not subject to the authority of the central government were, accordingly, to be withdrawn. Provincial administration and powers not delegated to national government were to be reserved to the provincial governments.

Second, the national government, again after consultation with the provincial governments and interested political groups, would present to the Parliament a new law to establish definitive arrangements for divisions of revenues between the national and provincial governments and regulations and procedures for the use of foreign exchange. United Nations experts were also to assist in the preparation of that law. Until that process was completed the national government and Katanga were to agree to share revenues, duties, and royalties equally, and all foreign exchange earned by any part of the Congo was to be paid to the Monetary Council of the national government or any other agreed-upon institution.

Third, the national government would ask the International Monetary Fund to help with a plan for national currency unification, which would be implemented within the shortest possible time.

Fourth, rapid integration and unification of all military, paramilitary, and gendarmerie units was to be accomplished.

Fifth, there was to be a proclamation of general amnesty.

Sixth, all Congolese authorities—national, state, and local—were to cooperate fully in carrying out UN resolutions.

Seventh, the central government was to be reconstituted to provide a suitable representation for all political and provincial agencies.[56]

As the provisions indicate, the constitution that the legal experts were to draft formed part of the arsenal of the UN Plan of National Reconciliation for the Congolese Republic. Prime Minister Adoula accepted the plan but reserved his "freedom of action in the event that the Plan, although acceptable in substance, proved to be deficient in its application." [57] Tshombe enthusiastically hailed the UN proposals as offering "the basis of an acceptable settlement" and said that he and the Katanga authorities "adhered whole-heartedly to the Plan as a whole, particularly that part of it concerning a federal constitution." [58] There was thus a discernible feeling for a reconciliation of constitutional, if not political, views among the Congolese when the jurists arrived in the Congo. The experts had sufficient guidelines on which to base their work: the Loi fondamentale; the 1961 draft constitution; Adoula's proposals for a federal constitution; laws promulgated in August by President Kasavubu converting the five provinces under the control of the Léopoldville government into sixteen new provinces along ethnic lines; and the U Thant Plan of National Reconciliation for the Congo. In addition the experts had consulted with all relevant Congolese authorities to further ascertain their views and wishes.

In expressing their views on the drafting of the constitution, Tshombe and the Katanga authorities reiterated their basic beliefs that the only form of federalism suitable to the Congo was that of a fully decentralized federation. They held that the only powers that might be vested in the federal authority were those listed in the secretary-general's Plan of National Reconciliation; thus there could be no question of adding any other powers, in particular those called concurrent powers. They believed that all powers other than those expressly enumerated in the plan belonged, by right, to the component parts of the federation.

The legal experts warned against the dangers of dividing the Congo into provinces along ethnic divisions according to the laws promulgated by President Kasavubu. Dr. Elias pointed to the Nigerian experience. Nigeria, he said, was having problems even though its political divisions were not based on lines of ethnic origins. He also pointed out the Congo's acute shortage of personnel. The lack of personnel to man the provincial assemblies, he went on, militated against the division of the Congo into too many provinces. The experts therefore urged the Congolese leaders to subdivide the six original provinces into no more than twelve. [59] The Congolese, however, rejected the suggestion and created twenty-one provinces. (In 1966 Mobutu reduced the number of provinces to twelve and proved the efficacy of the recommendation of the constitutional experts.)

The jurists also paid particular attention to the need for unity and harmony between Katanga and the central government. The problem of Union Minière was recognized as a real one, and Tshombe's attitude was also considered crucial to the work of the panel. These last two considerations were reflected in the provision of the Thant Plan that required the central government to discuss matters of mutual interest with the mining company and in the elaborate system of revenue allocation worked out for the Congolese by the experts.

With regard to the views of Tshombe and the Katanga authorities on the allocation of powers, the experts pointed out that the Plan of National Reconciliation had mentioned only those powers that were of crucial importance. In addition to those, there were in every federation powers which, though less important, could be exercised only by the federal authorities, such as matters of nationality; the federal civil service; the constitutional court and the federal courts and tribunals; and international and interprovincial communications. As for concurrent powers, to which the Katanga authorities had raised strong objections, the experts explained that their existence was recognized, either explicitly or implicitly, in all federations.

Finally, the experts, having paid due attention to all opinions expressed by all relevant Congolese authorities and to the UN Plan of National Reconciliation for the Congo, produced a draft federal constitution which was as decentralized as possible without endangering the national unity of the Congo. They also formulated an elaborate system of revenue allocation and a revised judicial system. The revision of the judicial system involved reorganizing Congolese courts by combining the best elements of a continental European system of administration of justice with the Anglo-Saxon system as practiced in Nigeria, India, and Canada.

Their work finished, members of the constitutional panel asked Dr. Elias to compose an explanatory memorandum to accompany the draft constitution, to describe the document in clear language for the layman. The draft federal constitution together with the explanatory memorandum was submitted on 27 September 1962 to Adoula, who transmitted it to the bureaus of the two chambers of Parliament on 13 October 1962. A copy was also submitted to a conference of provincial presidents (boycotted by Tshombe) held at Léopoldville (16–23 October 1962).

Dr. Elias's active participation in drafting the federal constitution demonstrated again Nigeria's eagerness to help the Congolese, under the auspices of the United Nations, solve their problems. As in the case of Francis Nwokedi, Dr. Elias's presence in the Congo created a feeling of personal trust among the Congolese leaders with whom he dealt.

The Royal Nigerian Army with the UN Operations
in the Congo

As Nigeria participated very effectively in the UN civilian operations in the Congo, so did its troops play a distinguished role in the military operations in that strife-torn republic. Before its independence Nigeria had placed an airport at Kano at the disposal of the United Nations in order to assist in the transport of troops and matériel to the Congo. Two platoons of the Fifth Battalion of the Royal Nigerian Army aided the UN troops during their stopover at Kano. Food was provided by the Kano Canning Company, and arrangements for the accommodation of the UN soldiers were made by the Nigerian Army detachment in Kano.

In keeping with his policy that international assistance to the Congo should first be given by its sister African states as an act of their solidarity, Secretary-General Hammarskjöld approached Nigeria's prime minister, about a month before Nigeria's independence, for a contribution of troops to the UN force in the Congo.[60] The prime minister, cognizant of the position of his country and its peoples' aspirations in Africa, acceded to the request. Nigeria was eager to undertake an international commitment for which its armed forces had earlier been enlarged and modernized.[61]

On learning that Nigeria would contribute to the UN force in the Congo, the *West African Pilot* expressed a view shared by the Nigerian political elite. The newspaper said it was a proud assignment for Nigeria's manpower and financial resources to be made available to aid an African state in need. "But," asked the daily, "whom are we to aid? Must it be the UN which is weak and lifeless? Are we to go to the aid of Lumumba whose present whereabouts are not clearly known? Or should it be Ileo and his master Kasavubu? Or Moise Tshombe, or Congolese Army Chiefs Lundula, Mobutu and many political upstarts which the Congo crisis has produced."[62] The people, the newspaper concluded, should be assured as to which of the Congo governments their nation would be aiding. This was the forerunner of the criticisms that Nigerian parliamentarians of all political shades, the leading Nigerian dailies, and university students came to make of both the United Nations and the Nigerian federal government with regard to the use of Nigerian troops in the Congo.

While no Nigerian questioned the propriety of sending Nigerian troops to help an afflicted sister African state, Chief O. A. Fagbenro-Beyioku, an Action Group senator, warned against the use of Nigeria's

army in the Congo "without the authority of Parliament."[63] In a letter
to the prime minister, the senator said that while he was in complete
agreement that Nigeria should play a leading role in the restoration of
law and order in the Congo he believed that sending Nigerian troops
for action in any foreign country after "our independence" was a matter of vital importance that should be authorized only by Parliament.
Other Action Group politicians expressed similar protests, arguing that
the Parliament as the constitutionally supreme authority of the land
ought to be given an opportunity to debate the call for troops.[64] Although the prime minister ignored these demands they indicated that
his foreign policy choices would be under parliamentary control and
scrutiny. Eventually the federal legislature was given the opportunity
the parliamentarians had demanded, but only after Nigerian troops
were already in the Congo. Events had been moving so fast that on the
same day Nigeria was admitted to the United Nations, the secretary-
general announced that Nigeria had promised to provide a battalion for
the UN forces in the Congo. Nigeria thus became the fourteenth country to provide troops for the force.[65]

Before the departure of the Nigerian contingent, B. C. Okwu,
Eastern Nigeria minister of information, asked the prime minister to
ensure that the Nigerian troops were kept out of international politics.
In a release issued at Enugu, Okwu suggested that the army officers
should be given definite and "clear-cut instructions to resist any attempt by either Eastern or the Western bloc to use our troops to further
its cold war ambitions and interests in the Congo."[66] This was not a
misplaced fear because, among other things, the major cold war com-
batants, although they contributed neither troops nor administrative
personnel to the military operations in the Congo, had subtle ways of
manipulating events and individuals through intelligence networks and
bribery.[67]

Adding to Okwu's words of admonition to the troops, the *West African Pilot* urged them to adhere to the rules of strict impartiality in
their Congo mission. Nigeria, the newspaper said, was not at war with
any of the factions in the Congo. The country's role was instead that of
a peacemaker who, in a fight where swords were drawn, would never
brandish his own "matchet" and gun in the face of either of the warring factions.[68] The Nigerian prime minister added a few words of advice when, on the eve of the soldiers' departure to the Congo, he told
them that they were going to the Congo as soldiers, "nothing less,
nothing more." Their duty, he said, was to listen and to obey the UN

Table 5.1 Nigerian UN troops: chief areas of deployment in the Congo

Military units	Provinces where deployed	Period of service	
		First tour	Second tour
First Battalion	Kasai and Léopoldville	Nov. 1961–May 1962	Nov. 1963–June 1964
Second Battalion	Kivu, Kasai, and Léopoldville	May 1961–Nov. 1961	Nov. 1962–May 1963
Third Battalion	Kasai, Katanga, and Léopoldville	June 1961–Jan. 1962	Sept. 1962–May 1963
Fourth Battalion	North Katanga and Léopoldville	Nov. 1960–June 1961	May 1962–Nov. 1962
Fifth Battalion	Kivu and Léopoldville	Nov. 1960–May 1961	Jan. 1962–Oct. 1962
Recc. Squadron	Kasai	Nov. 1960–Sept. 1961	
Field Squadron	Kivu and North Katanga	Nov. 1960–Sept. 1961	
Third Nigeria Brigade	Kasai and Katanga	Nov. 1960–Sept. 1961	

command. He charged them to have no interests whatsoever in the domestic affairs of the Congo.[69]

Before the contingent left Nigeria, a party of the Royal Nigerian Army led by the general officer commanding Nigerian military forces, Maj. Gen. N. L. Foster, conducted a reconnaissance mission in the Congo. Upon the advance party's return to Nigeria, the first units of the Nigerian contingent were flown to the Congo between 8 and 22 November 1960. The tour of duty for the Nigerian units was fixed at six months, after which those in active service were relieved by other Nigerian units. Thus five battalions of the Nigerian Army each had two tours of service of six months' duration in the Congo. During those tours they were deployed in four of the six original Congolese provinces—Kasai, Kivu, North Katanga, and Léopoldville. (See table 5.1 and map 2.1.)

The United Nations Operations in the Congo, under which the Nigerian contingents served, was charged with the primary responsibility of assisting the Congolese authorities in the maintenance of law and order. In seeking to prevent minor clashes and large-scale war among the various Congolese factions, clashes between the Nigerian UN contingents and various Congolese troops, ethnic groups, and mercenaries whether pro-Lumumba, pro-Kasavubu-Mobutu, or pro-Tshombe were unavoidable. While separating warring groups, or in the line of duty, Nigerian UN contingents were attacked and quite naturally they defended themselves.[70] (While it is clear that there were indeed Nigerian fatalities, the official statistics do not enumerate them.)

In addition to military skirmishes encountered in the line of duty the Nigerian troops bravely and tactfully executed several other military and civilian tasks. They sustained the morale of the civilian population against intimidation and fear of violence; they reduced inter-ethnic and interfactional clashes; they assisted the civil authorities, the Congolese Army, and the gendarmerie in working together and acted as trades-dispute arbitrators and as magistrates by participating in fair trials of those who had been imprisoned without summary trial or due process of law; and they offered protection to Congolese as well as foreign administrators and public utility workers, thus allowing them to function unmolested by rebel Congolese soldiers or partisan ethnic groups. They fulfilled this last part of their mission by means of guard duties at key Congolese installations, like mines, vital airstrips, factories, power stations, waterworks, and railway stations.

A great deal of the troop effort was also directed at rescuing and protecting stranded European and African refugees at isolated locations and arranging their repatriation. In addition, the troops helped to minimize disorder arising from unemployment, lack of food, and failure of public utilities. They assisted in driving railway trains; distributed food and medicine to schools, hospitals, and refugee centers; escorted World Health Organization officials; aided engineers who repaired roads and bridges; guarded various public buildings where Congolese leaders held summit meetings; and in several instances they supervised schools and hospitals.[71] They also participated effectively in the UN military operations carried out between 24 December 1962 and 21 January 1963, which led to the complete liquidation of the gendarmerie of Katanga as an organized fighting force and the termination of the secession of Katanga. Nigerian troops were instrumental in the completion of the UN military disengagement in the Congo, which had been expected to take place on 31 December 1963, about a year after the termination of the secession of Katanga.

But stability, a major objective of the UN mission to the Congo, did not return to the republic immediately after the end of the secession. On the contrary, there remained serious uncertainties relating to a possible recrudescence of secessionist and dissident activities in Ka-tanga. Also, the exercise of governmental authority in many other areas of the country remained very inadequate, and the Congolese army and police still lacked the discipline to assume full responsibility for the maintenance of internal law and order. Consequently, and pursuant to Prime Minister Adoula's request, the United Nations authorized the continued presence of 3,000 UN troops in the Congo until June 1964.[72]

Nigerian troops formed part of the UN force that remained to meet the needs outlined by Adoula. Brigadier B. A. O. Ogundipe served as chief of staff of the remaining force until 31 December 1963. Major General J. T. U. Aguiyi-Ironsi, another Nigerian, became commander of the force from 31 December 1963 to the last day of UN military activities in the Congo. His appointment to the command was not only a recognition of his competence but also a tribute to Nigeria's role in the Congo mission.

Major General Aguiyi-Ironsi executed "Operation Stayput" (7 March–31 May 1964) which carried out emergency evacuation of UN Educational, Scientific, and Cultural Organization (UNESCO) teachers, Food and Agricultural Organization (FAO) experts, and World Health Organization (WHO) doctors and their dependents from Kik-wit, Kwilu Province, to Léopoldville. Resurgent supporters of the former minister of education in Lumumba's government had carried out a series of raids in an effort to paralyze the area's economic activity and administration. In "Operation Cornelius" (19 March–14 April 1964), Maj. Gen. Aguiyi-Ironsi persuaded 3,500 Kasai to return to their homes, which they had abandoned because of terrorist activities.

Relations between the officers and men of the Congolese army and the UN force at this concluding period of the UN Congo operations were cordial. A great deal of confidence and some measure of discipline had returned to the army. The Congo had become more peaceful, its prospect for embarking on the road to true independence comparatively brighter. The UN military operations in the republic ended on 30 June 1964. Major General Aguiyi-Ironsi and Capt. Ohawady Alily, the Nigerian liaison officer at the UN Operations in the Congo headquarters, were the last of the UN troops to leave the Congo on that day.[73]

The presence of the Nigerian troops in the Congo enhanced the prestige of Nigeria in the eyes of the world and helped to establish friendly relations between Nigeria and the Congo.[74] The meticulous preparation and reconnaissance activities that had preceded their dispatch to the strife-torn republic was a tribute to the Ministry of Defense and the Nigerian military high command, who appreciated the political and military importance of the mission and left nothing to chance. Nigeria was confident that it could fulfill its "historic mission" in Africa and was satisfied with the "most honourable role the Nigerian troops had played in projecting Nigerian personality abroad." [75]

The Nigeria Police Force contingent
with the UN Operations in the Congo

Just as the Nigerian Army participated very effectively in the military operations, so did the Nigerian Police. [76] In November 1960 the secretary-general sent an urgent request to Nigeria for 300 policemen to assist the United Nations in the maintenance of law and order in the Congo. The Nigerian government promptly acceded to the request. [77]

On 21 December 1960, shortly after the return of a reconnaissance mission, the first contingent, comprising 400 officers and men, left Nigeria for the Congo under the command of Louis O. Edet, then deputy commissioner of police. It was airlifted to Léopoldville, the contingent's main base, in giant American Globemasters to replace companies of Ghanaian police, which were being withdrawn after six months' service. On the eve of the departure, the Nigerian prime minister expressed his confidence that members of the contingent would bear in mind that their reputation and that of Nigeria lay in their hands. He said to the policemen:

> The call [to help a sister African state] has come soon after our attainment of independence and signifies the responsibilities of sovereignty and the interdependence of nations, one with the other in times of trouble. You all know you are going to the Congo, a sister country . . . which needs help. You are going there under the auspices of the United Nations . . . whose main purpose is the preservation of peace. Yours is, therefore, a peaceful mission and one that will commend itself everywhere to men of goodwill. . . . It will not be your concern to interfere in any way in the domestic affairs of the country. [78]

The prime minister believed it was prudent to emphasize publicly his policy of noninterference in the domestic affairs of the Congo because the Congolese had accused the Ghanaian policemen, who were consequently to be replaced by their Nigerian counterparts, of interfering in their national affairs.

Units of the contingent stationed at Léopoldville, Luluabourg, Stanleyville, Bukavu, and Kindu lost no time in adapting to local conditions and making friends with the Congolese. After only two months, most of them spoke some passable French and Lingala, a native Congolese language. This breaking of the language barrier ingratiated the policemen to the Congolese people and facilitated their efforts toward the restoration and maintenance of law and order.[79] The contingent posted men on beats around the clock, investigated crimes, controlled and regulated traffic, and guarded the premises of UN officials. Despite the explosive possibilities of the assignment, the policemen performed these duties, even the street patrols, unarmed. This tradition made a tremendous impression on the Congolese, who had previously connected the forces of law and order with brutal methods of suppression.

The Léopoldville authorities faced the major task of building an entirely new police service while simultaneously using available resources to control the wanton acts of lawlessness which menaced the country's economic and social life. To address the problem the Nigeria police contingent organized a rapid and intensive refresher course for Congolese police officers and a long-term comprehensive training program for recruits at the Police College in Léopoldville; they also undertook an administrative reorganization of the Congo Police Force. The training program included demonstrative exercises (ranging from riot control and first aid practice to criminal investigation) as well as collaboration among members of the Nigerian contingent and their Congolese counterparts in all duties they performed.[80]

Units of the Nigerian contingent served in the Congo for five years, during which they helped the republic on its way to recovery and further cemented the bond of friendship between the two countries. Their introduction of the practice of criminal investigation into the Congo reduced the crime wave in the major cities considerably. Their practice of patrolling on foot unarmed, which was introduced into the Congolese police set-up, similarly inspired confidence in a hitherto fearstriken Congolese public. The collaboration between men of the contingents and their Congolese counterparts improved the discipline of the Congolese constabulary.[81]

In a farewell address to the last contingent, Congolese Minister of Interior Etienne Tshisekedi said that while the government and people of the Congolese republic were sad at the departure of the Nigeria Police contingent, they were nevertheless happy, too, because its services in the Congo had strengthened Congo-Nigeria relations. The fact, he said, that the Nigerian policemen were among the first to respond to the Congolese call for assistance but were the last to depart was a tribute to the policemen and an indication of the trust that the Congolese people and government had developed in their Nigerian counterparts. "Nigeria's role in the Congo," the minister affirmed, "had proved how African countries could cooperate, not by shouting empty slogans but in practical ways." [82] Earlier, Réné Bavassa, chief of protocol, Congolese Ministry of Foreign Affairs, had expressed similar views. He said that although the general impression of the Congolese was that many participants in the UN operations in the Congo had used the occasion to entrench their politicians in Central Africa, the Nigerian policemen had not in any way sought to further their country's politics in the Congo. Rather, "they, like us," he said, "know that if we arrive at a solution of our problems, Nigeria and the Congo will be two great countries of Africa, and that they will remain friendly." [83]

In a message to the commanding officer of the tenth and last Nigerian police contingent in the Congo, David Owen, executive director of the UN Technical Assistance Board, conveyed the gratitude of Secretary-General Thant for the invaluable services rendered by the Nigeria Police in the Congo. He said that during the most trying times of the UN Operations in the Congo and later under the administration of the UN Technical Assistance Board, the Nigeria contingent "stood as a pillar of strength, courage and discipline. It served in a spirit of dedication to the cause of peace and international cooperation." [84]

The Nigerian federal government was pleased that the policemen had enhanced Nigeria's prestige in the Congo and before the world. In his welcome-home address to the policemen the Nigerian prime minister said that his government had acceded to the UN request for Nigerian policemen to participate in the Congo operations for two reasons. First, Nigeria was deeply concerned about peace in the world and was prepared at all times to support genuine efforts in that direction. Second, Nigeria's African policy, subject to the limitations of the government's resources, was fully committed to assisting any African country that requested help. The prime minister elaborated:

We do not do this to win favour as we sincerely believe that aid should be given without strings or fanfare. We are convinced that this sort of mutual assistance is a practical way towards greater understanding and unity in our continent.

It is in this context that I and my Government have derived the greatest joy with the contingents, the last of whom we are welcoming home today. These Ambassadors of peace have through their performance brought the peoples of the Congo and Nigeria together.[85]

Finally, the prime minister said that the return of the Nigerian policemen did not mean the end of the cooperation between Nigeria and the Congo. Rather, he expected a new era of greater cooperation and understanding to begin. It was his wish that the link the policemen had so worthily forged between the two peoples would endure to the furtherance of African unity.

Nigeria's financial contribution to UN Operations in the Congo

Financing its operations in the Congo was one of the major problems the United Nations had faced since its inception.[86] By 30 June 1964, when the Congo operations were concluded, the United Nations had spent about $419,208,771 on both the military and the civilian aspects of the undertaking.[87] A number of the member states, notably the Soviet Union and France, refused to pay their share of the costs according to the provisions of Article 17 of the UN charter. Nigeria, on the contrary, paid her regular assessment, 0.21 percent of the organization's budget, and in addition made voluntary donations to help meet the expenses of the operations.

Under the General Assembly's resolution of 20 December 1960 the acting secretary-general, U Thant, was authorized to issue UN bonds to a total of $200 million in order to alleviate the serious financial crisis that confronted the organization chiefly as a result of its operations in the Congo and the Middle East. Nigeria was one of the first nineteen member states to purchase bonds; its subscription to the issue was $1 million, more than double its share on the basis of the scale of assessments for the regular budget of the United Nations.[88] There was no fierce legislative battle in Nigeria over the subscription to the bond issue as had been the case, for example, in the United States and the United Kingdom. In making the subscription the Nigerian government emphasized its strong support for the United Nations and its faith in the organization as the most potent factor in international cooperation. It expressed renewed confidence in the ever-increasing role the United Nations would be called upon to play in ensuring political stability for the world at large and economic development for the new states in particular.[89]

In August 1963 the secretary-general again called upon a number of the UN member states that had in the past helped to finance the UN civilian operations in the Congo to make good the operations' deficit, estimated at $3 million; Nigeria was one of the eight to whom he appealed. Nigeria's permanent representative at the United Nations, Chief S. O. Adebo, persuaded some reluctant member states to support the need to liquidate UN financial obligations incurred in the Congo operations.[90] He negotiated with the major powers and with other African states and succeeded in steering through the Fifth (Administrative and Budgetary) Committee and the General Assembly a plan that ensured the continuation of the Ad Hoc Account for the United Nations Operations in the Congo until 30 June 1964.[91]

In addition to these efforts Nigeria contributed $626,000 to the UN Congo Special Fund and other aspects of the Congo operations by 30 June 1964. The initial cost to Nigeria arising from items of stores and equipment dispatched to the Congo in 1960–61 amounted to $1,800,000. The Nigerian government also paid the salaries and allowances of all personnel of the Nigerian UN troops and police contingents throughout the duration of the UN operations in the Congo.[92] It is estimated that the salary and special family allowances paid to the 2,000 troops during their three and a half years' service in the Congo cost $12,360,000. The cost to Nigeria of maintaining its 4,000 policemen who served for five years in the Congo was $29,580,000. Thus for Nigeria the estimated cost of the Congo operations was $44,366,000, which does not include Nigeria's $1 million subscription to the UN bond issue of 1962 or the intangible cost of lives lost. For contemporary Nigeria this expense was a sacrificial contribution to the insurance of stability in the Congo.

Nigeria, the United Nations and the Congo:
An appraisal

Nigeria's use of the United Nations as its major avenue of foreign policy relative to the Congo crisis was not, in the end, wholly satisfactory. Among other complications that impeded speedy resolution of the crisis the United Nations was often paralyzed by cold war differences and the requirements for big-power unanimity in the Security Council. These complications tended to relegate the political and constitutional problems of the Congolese to the background. Thus the UN experience emphasized for Nigeria and sister African states the urgency of creating an indigenous organ that would work to resolve crises in Africa. Provision was made for such a unit in the charter of the Organization of African Unity established in 1963. Sir Abubakar, in an appeal to the Organization of African Unity foreign ministers, meeting in Lagos in February 1964, characteristically urged the ministers "to devise ways and means of resolving crises in African countries within our Organisation without resorting to outside help, with all its complicating consequences. The OAU . . . should seek as speedily as possible to establish its authority and effectiveness in the ordering of our affairs." [93] Whether the Organization of African Unity could have successfully handled the Congo crisis, had it been in existence in 1960, and given its record in such later matters as the Nigerian civil war of 1967–70 and the Angolan civil war of 1975–76, is a different and speculative matter.

The Nigerian experience in the UN mission to the Congo pointed to both external and internal constraints on Nigeria's foreign policy, but the constraints were fundamentally all internal because any external constraints had been internally induced. For example, Nigeria had to rely on British seconded officers to command some of the Nigerian military contingents to the Congo because of the local dearth of experienced military officers. British nationals predominated in the officer corps of the Royal Nigerian Army until independence, and the Nigerian prime minister had been slow in urging the promotion of indigenous commissioned officers. The dissatisfaction of some of the Nigerian soldiers with their British commanders was a potential source of great embarrassment to Nigeria in the event its soldiers mutinied while on duty in the Congo. The use of such commanders in a situation where their own government's attitude was indifferent at best, if not actually hostile, was equally a source of embarrassment to Nigeria. [94]

Because of internal weakness in transportation facilities, Nigeria also had to rely on the United Kingdom and the United States to move its military and police contingents, stores, and equipment to the Congo. We do not know what, if any, quid pro quo those two governments demanded for their services. We do know, however, that both countries had economic and thus political and strategic interests in the Congo and that a state of dependency induces constraints on foreign policy options.

Participating in the UN mission provided Nigerian soldiers worthwhile experience in combat, however, helping to increase their prestige at home and abroad. The effective role of Nigeria's military and police contingents in the Congo operations gave leverage to Nigeria's voice and counsel within the UN Secretariat, Security Council, and General Assembly. That voice was particularly forceful after October 1962 in urging strong UN action to expel mercenaries from Katanga and to support the Adoula government in its efforts to reintegrate the province into the Congo republic. Thus the Congo experience strengthened the conviction of Nigeria and other African states that their membership in the United Nations could be used to redress the wrongs former Western colonial powers had inflicted on Africa.

As a participant in the UN mission to the Congo, Nigeria deliberately fulfilled its international obligations as a member of the United Nations and as an African country. The outspokenness of its representatives at the United Nations introduced a note of directness which contrasted with the slower, more subtle, and formal diplomacy of the older nations. In all, Nigeria played a constructive, consistent, peace-promoting role, and contributed money, soldiers, policemen, and legal and administrative experts to accomplish the objectives of the mission.

The seriousness with which Nigeria viewed its role in the mission is attested to by the caliber of representatives it sent to the United Nations and the UN Operations in the Congo—men such as Chief S. O. Adebo, Edwin Ogbu, Dr. T. O. Elias, Godfrey Amachree, Francis Nwokedi, and the Hon. Jaja Wachuku. Together, the ambassadors, the legal and administrative experts, and the soldiers and policemen all performed their assigned duties with commendable dedication. Significantly, there is no evidence that Nigeria sought to use its involvement in the UN mission to advance a totally parochial foreign policy interest. Nor is there any evidence that Nigeria as a moderate state allowed itself to be used in any appreciable degree as a surrogate by the Western powers to advance their own interests in the heart of Africa. The record of Nigeria's participation in the UN mission to the Congo thus established that Nigeria could adequately mobilize its national resources in the implementation of any foreign policy that its leaders conceived to be in the national interest.

On the whole, therefore, Nigeria's performance in the UN mission to the Congo established its positive image and constructive presence in world affairs, confirming that Nigeria has the potential to become an effective power for good on the international scene. Such a potential, based on the Congo experience, augured well for the overall interest of Africa. Seen from this perspective, Nigeria's record in the Congo should dispel any fears among its neighboring states that Nigeria, through the magnitude of its population and economic potential, would dominate them. Accordingly, Nigeria should no longer consider its size and economic resources as constraints against its leadership within Africa.

Nigeria's conduct in all the UN bodies involved in the Congo mission convincingly indicates that Nigeria perceived itself, and accordingly acted, as a responsible member of the world system from whom nothing but correct international behavior was expected. This perception required Nigeria's reliance on international law, invocation and application of customary usages, and use only of approved channels. Thus, no serious decision maker in Sir Abubakar's government in 1960 perceived Nigeria as a catalyst for the "revolutionary" transformation of the international system. None questioned the contemporary international order, particularly as represented by the United Nations.[95] Thus Nigeria eagerly worked within and through the United Nations to strengthen world peace, an undertaking that was perceived to be conducive to the political integration and social and general well-being of its nationalities.

6

Avenues of Policy Implementation:
Bilateral Aid

NIGERIA RELIED on both the United Nations and African groups for help in achieving its objectives in the Democratic Republic of the Congo. Its comparatively greater efforts through the United Nations were more productive, however.[1] But the use of bilateral African aid also produced concrete results which enhanced the achievements obtained through the United Nations.

Many political analysts and practitioners consider bilateral (or foreign) aid as an instrument of foreign policy. This attitude was particularly prevalent during the 1950s because the Eastern and the Western power blocs, the major donors of foreign aid, used such aid as a cold war weapon, looking upon their programs as means of ensuring their security. The United States and its allies have used foreign aid as a prophylactic against the spread of communism and as a means of retaining the sympathy, resources, and strategic locations of the newer and the older but weaker states.[2] The Soviet Union and its allies, on the other hand, use their aid as an instrument of communizing the newer states and upsetting the existing political order there, particularly if such order seemed to favor the Western bloc.[3] As a consequence both Eastern and Western power blocs have invariably attached political strings to all substantial aid they make available to the newer nations. They have also tended to use cooperating newer nations as channels of such aid to other newer states.

The Democratic Republic of the Congo—with its resources and strategic location—provided an excellent setting for such maneuvers. This being the case, an examination of the motives of Nigeria's bilateral aid to the Congo is in order.

Nigeria's aid to the Congo was based on the principles underlying its aid to sister African countries generally. Any aid from Nigeria had to be specifically requested. Thus there had to be a genuine need and Nigeria would "have to be approached." Nigeria would "not impose [itself] on other people, but . . . wherever a request for assistance is made for [its] time, and resources, Nigeria will always be willing to give whatever assistance it can to other countries in Africa."[4]

The aid given had to be such that Nigeria could afford it without jeopardizing its own economic, political, or social conditions. "We must be careful," emphasized Minister of Mines and Power Maitama Sule, "not to make promises that we cannot fulfill, promises of financial or technical aid to our sister African countries, for we have not enough of these valuable assets ourselves as yet."[5]

No political strings were to be attached to Nigeria's aid to any other African country. The Nigerian prime minister elaborated on this principle in an address to the Plenary Session of the Conference of Heads of African States and Governments at Addis Ababa on 24 May 1963:

> When we give assistance to another [African] country which is fighting for its independence, some of us are in the habit of imposing obligations on the States. That is wrong. If we give assistance to African people . . . we should not ask for any obligation on their part. . . .
>
> If we assist any dependent territory in Africa, we must see to it that we do not attach conditions to our assistance. This is very, very important if we want to establish the solidarity of the continent of Africa, to make sure that any form of assistance we give is free.[6]

To attach political strings to any aid Nigeria made available to a sister African state would negate the stand Nigeria had taken against the alleged policy of those non-African states that did attach such conditions to their aid to the developing nations of Asia and Africa.

The aid should contribute to the welfare and the political and economic stability of the recipient state and to the solidarity of African countries and peoples in general. With particular reference to the Congo, it was hoped that the aid would contribute to the solution of Congolese political and trained-manpower problems. The aid program was designed to ensure stability in the heart of Africa and enhance the bond of friendship between the Congo and Nigeria as well as to contribute to their strength and mutual security. Given their potential, it was believed that mutually beneficial trade relations would develop between the two countries.

On the whole, these principles are characteristically pragmatic. In keeping with them Nigeria seconded experts to Congolese Prime Minister Adoula to help him find solutions to some of the administrative and financial problems. But the first tangible aid Nigeria extended to the Congo was medical.

Medical aid

The Congo had been plagued with a terrible shortage of doctors and medical personnel and with epidemic outbreaks of disease unleashed by the July 1960 crisis. To help combat the situation, Nigeria's federal Ministry of Health sent Mrs. S. George, matron of the Lagos Island Maternity Hospital, who had had some experience in flood relief work, to the Congo to discuss the problem of medical aid. On the basis of her report, the Nigerian federal government shipped supplies to the republic amounting to one million doses of smallpox and yellow fever vaccines. The Ministry of Health later sold 250,000 doses of vaccine to the World Health Organization to enable that organization to sustain its services in the Congo.[7] The vaccines, used in immunization campaigns, proved to be of immense benefit to the people of Coquilhatville, Stanleyville, Bukavu, and Luluabourg.

The Congo Relief Fund

The suffering of masses of Congolese people from famine and disease elicited widespread sympathy in Nigeria. A number of Nigerians, however, tended to exaggerate the overall situation in the Congo, telling such pathetic stories of the distress and sufferings of Congolese men, women, and children that Nigerians—whether in the cities or in the rural areas—were rendered susceptible to suggestions for alleviating the woes that had befallen the Congolese people.[8] Having thus created the necessary atmosphere, the enthusiasts launched an appeal for a Congo Relief Fund and forthwith published a list of the fund's officers, all prominent Nigerians.[9]

Nigerians, poor and rich alike, responded favorably to the appeal. Donations came from private individuals and public figures, indigenous and foreign-owned business establishments, Christian and Muslim movements, colleges and universities, municipal councils, and clubs. People in the rural areas—Ogoja and Abakikili provinces, the granary of Eastern Nigeria, in particular—donated food.[10] The governing committee of the Relief Fund organized dances, soccer matches, and lectures in its drive to raise funds.

By the middle of February 1961, the Congo Relief Fund contained about $7,500. Zeal for the fund abated, however, when the murder of Patrice Lumumba was reported. Eventually, a total of about $10,500 was raised.

The amount donated by Nigerians to the Congo Relief Fund was, in comparison to Nigeria's population of about forty million in 1961, very small. But the fact that the appeal for funds met no opposition and evoked a favorable response from all sectors of the Nigerian public demonstrated that the people could answer any request made to them by a legitimate authority in the name of a national ideal or Pan-Africanism. On the other hand, the meager amount donated to the fund demonstrated the poverty against which both the Nigerian public and their government had to contend.

University and secondary-school scholarships

Nigeria's desire to provide educational opportunities for the Congolese people took the form of scholarships in the belief that such help would strengthen the foundations for political and economic stability in the Congo.[11] A large sector of official Nigeria held an almost uncritical belief in education as a panacea for most of society's ills. The federal government spent no less than 20 percent of its annual budget on education; the regional governments spent even more. The north, which said it would not forgive the British for letting it lag behind the other regions in education, spent 25 percent of its annual budget on education; the east and west each spent 45 percent of their annual budgets on education. This faith in education prompted the federal government to appoint the Ashby Commission on postsecondary education. The recommendations of the commission, whose report had been published in October 1960, were fresh in Sir Abubakar's memory when he proposed to the UN General Assembly that African states should join Nigeria in providing places for higher education for some hundreds of Congolese young people.

Accordingly, the Nigerian federal government in the period 1960–65 awarded thirteen university and secondary-school scholarships to Congolese students to attend various institutions of higher learning in Nigeria. The regional government of Eastern Nigeria also awarded five university and five secondary-school scholarships tenable in the region's university and secondary schools.

There is some irony in Nigeria's scholarship aid to the Congo. There were over a hundred Nigerian students at Lovanium University in the Congo during the period 1961–66; by special arrangement all attended Lovanium on a scholarship program. When the Congo crisis threatened to jeopardize the future of the university, the Ford and Rockefeller foundations provided grants to enable the institution to remain open. In addition to these grants, the U.S. government under its Agency for International Development program provided the Congo a number of scholarships tenable at the university. The Congolese were unable to absorb all the scholarships because of a dearth of qualified students, so the university was allowed to recruit students from other African states.[12] The United States believed this would promote an inter-African student exchange and hoped that participating students, in addition to benefiting from the excellent French language program at Lovanium, would develop greater appreciation of the complex problems of the Congolese people.

The Congolese government and Lovanium University gave priority of scholarship consideration to Nigeria. Thus more than a hundred Nigerians became part of the academic community of Lovanium. The bond of friendship that was developing between the Congo and Nigeria and certainly the United States' relative approbation of Nigeria's policy of moderation were important factors for this concession to Nigeria. There were other considerations, such as the fear of possible subversive activities by students from radical African states. It was also hoped that the enrollment of the Nigerians at Lovanium would enrich the university's academic and cultural climate. The experiment proved beneficial to the participants and to the academic community in Léopoldville.

Modernization of the Congolese police force

Efforts at modernizing the Congolese Police Force represented the last stage of Nigeria's bilateral aid to the Congo during the period of the UN mission. Adoula's government, wanting Canada, Italy, Norway, Israel, and Belgium to undertake the modernization program in cooperation with the United Nations, had expected that the United States would provide the equipment necessary to ensure the success of the

program and no more. But Robert K. Gardiner, officer in charge of the
UN's Operations in the Congo at Léopoldville, suggested to Adoula
that Nigeria, Ethiopia, and Tunisia be included in the international assistance program to make it a truly UN mission. Adoula agreed. The
major purpose of Dr. Gardiner's suggestion, however, was to forestall
possible objections to the proposed program by Communist and nonaligned states.[13]

The proposed technical assistance program was by its nature controversial. It implied the prospect of direct military assistance to the
Congo and a violation of the General Assembly resolution of 20 September 1960, which had urged "all States to refrain from direct and
indirect provision of arms and other material of war and military personnel [for the Congo while the UN forces remained there] except
upon the request of the UN." Furthermore, the association of the name
of the U.S. government with the proposed program raised the question
of big-power involvement. Hence, despite Dr. Gardiner's foresight, the
proposed assistance program soon ran into difficulties. A number of
African countries objected to the program mainly on two grounds.
First, they were opposed to the inclusion of Belgium and Israel—Belgium because of its past record and abiding interest in the Congo, and
Israel because of Arab opposition. Second, they argued that paragraph
six of the 20 September 1960 resolution 1474 (ES-IV), quoted above,
urging UN member states to withhold military assistance unless specifically requested by the United Nations, still applied.

The representative from the Soviet Union also raised serious objection to the proposal, which he labeled a "NATO design to impose colonial shackles" on the Congo. Eventually, the secretary-general, after
consultation with the Advisory Committee on the Congo, informed
Adoula that he and the committee did not see the advisability of the
United Nations assuming sponsorship of an essentially bilateral military assistance program by a particular group of states. Adoula countered by stating that the Congo as a sovereign state had the right to
negotiate bilateral agreements and would do so. Consequently the
technical assistance program was no longer carried out under UN auspices.

But in deference to the United Nations, after the heat of the debate
had subsided, Adoula informed the secretary-general on 18 May 1963
that his government's request to the Nigerian government for technical
assistance in the retraining of the Congolese Police Force had received
a favorable response. He explained that the performance of the Nigeria

Police Force in his country up to that point, the high reputation of the senior ranks of the force, and the willingness of the Nigerian government to bear the cost of the aid program met the conditions that governed the choice of countries from which his government sought technical assistance.

In his appraisal of the modernization of the Congolese Police Force by Nigeria, Secretary-General Thant explained to the Security Council:

> The question of training of the ANC [Congolese National Army] would have lesser importance if law and order could be protected in various [Congolese] localities by the local police force. Unfortunately, those forces tend to be badly organized, poorly paid, and highly sensitive to political influence. In Léopoldville itself a police revolt occurred in May [1963].
>
> It is very satisfying, therefore, that the Nigerian Government has now undertaken to help the Congolese Government in the reorganization of the Congolese police force, which in the long view is also a vital necessity for the country.[14]

Indeed, talks about Nigeria's part in the program had begun as early as December 1961, but agreement was not formally reached until May 1963 when Adoula visited Nigeria.[15] According to the agreement Nigeria initially seconded six police instructors to the Congolese National Police College in Léopoldville. E. E. James of the Nigeria Police Force served as the first Nigerian technical director of the modernization program, followed by F. Okoye, another Nigerian police officer. Considerable success was achieved; as a result the Congolese government requested and received twelve more Nigerian police instructors. The new contingent enabled substantial expansion of the training program throughout most of the country.

As part of the modernization, a number of Congolese police officers visited Nigeria for special studies and observation for periods of from three to six months. During this time they received instruction at the Advanced Training Wing of the Southern Police College at Ikeja-Lagos. The trainees also visted the various regional headquarters of the Nigeria Police Force to enrich their training experience. The Nigerian government provided their food, lodging, and uniforms, but their own government paid their salaries.

By the end of 1964 the first two groups of Congolese officer trainees, totaling forty men, had graduated and returned to Léopoldville; by the end of 1965 more than sixty Congolese police officers had been trained at the Advanced Wing of the Southern Police College. These men formed the nucleus of the new breed of Congolese police officers who energetically played their part in building a virile police force for their country. The training program did much to increase the effectiveness of the Congolese constabulary.[16]

Summary

In implementing its Congo policy Nigeria pragmatically expended greater efforts, with appreciable results, through the United Nations and bilateral aid than through collective action by African states because collectively, outside the United Nations, African states could not appreciably influence the outcome of the Congo conflict as much as could the great powers, which believed they had vital interests to protect in the Congo. Also, the prerogatives of newly won sovereignty which individual African states guarded so jealously made collective action very difficult. In addition, at this time African states not only lacked experience in the intricacies of international politics but were also political strangers to one another. Mutual confidence developed only with time and experience. The tendency of sovereign African nations during the period of the Congo crisis to tread the path of the former colonial powers on issues before the United Nations gradually changed to a tendency to vote as a bloc, more so than any other group of states within the organization.

Nigeria's use of bilateral aid produced concrete results because it involved aspects of the Congo's troubles that were less political and less controversial than the conflict itself. Nor did the great powers perceive such aid as detrimental to their own interests in the Congo, and so they raised little or no opposition. The effort was truly bilateral. Throughout, Nigeria adhered strictly to the general principles governing its aid program to all sister African states. Nigeria never became a conduit of aid from any third power, thus maintaining the integrity of the bilateral process and advancing its objectives.

7

Congolese Appraisal of Nigeria's Role

VERY SELDOM are military men who leave their country for military or peacekeeping operations in another country admired by citizens of their host country. The UN force in the Democratic Republic of the Congo was no exception. To many Congolese, particularly the Lumumbists and the Tshombists, the force was an army of occupation and a resented foreign presence. Throughout the period of the UN military operations in the Congo the relationship between the UN command and General Mobutu was characterized by mutual distrust, whereas friction characterized the relationship between the UN force and the major Congolese rivals for power—Lumumba, Kasavubu, and Tshombe. From Tshombe there was open hostility. Most of the Congolese were particularly antipathetic not only toward Indian troops and Indian representatives of the secretary-general, such as Ambassador Dayal and Lieutenant-General Indrajit Rikhye, but also toward the troops from radical African states.[1] In fact, when Major General Aguiyi-Ironsi of Nigeria led the last troops of the UN force out of the Congo on 30 June 1964, not one Congolese official went to the airport to pay his respects. There were, however, some Congolese nationals and European residents in the Congo who regarded the force either as a protector or as a necessary evil. And occasionally the relationship between the troops and the Congolese army officers was cordial.

Despite the general situation, the presence of Nigerian soldiers and policemen in the Congo did foster friendly relations between the Congolese government and its people on the one hand and Nigeria on the other. Although Nigeria was just one of the African states that answered the call to help the Congo, the cordiality of relations which immediately developed between it and the Congo was unsurpassed.

The explanation for the degree of cordial relations lies in the manner of Nigeria's participation in the UN mission. With a host of its own problems of nation-building, Nigeria had no imperialistic ambitions in the Congo. Its paramount interest in the UN mission was to achieve stability in Central Africa, the peace and security that the Congo and Africa as a whole needed for social, political, and economic development. The Nigerian federal government stressed that it was not interested in Congolese personalities and factions but in legality and what was right for the Congolese people. Although these goals were difficult to reach, particularly since the concepts of legality and "what is right" in a controversial situation are capable of various interpretations, Nigeria did maintain commendable objectivity with regard to endorsing any of the mushroom governments that the Congo crisis produced. It remained characteristically silent on that question. It did not recognize the Kasavubu-Ileo government. It rejected recognition of Tshombe's Katanga regime, Gizenga's Stanleyville government, or Albert Kalongi's "Diamond State" as tantamount to recognizing the splitting of the Congo into nonviable states. Nigeria worked to bring about a reconvening of the elected Parliament of the Congo which Kasavubu had unilaterally dismissed. In August 1961 the reconvened Parliament selected its government and a prime minister—Cyrille Adoula.[2] On this occasion the acting governor-general of Nigeria, Chief Dennis Osadebay, sent a congratulatory message to Kasavubu in which he prayed that the formation of the new government might be the turning point in the history of the Congo republic and the end to the unsettled period there.[3] Nigeria thus granted recognition to a government that represented the collective will of the Congolese people.

One significant event that led to the formation of the Adoula government was the UN rejection of Lumumba's claims. That rejection eventually led to the total removal of Lumumba from the Congolese political scene. Nigeria's performance in that event naturally did not impress all Congolese factions. Its delegation had refrained from voting on the question of seating the Congolese delegation at the United Nations. Its representative, who was also chairman of the Congo Conciliation Commission, had failed to prevent the murder of Lumumba. Unlike the radical African states, the Nigerian government failed to recognize Gizenga, former deputy premier of the Congo, who claimed to represent the legitimate government after Lumumba's removal from Congolese politics. Hence, while the record of Nigeria's performance satisfied the government that was established in Léopoldville by the grace of the United Nations, it naturally disappointed the pro-Lumumba forces in and outside the Congo. The net result was that while good relations developed between the Nigerian government and the established government in Léopoldville, the Nigerian government remained suspect to the Lumumbists, whose struggles to regain authority in the Congo continued without any appeal to Nigeria for support. Although Lumumbist leaders were among those protected by the Nigerian troops during the various conferences of Congolese political leaders, they and their official organs, unlike other Congolese factions and their dailies such as *Actualités Africaines* and *Le Courrier d'Afrique,* were less enthusiastic in paying tribute to the work of the contingents in their republic.

Although the Nigerian government refused to recognize the Tshombists, it never openly denounced Tshombe and his forces. Hence its policy did not earn the wrath of the Tshombists. Most Congolese leaders, with the exception of the staunch Lumumbists, appreciated Nigeria's help in resolving their republic's crisis. Whereas they denounced Ghanaian, Guinean, Moroccan, Tunisian, and Sudanese troops for both "interfering" in their domestic affairs and "committing acts of brigandage," Congolese leaders commended the "impartial manner" in which the Nigerian army and police contingents had conducted themselves everywhere in the Congo.[4] There were, of course, those who, having lost their loved ones as a result of military skirmishes, were not so enamored of the Nigerian troops.

Tshombe's cablegram to Sir Abubakar in December 1962, despite open denunciation of Tshombe by a majority of unofficial Nigeria, tells much about official Nigeria's attitude toward the Congo conflict. Nigerian troops had intervened to save Tshombe's life (18 April 1962) from Congolese troops, who had surrounded his plane when he attempted to leave Léopoldville after his negotiations with Adoula's government had broken down. They had also protected him during a series of other negotiations with the Léopoldville authorities. And in December 1962, when the UN Operations in the Congo was about to mount the military actions that finally ended the secession of Katanga, Tshombe cabled to the Nigerian prime minister the following complaint and appeal against the United Nations:

> The Government of Katanga presents its complaints to you and has the honour to bring to your knowledge that the United Nations Organisation under the influence of the USA are preparing for a third war in Katanga with a view to exterminating the black people of this Region of Africa under the guise of Congo unification.

USA desires to monopolise the wealth of Katanga and thus
paralyse the economic advancement of Africa.

We have the hope that you will not remain inactive in view
of these preparations to massacre a brotherly people.

High considerations.[5]

Three major factors encouraged Tshombe to send this cable to Sir
Abubakar. First, Nigerian soldiers, the Third Battalion, were among
the UN force deployed in Katanga at this time. Second, Tshombe realized that the United States and other Western powers that were wield-
ing great influence in the United Nations had high esteem for Sir
Abubakar, who had been dubbed by Western propaganda as "the
Golden Voice of Africa," and that his action would help to moderate
what Tshombe described as "preparations to massacre a brotherly people." Third, official Nigeria's attitude toward Tshombe contrasted
greatly with that of the more radical African states, which had openly
taken a stand against him. In none of his speeches on the Congo conflict, whether in the UN General Assembly or in Nigeria's federal legislature, did Sir Abubakar deplore Tshombe's activities or even the
maneuvers of those foreign economic interests that proved to be the
bulwark of Tshombe's intransigence. This failure to criticize does not
suggest that Sir Abubakar condoned secessionist moves; he was sym-
pathetic not with the ambitions of Congolese political leaders and their
factions but with the Congolese people because of the complexity of
their situation, which had become compounded by international politics. Initially his concern with legality and uncertainty over the confused situation in the Congo made it difficult for him either to appor-
tion blame or to exonerate any of the Congolese leaders and their
factions.[6] He desired to play the role of mediator rather than intruder in
the affairs of a sister African republic. This attitude, which avoided his
open condemnation of Tshombe and the other parties to the conflict,
facilitated Sir Abubakar's endorsement of Tshombe as Congolese premier after the UN termination of the Katanga secession and the expira-
tion of Adoula's term of office.[7] The endorsement had been recommended by Nigerian diplomats to the Congo.

Again, to adopt a policy of publicly denouncing the foreign economic interests in Katanga was not Sir Abubakar's style. He was not
the statesman to alienate in that manner Nigeria's old friends and principal trade partners and investors, given his country's needs for economic development and political stability. For this policy, certainly, Sir

Abubakar was assailed by the opposition in the Nigerian federal legislature and by segments of the Nigerian intelligentsia for being unduly pro-West.

Resulting Nigeria-Congo relations

Because of the confidence the Congolese government had come to place in Nigeria's federal government, cordial relations between the sister states began to take shape. By the time the Congo was able to begin reconstruction and national consolidation the two countries had already established mutual diplomatic relations on the ambassadorial level. Nigeria had not planned to open one of its ten initial diplomatic missions in Léopoldville, but rapid developments in the Congo, with international ramifications, compelled Nigeria to send a chargé d'affaires to that capital in November 1960. The official, O. Ogunsulire, was instrumental in the arrangement of diplomatic exchanges and visits between Lagos and Léopoldville.

Kasavubu's proposed visit. — What was to have been the first visit of a Congolese political figure, President Kasavubu, to Nigeria did not materialize. The president had expressed his desire to visit Nigeria on his way home from a visit to the Ivory Coast, and the federal government welcomed the proposal in the hopes that the visit would afford an opportunity for an exchange of views between Kasavubu and administration officials.

But the visit proposed for 9 August 1961 was badly timed for a number of reasons. The strong Lumumba sentiment that led to riots in Lagos in February 1961 had not abated. It was too early to expect that Kasavubu would be accorded a warm public reception in Nigeria after the occurrences in the Congo. In addition, such a visit would further alienate the Nigerian government from pro-Lumumba forces in and outside Nigeria. It would have provided ammunition for those critics who saw the Nigerian government as a puppet of the Western powers who had enthroned Kasavubu in Léopoldville for their own parochial interests.

Accordingly, news of the projected visit touched off heated political controversy in Lagos. Leaders of the Nigerian Youth Movement and Nigerian Pan-Africanists sought to prevent the visit because they believed it would minimize Nigeria's international reputation. The *West African Pilot,* often reflecting the views of the National Council of Nigeria and the Cameroons, the minority party in Sir Abubakar's coalition government, denied the expected visitor the customary words of welcome. "Nigeria could not forget," said the paper, "that this man, Kasavubu the intriguer, is a cold-blooded murderer, . . . who cannot fight fair, . . . [who] sent Patrice Lumumba to his death." Nigerians, the paper went on, "do not welcome Mr. Kasavubu. . . ."[8] Certainly, Kasavubu was privy to plots to assassinate Lumumba. United States Central Intelligence Agency agents discussed with him the assassination of Lumumba. He seems to have consented to the plot with a great deal of reluctance, arguing that there was "no other leader of sufficient stature to replace Lumumba."[9]

A letter to the *West African Pilot* regarding the editorial on the proposed Kasavubu visit said that the paper spoke the mind of the people of "this great African nation"; the letter claimed that those who planned Kasavubu's welcome owed the entire nation an apology "regardless of their political or personal idiosyncrasies."[10] Numerous other releases on the occasion, reinforced by the memory of the Lumumba riots in Lagos, caused the federal government increased concern over the proposed visit. Lagos was eventually relieved of the problem: Kasavubu failed to appear after every preparation had been made for his reception. The only explanation from Léopoldville was that since President Kasavubu had not visited Abidjan as planned, he could not visit Lagos.

Inauguration of an air link between Lagos and Léopoldville. — In February 1962, shortly after the Lagos African Summit (Monrovia Powers), Congolese Foreign Minister Justin Bomboko led a cultural group to Nigeria on the occasion of the inauguration of an air link between Lagos and Léopoldville. Bomboko declared that the link showed that Nigeria and the Congo had begun to effect the recommendations of the conference at Lagos on cooperation, fraternal relations, and unity. He also said that if the Congo was the heart of Africa, Nigeria was the head, and the two could spearhead cooperation among African states.[11] The O.K. Jazz Band, which had accompanied Bomboko on the inaugural flight, spent ten days performing in Nigeria.

Just as Bomboko had indicated, both the air link and the visit of the Congolese cultural group to Nigeria were historically, economically, and culturally important. The air link was a historical breakthrough, for no such connection had ever before existed between any former British West African colony and a former French or Belgian Central African territory. It was bound to promote the growth of economic and cultural relations between the two countries. The visit of the jazz band opened the way for more such cultural exchanges between the peoples of the two countries.

The delegation of Nigeria's foreign minister to Léopoldville. — About a year after the inauguration of the air hookup, Nigeria's foreign minister, Jaja Wachuku, led a sixteen-man delegation (2–7 March 1963) to the Congo. The major purpose was to discuss with the Congolese authorities matters of common interest in which the two countries could cooperate. The salient matters were transport, telecommunications, trade, finance, education, and cultural and technical exchange.

On this occasion a leading Congolese daily, *Le Courrier d'Afrique,* described Nigeria and the Congo as "two pilot nations" in Black Africa that "have every reason to establish very close relations between themselves." [12] The Congolese, the paper said, have nothing to fear from their Nigerian friends to whom they certainly could not attribute either expansionist or imperialist intentions. Nigeria and the Congo, the daily went on, have many possibilities and a future in the economic field. It referred to the new air connection between the capitals and asserted that both countries could be leaders in other fields as well. They could become the centers of a purely African telecommunications network which eventually would allow Africa to liberate itself from an unfortunate foreign dependence and guarantee relations among all African states.

Officials of the Nigerian delegation, drawn from the ministries of external affairs, commerce and industry, communications, transport, education, finance, and establishment, discussed with their Congolese counterparts various aspects of the Congo's reconstruction problems and agreed on the basis for mutual cooperation and assistance. Out of the discussions was born a bilateral Nigeria-Congo agreement that provided for economic and cultural cooperation between the two countries. This pact was in keeping with Nigeria's stress on practical cooperation as the best means of fostering African unity. Another outcome of the discussions was the Congo-Nigeria Aviation Pact signed on 27 September 1963. Finally, with the cooperation of UN technical experts, a telecommunications link, agreed upon by officials of the two countries during the mission, was inaugurated between Lagos and Léopoldville in January 1964.

General Mobutu's visit to Nigeria. — Shortly after the return of the delegation to the Congo, General Mobutu paid a nine days' good-will visit to Nigeria at the invitation of the Nigerian Army and the Ministry of External Affairs. Mobutu observed the proceedings in the federal House of Representatives in Lagos; he inspected military and naval establishments to familiarize himself with their structure. He also visited the regional capitals and held discussions with the regional premiers and governors. The Nigerian governor-general, the prime minister, and the minister of defense provided encouragement regarding the problems of reconstructing and consolidating the Congo. But Mobutu was, on at least two occasions during the visit (26 March–3 April 1963), greeted by Nsukka and Ibadan student demonstrators who protested his alleged involvement in Lumumba's murder.

Prime Minister Adoula's visit to Nigeria. — Mobutu's visit was followed by Prime Minister Adoula's four-day visit (5–8 May 1963). Unlike Mobutu and Kasavubu, whose names evoked bad memories and misgivings among Lumumba's hero-worshipers in Nigeria, Adoula had a clean record. Jaja Wachuku believed Adoula was the one Congolese leader who was genuinely interested in the Congolese people. Adoula's government was the one the Nigerian government readily endorsed. His report to the Lagos Summit Conference of African states regarding the situation in his country had been reassuring. Under him the Congo had reunited. It was, therefore, not surprising that he was enthusiastically received by all sections of Nigeria.[13]

In a brief welcome address to the Congolese premier, the Nigerian prime minister emphasized the sovereign equality of all African states and expressed appreciation of Adoula's "tact, courage and wisdom to bring stability to the Congo and towards establishing African unity"[14] Sir Abubakar added that Nigeria and the Congo had many similarities, and he hoped that Adoula would confirm them during his visit to Nigeria.

Replying to the welcome address, Adoula referred to Sir Abubakar's belief in the sovereign equality of all African states as "a great comfort"; he said it was frank and polite declarations that should take first place in the relations of states that aspire to unity. He paid tribute to the work of the Nigeria Police in the Congo and stated that the visit of a number of Congolese police officers to Nigeria had been very useful to his country. Adoula finally declared: "Our dearest wish is that the Congo experience should not be lost on Africa. Our misfortunes must stand as a lesson and our reconciliation as an example."[15]

Sir Abubakar and his cabinet might have learned more than they did from this prophetic warning, but it was lost on them. Their domestic policy of drift and vacillation rendered them unable to deal with the realities of the political situation brewing within their own country.

Adoula's visit was significantly timed to take place a few days before the Addis Ababa Conference of African Heads of State and Government (22–27 May 1963). The major objective of that conference was to bridge the gulf between the Casablanca and Monrovia groups and to lay a firm foundation for African unity and for collective confrontation of the continent's major problems. Adoula conferred with Sir Abubakar regarding the summit conference to the effect that Nigeria and the Congo might work together to ensure its success and to prevent further dissipation of Africa's energy and resources. The two premiers also reviewed the problem of colonialism in Africa with particular reference to Angola, Southern Rhodesia, South West Africa, Mozambique, and South Africa. In a communiqué issued at the end of the visit, Adoula and Sir Abubaker noted with satisfaction the complete identity of views and common attitude adopted by their governments in relation to the important problems in Africa. They expressed their determination to do their utmost to ensure the success of the planned conference at Addis Ababa.[16]

Adoula, in an earlier statement, had called on Nigeria and the Congo to initiate plans for the formation of an African Common Market and had asserted that it was expedient for the two countries to form the nucleus of such a scheme designed to promote the economic stability of Africa.[17] In the end, regrettably, nothing came of these proposals.

Sir Abubakar's visit to the Congo. — To reciprocate Adoula's visit, Sir Abubakar paid an official visit to the Congo (12–15 September 1963). He and his entourage—the minister of external affairs, the permanent secretary to the ministry of external affairs, and the head of the Africa Division of the External Affairs Ministry—were accorded a grand welcome by the Congolese government and people. Sir Abubakar and Prime Minister Adoula, together with other officials of both governments, conferred at length in an attempt to strengthen the foundations that had been laid for cultural and economic cooperation between their two countries.

On this occasion Adoula said that Nigeria and the Congo had never lost sight of the mission of African states: to achieve and foster African unity, to develop the material and moral forces of Africa, and to fashion them into its striking force. These objectives, he said, constituted the very basis of their understanding and friendship. Adoula went on to assure his Nigerian visitors that he was happy "our present talks have served to confirm our identity of views and to reinforce our convictions on this subject [i.e., the mission of African states]." [18]

Adoula's remarks, with respect to Nigeria, may be justified on two grounds. First, the occasion called for such a flattering tribute to those who had contributed to the UN efforts to install his government in power. Second, most Nigerian nationalists were strong believers in the mission of African states. Dr. Azikiwe's speeches, in particular, have constantly articulated this belief. But with respect to creation of active and concrete measures toward the fulfillment of the mission, the tribute, at least at the time it was made, was an exaggeration. Only a few African nationalists, even in the Congo and Nigeria, would have shared Adoula's sentiments. Sir Abubakar's government, regrettably, was not the one to develop the material and moral resources of Africa and to fashion them into a striking force. Contrary to the early optimism of many, his government came to manifest a lack of the adventurous spirit and decisiveness such a task demanded.

Nigeria-Congo relations from conclusion of the UN Operations in the Congo to December 1965

The cordial relations established between Nigeria and the Congo continued to flourish after the conclusion of the UN operations. The Congolese government and people had eventually come to repose such confidence in Nigeria that, by specific request of the Congolese government, first under Adoula and later under Tshombe, Nigeria represented Congolese interests in the Soviet Union (where the Congo had established no diplomatic mission) and in the United Arab Republic following the rupture of diplomatic relations between Tshombe's Administration and President Nasser in 1964.

It is pertinent that Tshombe's accession to power in the Congo was a source of conflicting pressures upon the foreign policies of African states. Having led a secessionist movement and having been regarded by contemporary African radical nationalists as a "stooge of Belgian imperialists and Western exploiters of Africa," Tshombe was anathema to many African states and not popular in any. There was thus some conflict among African states when he acceded to power; should they shun him or help Congolese rebels overthrow him? Nigeria maintained its usual position of noninterference in the affairs of another state. Unlike most other African states, Nigeria consistently opposed the exclusion of Tshombe from the Cairo conference of nonaligned states in 1964 and, to the dismay of Nigerian Pan-Africanists, was the only African state that openly defended the United States–Belgian paratroop drop into Stanleyville in November 1964.[19] Nigeria's argument for its position was that the drop had been requested by the legitimate government of the Congo and that the republic's sovereignty should be respected by other African states.

But Nigeria's insistence on legitimacy notwithstanding, General Mobutu, soon after he had ousted Tshombe and Kasavubu from office in November 1965, sent a special message to Nigeria's prime minister on 4 December 1965. The message, handed to Sir Abubakar by Mobutu's special envoy, Marcel Lengema, in the company of the Congolese Ambassador Bahizi, expressed Mobutu's appreciation for "the distinterested aid which Nigeria had been giving to the Congo, both through the United Nations Organisations and bilaterally."[20] Mobutu expressed the hope that Nigeria, as "a friendly country, a tried and sincere partner," would view with sympathy and understanding the steps his new government had taken and that the two countries would continue and even intensify the numerous ties uniting them.

There is another side to this message. It was essentially a maneuver intended to gain Sir Abubakar's recognition of Mobutu's already accomplished coup d'état. A similar message was sent, via the same envoy, to Ghana's president, Dr. Nkrumah, whom Mobutu and other pro-Kasavubu forces had consistently accused of being an incorrigible Lumumbist interfering in Congolese affairs.[21]

8

Conclusion

IN THE FOREGOING discussion we presented a record of Nigeria's participation in the UN mission to the Democratic Republic of the Congo. In this final chapter we undertake two major tasks: we attempt to evaluate Nigeria's participation in that mission, and, with regard to the importance of this study in general, we address the following questions. First, how may it contribute to our understanding of international politics; second, what insights does it provide into Nigeria's behavior during its first significant opportunity to participate in international conflict resolution; and third, what does this study reveal about the determinants of Nigeria's international behavior and foreign policy.

The UN mission to the Congo, by far the most complex operation the world organization has ever undertaken as well as its first major conflict resolution task in Africa, achieved a significant measure of success, particularly the restoration of the territorial integrity of the Congo and the preservation of the republic's political independence. The mission provided opportunity for gaining a considerable body of new and valuable experience, both for the United Nations and for the new states of Africa.[1] But its achievements could have been accomplished with less violence, in less time, with less expense, and without the murder of Lumumba. As it turned out, the mission was controversial, protracted, expensive, and only minimally efficient, all these because of a number of factors:

First, the objectives in the Congo crisis of UN member states were not African objectives; some member states sought to use the mission for their parochial interests. The great powers' struggle for mastery in the Congo was the most significant part of those interests and contributed much to the controversy and protracted duration of the mission. The West had a definite advantage in that struggle; the odds were overwhelmingly against the Soviet Union and those it supported in the Congo conflict. The West had earlier established a legitimate, all-encompassing presence in the Congo and in Africa, which shielded the Western powers and their actions from the blatant suspicion, if not scrupulous examination, to which Soviet actions were subjected. Despite those odds the Soviet Union and its supporters made determined but vain efforts to establish a new order in the heart of Africa.

Second, Belgium, South Africa, and other foreign economic interests in Katanga never completely gave up their maneuvers in support of Tshombe and his secession attempt. Belgium in particular had only a poor understanding of the trends and force of nationalism in Africa and was unprepared for the measure of influence the new African states were determined to exert in world affairs. The Western powers, although appreciative of nationalist trends, were unable to prevent Belgium from precipitating the actions that fostered and triggered the Congo crisis, partly because they too had economic and strategic stakes in the Congo and partly because the Belgians were unwilling for almost a year into the course of the conflict to accept the political realities in Africa and the world.

Finally, Secretary-General Dag Hammarskjöld, under whom the mission began, was accused (on many occasions justifiably) of taking sides in the conflict. He lost his life in the course of the mission in an aircrash in September 1961 at Ndola in Northern Rhodesia (now Zambia) on his way to meet Tshombe. Hammarskjöld's special representatives, Dr. Ralph Bunche and Ambassador Dayal, and later his successor, U Thant, were similarly assailed. The mission became a test for the very survival of the United Nations itself: it threatened the office of the secretary-general, and engendered a financial crisis for the organization.

In the course of a legitimate mission to the Congo, the United Nations exceeded both its mandate and its charter when it intervened in that country's internal affairs. Doing so set a precedent that should make African states wary of either precipitating or approving a not wholly African multilateral intervention to resolve an African conflict. While African states have shown concern for external intervention in wholly African conflicts (when, for example, after the second Shaba invasion in 1978 they flatly rejected a Franco-Belgian proposal for a Pan-African peacekeeping force), they have not yet developed the political will to effectively settle such disputes, which invite outside intervention.

Any evaluation of Nigeria's participation in the resolution of the Congo crisis must be made in the light of these circumstances and from three major perspectives: the effect of Nigeria's participation on the Congo; the effect on the collective interests of African states; and the effect on Nigeria's external relations and domestic conditions.

Effect on the Congo of Nigeria's participation

Nigeria's response to the Congolese call for help achieved some of Nigeria's objectives. A large measure of law and order was restored, and the territorial integrity and political independence of the republic were affirmed. In cooperation with other states with similar objectives, Nigeria participated to thwart the interests of those states that had sought to help Katanga become a separate sovereign state, or to balkanize the Congo, or to entrench an extremely centralized nationalist regime in Léopoldville. A moderate Congolese central government, amenable to the West and with a more or less feeble authority encompassing the whole republic, was established in Léopoldville. And the Congolese Police Force was reorganized to become a more reliable instrument of Congolese internal security.

The major failures of Nigeria's participation were in large part also the failures of the UN effort in the Congo. The Nigerian prime minister's equivocal support for the first Congolese premier was apparently influenced by two factors: the Western powers' (particularly the United States') dislike of Lumumba's political orientation, and concessions made by Sir Abubakar to accommodate perceived Nigerian interests. Sir Abubakar's speech on the Congo crisis before the United Nations General Assembly in October 1960, particularly the call for new Congolese elections, was a subtle rejection of the legitimacy of Lumumba's government. It is little wonder that Nigeria's participation in the Congo operations failed to save Lumumba and his government.[2] Rather, it helped to install the opponents of Lumumba, namely, Kasavubu and Tshombe, in power. Then it failed to eliminate subsequent serious challenges posed by rebel movements to the authority of Tshombe's central government,[3] especially in 1964. The installed Kasavubu-Tshombe administration was short-lived, swept away by Mobutu, who assumed dictatorial powers in his bloodless coup of November 1965. Even Mobutu, despite substantial support from the West, has not had completely quiet sailing since then.[4]

Nigeria's participation also failed to bring about the retraining and reorganization of the Congolese army. It was here that the UN Congo mission as a whole failed most woefully. As a result the Congolese Army, which had precipitated the crisis, remained almost as irresponsible and unreliable after four years of UN peace keeping as it had been when the mission began.[5] The intransigence of the Congolese government, which insisted on entrusting the reorganization program to one bloc of powers, shares responsibility for this failure.

The achievements of the United Nations in the Congo, including thwarting Belgian aims for an independent Katanga, reunifying the Republic of the Congo, and establishing the republic's independence, represented largely a holding action. The Congolese leaders that emerged from the crisis proved incapable of translating the achievements of the UN mission into benefits for the people. Nor has the Congo's dependence on the West decreased since the termination of the mission. Hence, the aspirations of the people remain largely unfulfilled, and their republic remains incapable of realizing the political role in Central and Southern Africa that African nationalists had anticipated for it.

Effect on the collective interests
of African states

The crisis provided African states their first significant experience in "practical Pan-Africanism." It was the first serious test of African solidarity and a crucial test of the collective ability of African states, through the United Nations, to influence events in Africa and to limit the extent of intervention by the major powers. Collectively, African states were unable to measure up to these tests. The crisis helped to widen already existing divisions among them that took three years to heal. The divisions were fundamental and ominous, relating to issues far beyond the UN mission and successful decolonization.[6] In spite of this the African states, in cooperation with Asian states, acted decisively to ensure that the United Nations undertook the peace-keeping mission, thus preventing direct military intervention in the Congo by the great powers.

The UN mission to the Congo introduced Africans into the inner workings of the UN Secretariat. In so doing, the mission helped to reduce the predominance of the West in that organ. Despite the effective participation of military and police contingents from Africa, however, the UN mission to the Congo underlined the powerlessness of the Af-

rican states and their consequent dependence on the United Nations for
their ability to influence world, including African, events. African
states have still to overcome this weakness.

The crisis gave Africa a foretaste of the struggle that lay ahead: to
eradicate, with or without UN help, residual colonialism and white supremacy, especially in Southern Africa. Thanks to subsequent indigenous nationalist struggles, assisted by individual African states and
sometimes the Organization of African Unity, formal colonialism in
Southern Africa is now a thing of the past, except in Namibia and
South Africa. The attainment of the same objective remains elusive in
these two Southern African countries, even though the United Nations
has been deeply involved since the early 1960s. African experience in
the two remaining colonial areas in Southern Africa reinforces the lesson of the Congo: African states should not rely on the United Nations
for their salvation.

In addition, the experience of the African states in the UN mission
to the Congo alerted them to the absolute need for clear specification of
relationships and responsibilities in the event of future invitations to
the United Nations in similar situations.

Nigeria's participation in the mission definitely enhanced the collective interest of African states. Sir Abubakar, in collaboration with
the other African chief executives, made frequent attempts (through
diplomatic channels, in the lobbies of the United Nations, and at various international gatherings) to end the division among African states.
Although those efforts were somewhat successful, Sir Abubakar's Nigerian critics asserted that his policy of moderation and "drift with the
United Nations" on the crisis was a negation of Nigeria's own objective to maximize collective African interests.[7]

To some critics, Sir Abubakar's application of quiet power was ill-
timed. A substantial segment of Nigeria's political elite, still inebri-
ated, as it were, with the heady atmosphere of independence, desired a
more forceful assertion in matters affecting Africa. To these Nigerians
Sir Abubakar's taciturnity and cautious approach lacked the dynamism
expected of the leader of Africa's most populous nation. These "faults"
may be viewed as shortcomings of Sir Abubakar's style rather than of
the substance of his policy, however. Despite Sir Abubakar's methods,
Nigeria's participation in the Congo mission, in cooperation with other
states, produced some beneficial results. The hopes of South Africa
and Rhodesia to extend their policies and influence beyond their borders through collaboration with an independent Katanga under Tshombe

were frustrated. Central Africa was spared the odium of becoming, like South Vietnam, the theater of armed confrontation among the world's elephants engaged in their ideological struggles. Neighboring states were spared the excessive burden of caring for waves of refugees such a proxy war could have triggered.

Nigeria used the series of inter-African conferences, at which the crisis was one of the major issues, to reiterate, in the collective interest of African states, three of the cardinal principles of her African policy: mutual respect for the sovereignty of all African states; noninterference in the domestic affairs of other states; and sincere cooperation among African states on the basis of absolute equality and reciprocity. Nigeria restated these principles as an article of faith to reassure her smaller neighbors and to forewarn potential violators.

With respect to the nuances of international politics, the Congo crisis put Nigeria's abhorence of bloc-politiking and her declared policy of pragmatic nonalignment to the test both in the Republic of the Congo and at the United Nations. With regard to the factions in the Congolese republic the policy apparently aligned Nigeria with the forces of moderation against those of extremism despite professions of strict impartiality. In the United Nations the policy tended to give the Western bloc the benefit of the doubt, due partly to the strong attachment of Nigerian political leadership to Western values, education, language, law, and other legacies of the imperial era. It was also due to the leadership's deliberate attempt not to rush into the unfamiliar terrain of the Eastern bloc.[8]

In 1960, however, the question was, given real-politik and its needs and circumstances, should Nigeria have sacrificed its bilateral relations with the Western powers for the pursuit of African nonalignment and the political sovereignty and stability of the Congo? We think not, especially since there was no such dichotomy: Nigeria's bilateral relations with the West and the political sovereignty and stability of the Congo were not mutually exclusive. In particular, the weakness of the economy Nigeria inherited at independence and the problem of consolidating nationalities in a rather difficult federal system inherited from Britain imposed severe restraints on Sir Abubakar's foreign policy options. As much as the Western powers needed Nigeria, Nigeria in 1960 needed them even more for its development. The situation has since changed, with Nigeria's economic expansion and the oil boom of the 1970s.[9]

The propensity of the Western powers to use disgruntled political elements (of which Nigeria had plenty in 1961–62) to destabilize any government that pursued a policy considered detrimental to Western interests is well known.[10] In the early 1960s it was necessary therefore for Nigeria to conduct its policy in a manner not unnecessarily obnoxious to the Western powers. Nigeria is stronger now; its leaders can forcefully demand, as they have on occasion, acceptable conduct from the Western powers.

Even so, the pro-Western tendency of Nigeria's foreign policy in the early 1960s pointed out some fundamental needs: a certain degree of cultural, economic, and psychological disengagement from dependence on the West and increasing demonstrations of the nation's independence. Deliberate steps have been taken in this direction, particularly since 1975.

Finally, the termination of the UN military operations in the Congo under the able leadership of Maj. Gen. Aguiyi-Ironsi of Nigeria as well as the thorough work of the Congo Conciliation Commission under the chairmanship of Nigeria's Jaja Wachuku had positive impacts. These events, of which Africans can be proud, established the ability and trustworthiness of Africans for similar international responsibilities in the future.

Effect on Nigeria's external relations and domestic conditions

The cordial relations that developed between Nigeria and the Congo were in keeping with Nigeria's interest in promoting common understanding and friendly association among African states. Thus Nigeria's conception of Pan-Africanism as a political union of African states to be achieved through a gradual elimination of its major obstacles— namely, cultural, linguistic, and economic differences—was put to work in the Congo. This approach led to economic and cultural cooperation agreements between the Lagos and Léopoldville governments and to air and telecommunications links between the two capitals. The two states need no longer communicate and trade with each other through the circuitous route of London and Brussels; they can now reach each other directly by telephone or by direct flight via national airways. This state of affairs embodies the essence of Pan-Africanism as conceived by Nigeria. If the Congo events were an important test of Pan-Africanism, Nigeria was thus the principal African gainer.

In terms of using the United Nations effectively as an instrument of its policy on the Congo crisis, Nigeria also gained. Although Nigeria was a new and less powerful nation, its future foreign minister was elected chairman of the UN Congo Conciliation Commission. One of its military officers, Aguiyi-Ironsi, served as a major general commanding UN forces in the Congo even before he attained that rank in his own country. Another Nigerian citizen was a member of the UN secretary-general's Congo Club; another took part in two Congo constitutional reviews. All things considered, Nigeria's participation in the UN mission enhanced its prestige before the administrative head of the United Nations and before those leading powers in the organization whose interests had best been served.

In some respects Nigeria obviously lost more than it gained, however. Its participation in the Congo mission tended to divert critical attention from indigenous currents that proved to be dysfunctional to political stability in Nigeria. Nigeria's Congo successes contrasted very sharply with domestic failures, perhaps because Sir Abubakar had a relatively free hand to deal with foreign affairs.

Domestic affairs fell under the influence of Sir Ahmadu Bello, considered the most powerful Nigerian politician of his time, and the leader of the Northern Peoples' Congress—the majority party in the Nigerian federal government coalition (1960–66). As Sardauna (scion and ruler of the royal house) of Sokoto, Sir Ahmadu had opted to remain in Sokoto to serve as premier of the Northern Region of Nigeria, then the country's largest region, allowing Sir Abubakar, deputy leader of his party, to become the prime minister of the Federation of Nigeria. He was assassinated in a military coup on 15 January 1966. When Sir Abubakar, regarded by some as Bello's lieutenant, was assassinated in Lagos on the same day, his government toppled.

Sir Ahmadu Bello and his domineering influence, among other domestic encumbrances, gave Sir Abubakar less flexibility on the domestic scene. This is not to imply that Bello did not seek to influence Nigeria's foreign policy, particularly with regard to relations with the Middle East and the Soviet Union: he was opposed to Nigeria's receiving a loan granted by Israel; he opposed opening diplomatic relations with the Soviet Union directly after Nigeria's independence; and he favored and called for the formation of a Muslim Confederation to embrace Nigeria, the Arab states of the Middle East, and Pakistan.[11] It was partly in consequence of domestic legal and constitutional encumbrances that those Nigerians who had helped heal the Congo were incapable of profiting from the experience by applying the lessons of the Congo to their own domestic conditions. Indeed, less than two years after the termination of the mission to the Congo, Nigeria suffered two military coups that led to the slaughter of thousands of its citizens (including the prime minister, Sir Abubakar, and Sir Bello), the displacement of over two million others, and finally the 1967–70 civil war that took two million lives.

It is hypothetical to claim that Nigeria could have prevented its own tragic crisis if it had spent more of its energy and resources at home; but it is also truly plausible that, had Nigerian political leadership seriously appreciated the gravity of the internal economic, political, and social realities, the lessons learned during the Congo experience might have been put to better use. Nigeria's political leaders failed to resist effectively those domestic forces that steadily threatened and eventually undermined their domestic peace and political stability. It is a sad commentary on the Nigerian leadership (1965–66 and immediately thereafter) that, by not using that same spirit of accommodation and compromise that characterized Nigeria's preindependence development and its policy toward the resolution of the Congo crisis, they failed to resolve the series of political crises that threw Nigeria into civil war. Thus while Nigeria sought to contain the political forest fires of other lands its political leaders allowed their own home to become a tinder box. The nation, engaged in a thirty-months' civil war, suffered a setback in the translation into reality of its leadership aspirations in Africa.

Significance of the study

This study of Nigeria's participation in the UN mission to the Congo, dealing as it has with Nigeria's first major involvement in complex international politics, provides insight into the foreign policy-making process and implementation in a new African nation. The Abubakar government, viewing its Congo policy as part of Nigeria's Africa policy, established pragmatic, general foreign policy principles for Nigeria. In the process of laying out these principles, Sir Abubakar and his government established a foreign policy tradition for Nigeria that, despite the criticism from the country's radical political intelligentsia, survived long after they were gone. The components of this tradition are pragmatism; caution and low profile; sensitivity to the suspicions and susceptibilities of sister African states; suspicion of the motives and operational techniques of the great powers, yet with pro-Western orientation (Nigeria will not forget its old friends); legalism and reliance on international law, and on invocation and application of customary usages; and deliberate consistency in seeking to fulfill international commitments.

One aspect of the tradition was the removal of foreign policy issues from domestic politics. There was no noticeable attempt by Nigerian politicians and aspirants to office to use Nigeria's participation in the mission to further their own political ambitions at home as Ghanaian politicians and civil servants had.[12]

Chief among the major factors that influenced the development of Nigerian foreign policy during the period was the experience and personality of the prime minister, Sir Abubakar: his perception of Nigerian and world conditions; the requirements of his coalition government; and the ideological exchanges and harmonization these brought about. Thus the formative stages of Nigeria's foreign policy bore the stamp of Sir Abubakar, a deeply religious, unassuming, and cautious man, a strong believer in honest diplomatic negotiations and legalism. He did not believe in slogans and ostentatious publicity as appropriate measures for conducting political affairs. Nigeria's policy on the Congo crisis not only reflected these characteristics, but was also marked by a spirit of compromise, pragmatism, and caution.

These characteristics, however, were also in no small measure due to the development and composition of Nigeria as a federation of several nationalities with diverse political cultures and differing political styles. In the Congo Nigeria pursued a policy of moderation and pragmatism because it knew what that policy meant at home.

An examination of Nigeria's foreign policy from 1966 to July 1975 reveals no sharp departures from the principles and traditions Sir Abubakar's government had established during the period of participation in the UN mission.[13] Nigeria's increased friendly relations with the Soviet Union during and after the civil war represented no sharp break in terms of foreign policy objectives and principles, because the change was mainly a redressing of the traditional negative imbalance toward the Soviet bloc vis-à-vis the West. Otherwise Nigerian foreign policy, by and large, was remarkably consistent and remained essentially pro-West both economically and politically from 1960 to 1975.[14] None of the domestic upheavals subsequent to Sir Abubakar's assassination on 15 January 1966 changed either the consistency in foreign policy or the ideological complexion of the governmental and business elite in Nigeria.[15] The successors of Sir Abubakar, particularly Major General

Aguiyi-Ironsi, Gen. Yakubu Gowon, and later civilian president Alhaji Shehu Shagari, deliberately chose to abide by the foreign policy objectives and principles and to continue along the paths he had established. Domestic political instability, exemplified by two military coups in 1966 and the thirty-months' civil war (1967–70), partly accounts for this trend. We believe, however, that the consistency and continuity of principles were due largely to the fact that Nigerian political and business elite accepted them as realistic. What critics objected to was the *tone* of official policy—its pro-Western orientation, the low-key, low-profile stance of Sir Abubakar—and the style of implementation.[16]

Sir Abubakar was accused of "elevating a low profile into a virtue and low-keyed personalities into heroes and saints" when he should have used Nigeria's human and material endowments to respond vigorously to the needs of forcefully asserting and projecting the African voice and personality. The low-profile stance irritated its Nigerian critics who were embarrassed that Nigeria's foreign impact was not commensurate with its size and that foreigners were perceiving Africa and what Africa stood for only in terms of Ghana and its foreign policy positions.[17]

A dynamic style and action orientation in the conduct of foreign policy would have satisfied the vast majority of the Nigerian intelligentsia. It was the lack of these characteristics in Sir Abubakar's foreign policy, not so much its pro-Western orientation, that we believe was the major cause of discontent with his foreign policy among the intelligentsia. As long as a policy serves the national interest, neither its orientation nor its style ought to be cause for disenchantment. Even so, given the Congo experience, the makers of Nigeria's foreign policy would do well to cultivate a sense of the moment and timing to enable them to seize the initiative, particularly on African affairs. They must also sustain such initiatives, avoid vacillation, and promote the country's postures and decisions with all the resources available to the nation. However, we must reiterate that we do not condemn a low profile per se as an approach to foreign policy as long as the objectives of the policy are clear and the political will to achieve them is evident, and particularly if the circumstances and national interest warrant such an approach.

In this sense one of the worst things that happened to Nigeria during its first three years of independence was the way the Nigerian intelligentsia perceived the performance of Kwame Nkrumah and his country, Ghana, in the realm of foreign affairs. They saw Nkrumah's radicalism, flamboyance, and precipitate actions as what Africa needed. They described the process as dynamism and prescribed it for Nigeria. They very seldom stopped to evaluate the results of the style and modalities of Nkrumah's foreign policy process they were admiring. In fact, Nkrumah had little real power to back up his policies.[18] The Nigerian critics of Abubakar's foreign policy did not consider that Nigeria and Ghana are two different nations, each with its distinctive national character and real power; that both radicalism and a low profile have their place in the conduct of foreign policy, considering the dictates of national interest and the particular circumstances of a foreign policy issue. Sir Abubakar's critics wanted dynamism for the sake of dynamism. They wanted to cast Sir Abubakar in the mold of Nkrumah and Nigeria in that of Ghana. Sir Abubakar, to his credit, rejected both assignments, for good reasons. Because of its size and potential economic power (in relation to all its neighbors in West Africa and to the vast majority of the other African states) and because of the fears of economic and political domination these advantages generated among sister African states, Nigeria, if it was to be an effective leader, had to lead with circumspection.[19] Sir Abubakar understood the sensitivities of Nigeria's sister African states, so he adopted his policy of diplomacy by quiet power that helped to lay the foundation of trust Nigeria still receives for mutual cooperation and effective leadership. Eventually Nigeria's low profile and deliberately consistent steps under Sir Abubakar not only prevailed over Ghana's radicalism and precipitate moves under Nkrumah but enhanced Nigerian status and respect in and outside Africa.[20]

Sir Abubakar's government made provision for extensive parliamentary debate of foreign policy issues as a regular feature of the activities of the federal legislature. Although this provision was appropriate (in order, among other reasons, to provide parliamentarians opportunity to constructively criticize the government and to impress their constituents), it should not have been regarded as a substitute for bipartisan consultation and briefing of key parliamentarians by the prime minister and his key cabinet ministers.

Even though Nigeria's needs and problems were recognized, no group in the country during the period of the UN mission to the Congo prescribed an isolationist policy for Nigeria so that it might first put its own house in order. Participation in the mission and setting its house in order were not seen as mutually exclusive. A very few did call (in 1961) for the withdrawal of Nigerian troops from the Congo, but that call was in protest against the circumstances of the assassination of Lumumba and what critics regarded as UN "fumblings in the Congo." Other critics charged, after the event and after Sir Abubakar's death, that the Nigerian prime minister had concentrated on foreign policy to the neglect of domestic affairs.[21]

Nigeria's foreign policy during the Congo mission showed that it operated within the parameters of the international system of 1960. Nigeria stressed legality, world peace, friendship, and cooperation because it genuinely believed that these were necessary for the interests of an emergent state. It projected into the international system the moral values of Nigeria's constitutional order and development, which extolled individual liberty, rule of law, and political sovereignty of the masses. Although these principles relate to normal processes of international relations that all states strive to uphold (when it serves their interests), Nigeria, by emphasizing them, sought "to leave the world in no doubt as to its capacity . . . to enjoy the rights and bear the responsibilities of statehood."[22]

Finally, we recognize that this study has limitations in terms of inferences regarding the entire spectrum of Nigerian foreign policy. As a single foreign policy issue, Nigeria's role in the Congo crisis does not provide us sufficient latitude to make categorical inferences about *all* the factors that show the limitations of Nigeria's strength and weakness in the achievement of its foreign policy objectives. The UN mission to the Congo was a multilateral international action, affecting Africa and Nigeria in general, the Congo in particular. (It would be an entirely different matter if the mission had involved Nigeria in particular, as the subsequent civil war did.) But given Nigeria's inexperience in the realm of world politics at the time of the UN mission to the Congo, then the record of its performance in that mission is a positive indicator of the potential in world affairs of a mature and maturing Nigeria.

Notes

Notes to "Introduction" (text pages 1–7)

1. Stephen R. Weissman, *American Foreign Policy in the Congo, 1960–1964* (Ithaca, N.Y.: Cornell University Press, 1974), pp. 23–40; M. Crawford Young, *Politics in the Congo: Decolonization and Independence,* pp. 17–18.
2. Conor Cruise O'Brien, "The United Nations and the Congo," *Studies on the Left,* 6(May–June 1966): 3–27; Catherine Hoskyns, *The Congo since Independence: January 1960–December 1961,* pp. 259–65; Weissman, *American Foreign Policy in the Congo, 1960–1964,* p. 88.

Chapter 1: Preparations for Independent Nigeria's Foreign Policy
(text pages 8–19)

1. See the Exclusive Legislative List, Part I, of the Nigerian Federal Constitution (1960).
2. J. S. Coleman, "The Foreign Policy of Nigeria," in *Foreign Policies in a World of Change,* ed. Joseph E. Black and Kenneth W. Thompson (New York: Harper & Row, 1963), p. 391; *Daily Times* (Lagos, Nigeria), 22 June 1960; *West African Pilot* (Lagos, Nigeria), editorial, 18 October 1962.
3. Federation of Nigeria, *House of Representatives Debates,* 2d sess., vol. 1 (1953), pp. 450–65. (Hereinafter cited as H/R Debates.)
4. Ibid., p. 452.
5. Federation of Nigeria, *The Training of Nigerians for the Representation of Their Country Overseas: A Statement of Policy by the Government of the Federation of Nigeria,* Sessional Paper No. 1, H/R Debates, 14 April 1956 (Lagos: Federal Government Printer, 1956), pp. 2–3, 87.
6. Ibid.
7. Ibid., p. 4. See also Sir Abubakar's answer to K. O. Mbadiwe's question on training of Nigerians for diplomatic service and in what countries in order of priority the government proposed to open embassies and consulates after independence, in H/R Debates, 5 August 1959, pp. 27–28.
8. See H/R Debates, 5 August 1959, pp. 27–28.
9. Ibid.
10. See Jaja Wachuku's question on this subject in H/R Debates, August 1959, p. 29.

11. See Chief S. L. Akintola's attack on the federal government's foreign policy in *Daily Times* (Lagos), 8 September 1960; H/R Debates, 1960–61, 1:208; *West African Pilot* (Lagos), 13, 25 October 1960.
12. Federal Ministry of Information, *Mr. Prime Minister: A Selection of Speeches Made by Alhaji the Right Honourable Sir Abubakar Tafawa Balewa, Prime Minister of the Federation of Nigeria* (hereinafter cited as *Mr. Prime Minister*), pp. 21–22.
13. Ibid.; *Daily Times* (Lagos), 7 August 1959.
14. *Daily Times* (Lagos), 20 January 1959.
15. *Mr. Prime Minister*, p. 21.
16. Ibid., p. 19.
17. See his speech on assumption of responsibility for Nigeria's external affairs, ibid., p. 35.
18. See, for instance, Nnamdi Azikiwe, *Zik: A Selection of the Speeches of Nnamdi Azikiwe*, pp. 62–63, 314; Claude S. Phillips, *The Development of Nigerian Foreign Policy*, pp. 11–13; K. W. J. Post, *The Nigerian Federal Election of 1959: Politics and Administration in a Developing Political System*, p. 307.
19. Nnamdi Azikiwe, "Nigeria in World Politics," reprinted in *West African Pilot* (Lagos), 6, 7 August 1959.
20. *Mr. Prime Minister*, pp. 28–29.
21. Ibid., p. 5.
22. For details on the foreign policy platforms of the three leading political parties, see Chief Obafemi Awolowo's presidential address to the 6th Congress of the Action Group of Nigeria, *Daily Service*, 15 September 1959; *Daily Times* (Lagos) 12, 18 September 1959; "National Council of Nigeria and the Cameroons Policy: Information," *Daily Times* (Lagos), 19 October 1959; "Why Independent Nigeria Should Join the Commonwealth," *Daily Times* (Lagos), 23 October 1959.
23. For various foreign policy statements during the period see H/R Debates, January–April 1960.
24. See *Mr. Prime Minister*, pp. 36–37.
25. H/R Debates, 12 April 1960, pp. 73–74; 13 August 1960, pp. 96–103.
26. Ibid., 13 April 1960, p. 101.
27. See "Foreign Policy of the Federation of Nigeria" (statement by the prime minister in the House of Representatives, Lagos, 20 August 1960), copy supplied by Nigeria's External Affairs Ministry, now in the private collection of the author. See also *Mr. Prime Minister*, p. 56; *Africa Digest* 8(2) (October 1960): 75–76; Phillips, *The Development of Nigerian Foreign Policy*, pp. 40–41.
28. See "Motion: United Nations Intervention in Congo Situation," in H/R Debates, April 1961, pp. 642–65; H/R Debates, July–September 1961, pp. 332–74.

Chapter 2: The Congo Crisis: Its Causes and Resolution
(text pages 20–52)

1. *Nigeria Army Magazine*, 1(1) (October 1963):18.
2. See Catherine Hoskyns, *The Congo, A Chronology of Events: January 1960–*

December 1961; M. Crawford Young, *Politics in the Congo: Decolonization and Independence;* Colin Legum, *Congo Disaster;* Conor Cruise O'Brien, *To Katanga and Back: A UN Case History;* Ernest W. Lefever, *Crisis in the Congo: A UN Force in Action;* King Gordon, *UN in the Congo: A Quest for Peace;* Rosalyn Higgins, *United Nations Peacekeeping, 1946–1967: Documents and Commentary,* pt. 3, "Africa" (Oxford: Oxford University Press, 1980).

3. United Nations, *Security Council, Official Records,* 15th Year. Supplement for July–September 1960 (Doc. S/4382: Telegrams dated 12 and 13 July 1960 from the president and the prime minister of the Republic of the Congo to the secretary-general), pp. 11–12. (*Security Council, Official Records* are hereinafter cited as *SCOR.*)
4. United Nations, *SCOR,* 1960 (Doc. S/4382), pp. 11–12.
5. Ibid.
6. Lefever, *Crisis in the Congo,* pp. 13–14; Stephen R. Weissman, *American Foreign Policy in the Congo, 1960–1964,* p. 57.
7. Quoted in Legum, *Congo Disaster,* p. 125.
8. See Bernard B. Fall, "Education in the Republic of the Congo," *Journal of Negro Education,* 30(3) (Summer 1961): 266–76.
9. See Young, *Politics in the Congo,* pp. 33, 36, 53.
10. Thomas Hodgkin, *Nationalism in Colonial Africa,* pp. 48–49.
11. Young, *Politics in the Congo,* p. 43.
12. Ibid., p. 44.
13. Legum, *Congo Disaster,* p. 43; Young, *Politics in the Congo,* p. 10.
14. Legum, *Congo Disaster,* p. 39; Lefever, *Crisis in the Congo,* p. 8.
15. Young, *Politics in the Congo,* p. 65.
16. Legum, *Congo Disaster,* p. 45.
17. See Belgian Congo and Ruanda-Urundi Information and Public Relations, *Belgian Congo,* 1: 439–42 (hereinafter cited as *Belgian Congo*).
18. There was a legally separate organization of education for Europeans in the colony who attended school. See Hodgkin, *Nationalism in Colonial Africa,* p. 49; *Belgian Congo,* 1: 441–42.
19. The two universities are Lovanium, a subsidized Catholic institution near Léopoldville, which opened in 1954, and the Government University, established at Elizabethville in 1956. *Belgian Congo,* 1: 451–52.
20. Legum, *Congo Disaster,* p. 39; Lefever, *Crisis in the Congo,* p. 6; Hodgkin, *Nationalism in Colonial Africa,* p. 51.
21. Hodgkin, *Nationalism in Colonial Africa,* p. 52.
22. Hodgkin, "Congo," *Daily Times* (Lagos), 30 January 1959.
23. Young, *Politics in the Congo,* p. 63.
24. Ibid., p. 37.
25. Young, *Politics in the Congo,* p. 57.
26. Besides this paradox of the whole colonial policy, Belgian administrators in the Congo, far from sharing the liberal attitude of the Belgian government at the Round Table Conference, occupied themselves with promoting the cause of Congolese politicians amenable to their interests.

27. Congolese political parties, mostly organized on the heels of the Brussels Round Table Conference, worked under enormous time pressure to prepare for the preindependence elections and the formation of the resultant coalition government. Such extreme compression of the political parties' preindependence life span was bound to have profoundly adverse consequences.

28. Comment, *Rand Daily Mail* of South Africa, 15 July 1960, quoted in *Africa Digest,* 8(2) (October 1960): 44.

29. Legum, *Congo Disaster,* p. 111.

30. Quoted in Young, *Politics in the Congo,* p. 315.

31. Quoted in *West African Pilot,* 3 April 1961, p. 4; *Africa Special Report,* August 1960, pp. 3–4.

32. Quoted in Young, *Politics in the Congo,* p. 315.

33. Lefever, *Crisis in the Congo,* p. 10; Young, *Politics in the Congo,* p. 316; Gordon, *The UN in the Congo,* p. 13; Weissman, *American Foreign Policy in the Congo,* p. 56.

34. See Stanley Hoffmann, "In Search of a Thread: The UN in the Congo Labyrinth," *International Organization,* 16(2) (Spring 1962): 332. Knowledge that American, British, and French consuls in Elizabethville had jointly and successfully urged the Belgian military intervention (see *New York Times,* 9 July 1960, p. 13; 11 July 1960, p. 2) raised the prospects of intervention by the Soviet bloc and made African nationalists more apprehensive of Western neocolonialism in Africa.

35. Gordon, *The UN in the Congo,* p. 14; Young, *Politics in the Congo,* p. 317.

36. United Nations, *SCOR,* 15th Year. Supplement for July–September 1960 (Doc. S/4382), p. 11.

37. Weissman, *American Foreign Policy in the Congo,* pp. 66–76, 231–32; Catherine Hoskyns, *The Congo since Independence,* pp. 140–50, 502.

38. Legum, *Congo Disaster,* p. 121; Gordon, *The UN in the Congo,* p. 33.

39. Legum, *Congo Disaster,* p. 122.

40. Professor Gordon relates that by the time of the Congo's independence, Tshombe had already appointed Belgian businessman Franz Scheerlink as ambassador-at-large for the state of Katanga—but the would-be ambassador was ousted from the country by the Belgian administration (Gordon, *The UN in the Congo,* p. 35).

41. United Nations, Docs. A/4711 and Add. 1 and 2, Report of the UN Conciliation Commission for the Congo, 20 March 1961, par. 104.

42. Ibid.

43. See *Africa Digest,* 8(1) (August 1960): 1.

44. H. F. Weiss, "The Tshombe Riddle," in *Emerging Africa in World Affairs,* ed. David K. Marvin (San Francisco: Chandler Publishing Co., 1965), p. 300 (this collection is hereinafter cited as "in Marvin"); Gordon, *The UN in the Congo,* p. 35.

45. Weiss, "The Tshombe Riddle," in Marvin,   pp. 300–301.

46. *New York Herald Tribune,* 29 July 1960, quoted in Note from the Minister of Foreign Affairs of Ghana to the President of the Security Council, 1 August 1960, *SCOR,* Doc. S/4415.

47. United Nations, *Introduction to the Annual Report of the Secretary-General on the Work of the Organization,* 16 June 1961–15 June 1962, p. 1.
48. See Weiss, "The Tshombe Riddle," in Marvin, pp. 298–300.
49. See Gerhard Everwyn, "Which Way in Katanga?" *African Affairs: Journal of the Royal African Society,* 61(243) (April 1962): 151; Sir Roy Welensky, *Welensky's 4,000 Days: The Life and Death of the Federation of Rhodesia and Nyasaland* (London: Collins, 1964), chaps. 9 and 10.
50. See Lefever, *Crisis in the Congo,* p. 101.
51. United Nations, *Report of UN Conciliation Commission for the Congo,* par. 62.
52. For a list of the principal minerals of the Congo, the percentage of world production they represent, and their main uses, see Everwyn, "Which Way in Katanga?" p. 153.
53. Ibid, pp. 147–57.
54. See Hoffman, "In Search of a Thread," pp. 358–61.
55. Hella Pick, "Towards Independence in the Belgian Congo," *Daily Times* (Lagos), 7 November 1959, p. 5.
56. In R. C. Good, "The Congo Crisis: A Study of Postcolonial Politics," in *Neutralism and Nonalignment: The New States in World Affairs,* ed. L. W. Martin (New York: Praeger, 1962), p. 42.
57. See Weissman, *American Foreign Policy in the Congo,* pp. 85–99.
58. Lumumba had appealed for and received Soviet aid for his attack (13–14 September 1960) on the Baluba people of South Kasai. See Hoskyns, *The Congo since Independence,* pp. 216–18; Weissman, *American Foreign Policy in the Congo,* pp. 79–80, 88.
59. See United Nations, *SCOR,* 15th Year. Supplement for July–September 1960 (Docs. S/4512, S/4517), pp. 164, 167ff.
60. Mobutu, who led the so-called peaceful revolution, was a creation of the U.S. CIA; he has maintained very cordial relations, bordering on dependence, with the United States since then. See Ghislaim C. Dabwit, "Zaire: The Roots of the Continuing Crisis," *Journal of Modern African Studies,* 17(3) (September 1979): 381–407; *New York Times,* 26 April 1966, p. 30; Andrew Tully, *CIA: The Inside Story* (New York: W. Morrow, 1962), pp. 220–22; Weissman, *American Foreign Policy in the Congo,* pp. 96–99; Hoskyns, *The Congo since Independence,* pp. 214–15.
61. See United Nations, *SCOR,* 15th Year. Supplement for July–September 1960 (Docs. S/4512, S/4517) pp. 169–71.
62. Quoted in United Nations, *General Assembly, Official Records* (Docs. A/4711 and Add. 1 and 2), *Report of the UN Conciliation Commission for the Congo,* par. 79. (The *General Assembly, Official Records* will herein after be cited as *GAOR*).
63. Ibid., par. 104.
64. See Lumumba's letter of 14 August 1960 to the secretary-general in United Nations (Doc. S/4417/Add.7:2).
65. See United Nations, *First Report of the Secretary-General on the Implementation of Security Council Resolution S/4387 of 14 July 1960* (Docs. S/4389 and Add. 1–6); *Second Report of the Secretary-General on the Implementation of Security*

Council Resolutions S/4387 of 14 July 1960 and S/4405 of 22 July 1960 (Docs. S/4417 and Addenda).

66. Legum, *Congo Disaster,* p. 126.
67. See United Nations, *SCOR,* 15th Year. Supplement for July–September 1960 (Doc. S/4387), p. 16.
68. United Nations, *SCOR,* 15th Year. Supplement for July –September 1960 (Docs. S/4389 and Add. 1–6), *First Report of the Secretary-General on the Implementation of Security Council Resolution S/4387 of 14 July 1960,* pp. 16–29.
69. For the role of the club, see Conor Cruise O'Brien, *To Katanga and Back,* pp. 50–51ff.
70. See United Nations, *GAOR,* 15th sess., part 1. Plenary Meetings, vol. 1, 1960 (A/PV. 864; Agenda Item 3), p. 3, and vol. 2, 1960 (A/PV. 924; Agenda Item 3), pp. 871–980; Weissman, *American Foreign Policy in the Congo,* pp. 106–7.
71. The commission actually consisted of representatives of eleven member states, four member states having decided to withdraw from it. See United Nations, *GAOR* (Docs. A/4711 and Add. 1 and 2), *Report of the UN Conciliation Commission for the Congo,* par. 2.
72. See United Nations, *GAOR* (Docs. A/4711 and Add. 1 and 2).
73. United Nations, *SCOR,* 16th Year. Supplement for January–March 1961 (Doc. S/4688/Add. 1), pp. 95–97.
74. See U.S. Senate, *Alleged Assassination Plots Involving Foreign Leaders* (Washington: U.S. Government Printing Office, 1975), pp. 1–70; Weissman, *American Foreign Policy in the Congo,* pp. 137–38.
75. See United Nations. *SCOR,* 16th Year. Supplement for January–March 1961 (Doc. S/4752/Add. 3), p. 199.
76. For the special arrangements made by the United Nations Operations in the Congo for reconvening the Parliament, see United Nations, *SCOR,* 16th Year. Supplement for July–September 1961 (Doc. S/4917), par. 3.
77. Hoskyns, *The Congo since Independence,* p. 497; Weissman, *American Foreign Policy in the Congo,* pp. 105–6, 106n, 149; Welensky, *The 4,000 Days,* p. 220.
78. O'Brien, *To Katanga and Back,* pp. 206–18.
79. United Nations, *SCOR,* 16th Year. Supplement for July–September 1961 (Doc. S/4940/Add. 1), p. 106.
80. O'Brien, *To Katanga and Back,* pp. 219–46.
81. See United Nations, *SCOR,* 17th Year. Supplement for July–September 1962 (Docs. S/5053/Add. 11), pp. 16–17. The plan had its genesis in the U.S. Department of State following lengthy negotiations involving British, Belgian, and French representatives (Roger Hilsman and Robert C. Good, eds., *Foreign Policy in the Sixties* [Baltimore: Johns Hopkins Press, 1965], pp. 258–60).

Chapter 3: Nigeria's Policy on the Congo Crisis (text pages 53–71)

1. H/R Debates, March–May 1960, p. 407; Claude S. Phillips, *The Development of Nigerian Foreign Policy* (Evanston: Northwestern University Press, 1964), p. 34.

2. See Sir Abubakar's statement to this effect in H/R Debates, 1960–61, 1:(251).
3. See Jaja Wachuku in United Nations, *GAOR*, 16th sess., Plenary Meetings, vol. 1 (Doc. A/PV. 1031, par. 7), p. 339.
4. Discussions of the crisis abound in the Nigerian dailies of late 1960 and 1961 through 1963. Also, a number of phonograph records, pamphlets, and dramas dealing with the crisis and with the murder of Premier Lumumba appeared during the later years. See, for example, F. N. Stephen, *Lumumba and Kasavubu in Congo Politics* (Onitsha: Njoku and Sons Bookshop, n.d.) and *The Trials of Lumumba, Jomo Kenyatta and St. Paul* (Onitsha: Njoku and Sons Bookshop, n.d.); Thomas Iguh, *The Last Days of Lumumba: The Late Lion of the Congo* (Onitsha: A. Onwudiwe and Sons, n.d.) and *Tshombe of Katanga* (Onitsha: A. Onwudiwe and Sons, n.d.).
5. See the *Daily Times, Daily Express, West African Pilot,* August 1960–April 1961, and particularly Dr. 'Tunji Otegbeye's piece on the crisis in *Daily Express,* 9 February 1961; text of a cablegram dispatched to Lumumba by the Nigerian Socialist Group in *West African Pilot,* 19 August 1960; "Africa Killed Lumumba," *West African Pilot,* 29 April 1961; "Nkrumah's Part in the Congo Crisis," *Daily Times,* 6 January 1961.
6. H/R Debates, 1960–61, 1:317.
7. Personal interview with Jaja Wachuku at Aba (August 1966); H/R Debates, 1960–61, 1:251.
8. Jaja Wachuku, in United Nations, *GAOR,* 15th sess., pt. 2, 1961, p. 318, par. 121.
9. "Congo's Impending Tragedy," *The Economist* (London), 25 June 1960, quoted in *Africa Digest* 8(August 1960): 1.
10. United Nations, *GAOR* (Doc. A/PV. 985, par. 99).
11. Hon. Jaja Wachuku, formerly Nigeria's Minister of External Affairs, is the source of the material in this paragraph.
12. Quoted in *Africa Digest* 8(3) (December 1960): 71; Gerhard Everwyn, "Which Way in Katanga?" *African Affairs,* 61(243) (April 1962): 151; Sir Roy Welensky, *Welensky's 4,000 Days: The Life and Death of the Federation of Rhodesia and Nyasaland* (London: Collins, 1964), chaps. 9 and 10, pp. 209–266; Rosalyn Higgins, *United Nations Peacekeeping, 1946–1947: Documents and Commentary,* pt. 3, "Africa," pp. 268–70; Royal Institute of International Affairs, *Survey of International Affairs 1961,* ed. D. C. Watt (London: Oxford University Press, 1965), p. 462; *Africa Digest* 8(2) (October 1960): 41, 47, 55.
13. Immanuel Wallerstein, "Africa, the United States and the World Economy: The Historical Bases of American Policy," in *U.S. Policy Toward Africa,* ed. Frederick S. Arkhurst (New York: Praeger Publishers, 1975), p. 31.
14. United Nations, *GAOR* (Doc. A/PV. 985, par. 115).
15. See H/R Debates, April 1961, p. 593; United Nations, *GAOR* (Doc. A/PV. 958[1960], par. 80).
16. Sir Abubakar, in H/R Debates, 18 April 1961, p. 649.
17. H/R Debates, 18 April 1961, p. 648.

18. Ibid., p. 592.
19. "No Foundation for the Rule of Law in the Congo," *Daily Times*, 5 January 1961, p. 5.
20. H/R Debates, 18 April 1961, p. 649.
21. Ibid.
22. Ibid., p. 648.
23. Ibid., pp. 648–49.
24. Ibid., p. 649.
25. See Michael Crowder, *The Story of Nigeria* (London: Faber & Faber, 1978), pp. 260–61; A. B. Oyebode, "Towards a New Policy on Decolonization," in *Nigeria and the World: Readings in Nigerian Foreign Policy*, ed. A. B. Akinyemi (Ibadan: Oxford University Press, 1978), pp. 104–7.
26. United Nations, *GAOR*, 15th sess., pt. 2, 1961, p. 316, par. 107 (emphasis added).
27. Ibid.
28. United Nations, *GAOR*, 16th sess., vol. 1, 1961 (Doc. A/PV. 1031, par. 39), p. 343.
29. These views resemble remarkably those of Nigerian parliamentarians as articulated in parliamentary debates after Sir Abubakar had declared his policy on the Congo in front of the UN General Assembly, 7 October 1960.
30. See United Nations, *GAOR*, 15th sess., pt. 1, Plenary Meetings, vol. 1, 1960 (Doc. A/PV. 893, pars. 171–202).
31. Ibid., pars. 175–76.
32. Ibid., par. 177.
33. United Nations, *GAOR*, 15th sess., 1960 (Doc. A/PV. 893, par. 181).
34. Ibid., par. 182.
35. D. C. Osadebay, *Daily Times*, 18 November 1960, p. 5.
36. *West African Pilot*, 10 August 1960.
37. For details see J. P. Mackintosh, *Nigerian Government and Politics*, pp. 71–74, 560–61.
38. United Nations, *GAOR*, 15th sess., 1960 (Doc. A/PV. 893, pars. 189–91).
39. Jaja Wachuku, "Nigeria's Foreign Policy," in *Africa: The Political Pattern*, ed. Miller Maclure and Douglas Anglin (Toronto: University of Toronto Press, 1961), p. 63.
40. David Williams, "Nigeria in the UN," *Daily Times*, (5 October 1960), p. 5.
41. Robert C. Good, "Four African Views of the Congo Crisis," *Africa Report*, 6(6) (June 1961): 3–4, 8.

Chapter 4: Formulation of Nigeria's Congo Policy: Factors and Determinants (text pages 72–84)

1. Richard C. Snyder et al., "Decision-Making Approach to the Study of International Politics," in *International Politics and Foreign Policy: A Reader in Research and Theory*, ed. James N. Rosenau (New York: Free Press of Glencoe, Inc., 1961), pp. 186–92.

2. H/R Debates, January 1960, pp. 25, 74.

3. For the impact of idiosyncratic variables generally on the formulation of foreign policy, see J. N. Rosenau, "Pre-Theories and Theories of Foreign Policy," in *Approaches to Comparative and International Politics*, ed. R. B. Farrell (Evanston, Ill.: Northwestern University Press, 1966), pp. 54–55.

4. Federation of Nigeria, "Foreign Policy of the Federation of Nigeria: Statement by the Prime Minister in the House of Representatives, Lagos, 20 August 1960." See also Sir Abubakar's statements in *Daily Times* (Lagos), 6 October 1960, *Daily Express*, 6 October 1960.

5. Although Dr. Wachuku had a great deal to do with the Nigerian government's comprehensive speech on the Congo crisis on 7 October 1960, the statement essentially reflected the personality of Sir Abubakar.

6. Interviews with Dr. T. O. Elias, formerly Nigeria's attorney general and minister of justice, and the Hon. Dr. Jaja Wachuku, formerly leader of Nigeria's delegation to the United Nations and Nigeria's minister of external affairs. These two cabinet officials of Sir Abubakar's government were generous in granting interviews (August and September 1966) and very helpful in providing details.

7. For demands that perceptive Nigerians were making for his removal from such a sensitive post see *West African Pilot,* 20 October, 2, 4, 5, November 1960; *Daily Express*, 4 November 1960.

8. Kalu Ezera, in H/R Debates, September 1961, p. 353.

9. Jaja Wachuku, "Nigeria's Foreign Policy," in *Africa: The Political Pattern,* ed. Miller Maclure and Douglas Anglin, p. 63.

10. See H/R Debates, 20 August 1960; Sir Abubakar, "What Happened at Addis Ababa," in Federal Ministry of Information (Nigeria), *Dawn of Africa,* pp. 10–14, 17–19.

11. Wachuku, "Nigeria's Foreign Policy," p. 73; O. Awolowo, "Nigeria's National Interest in the Three-Cornered World Contest," *Daily Times,* 24 September 1960.

12. Interview with Dr. T. O. Elias at Lagos, August 1966.

13. Interview with Hon. Jaja Wachuku at Aba, September 1966.

14. A. T. Balewa, quoted in J. S. Coleman, "The Foreign Policy of Nigeria," in *Foreign Policies in a World of Change,* ed. Joseph E. Black and Kenneth W. Thompson, p. 395.

15. Ken Post, *The New States of West Africa,* pp. 159–62.

16. *Mr. Prime Minister,* pp. 36–37.

17. United Nations, *GAOR*, 15th sess., Plenary Meetings, pt. 1, vol. 1, 1960 (Doc. A/PV. 839), p. 536.

18. H/R Debates, November 1960, p. 200.

19. H/R Debates, March–April 1961, pp. 21ff.; Claude S. Phillips, *The Development of Nigerian Foreign Policy,* pp. 108–10.

20. Sam Epelle, *The Promise of Nigeria,* p. 244.

21. H/R Debates, 1960–61, 1:240.

22. H/R Debates, November 1960, p. 40, and March–April 1961, p. 21; *Daily Times,* 8 July, 20 October 1960; *Daily Express,* 14 April 1960.

23. Federal Ministry of Information, *Dawn of Africa,* p. 18, and *Mr. Prime Minister,* p. 96; H/R Debates, January 1960, pp. 78, 96.
24. Based on interviews with officials of the External Affairs Ministry. Undetermined hundreds of Nigerians were resident traders in the Congo in 1960.
25. United Nations, *GAOR* (Doc. A/PV. 1031), pars. 41–43.
26. This state of affairs was part of the reason members of the opposition in the federal legislature declined the prime minister's invitation to accompany his delegation to the United Nations in October 1960 on the occasion of Nigeria's admission to the organization. The opposition said it had no idea of what the prime minister intended to say in the United Nations about some matters of topical international interest.
27. Joseph Frankel, *International Relations* (New York: Oxford University Press, 1964), p. 45.
28. Interview with Hon. Jaja Wachuku at Aba, Nigeria, September 1966.
29. The three major national dailies, *The Daily Times, West African Pilot,* and *Daily Express,* published letters to the editor to this effect (November 1960–February 1961 and thereafter).
30. The murder of Lumumba touched off demonstrations by Nigerian youths in Lagos and Enugu, which caused a great deal of damage to the British and U.S. embassies in Lagos and to the property of Lagos-based foreign companies.
31. The three major national dailies sent correspondents to the Congo to cover and report events there.
32. See *Daily Express,* 4 October 1960, 24 January 1961; *West African Pilot,* 10 October 1960.
33. Nkrumah of Ghana did a lot of this exploiting. See W. Scott Thompson, *Ghana's Foreign Policy, 1957–1966: Diplomacy, Ideology, and the New State,* pp. 119–61; Catherine Hoskyns, *The Congo since Independence,* pp. 28, 30, 62, 77, 80ff.
34. Interview with Hon. Jaja Wachuku at Aba, Nigeria (September 1966).

Chapter 5: Avenues of Policy Implementation: The United Nations
(text pages 85–118)

1. See, for example, the Charter of the Organisation of African Unity.
2. Established on 23 August 1960, the UN Advisory Committee on the Congo comprised the permanent representatives of UN member states that contributed contingents to UN Operations in the Congo. Its major function was to help the secretary-general to determine how best to implement Security Council mandates on the Congo. Two prominent Nigerians, Jaja Wachuku and Mohammad Ngileruma, among other Nigerians, served on the committee. Jaja Wachuku believed that it was his effective participation on the committee that earned him the appointment to the chairmanship of the subsequent UN Congo Conciliation Commission. Dr. Ralph Bunche, in an interview in New York in October 1966, confirmed this belief and also highly commended the participation of Mohammad Ngileruma.
3. The "Congo Club" was an informal but intimate group at UN headquarters in

New York, from which the secretary-general sought advice. The "Club" had considerable influence on the secretary-general and his determination of the direction of the Congo operation (see Conor Cruise O'Brien, *To Katanga and Back: A UN Case History,* p. 50). Initially the club was composed mainly of American international civil servants in the United Nations and as such was both suspected and denounced by the Soviet Union and Soviet-inspired press. To allay the suspicion and uneasiness the club's membership caused among Soviet and Afro-Asian member states of the United Nations, the secretary-general brought a number of Africans into the club. For instance, in 1961 Francis Nwokedi of Nigeria, who was already familiar with the situation in the Congo, became a member.

4. United Nations, *GAOR,* 15th sess., pt. 1, vols. 1, 2, 1960, Doc. A/PV. 864; Docs. A/PV. 917–24; United Nations, *Annual Report of the Secretary-General,* 16 June 1960–15 June 1961, pp. 22–24.

5. United Nations, *GAOR,* 15th sess., pt. 1, vol. 2, 1960, Doc. A/PV. 917–24.

6. Ibid., Docs. A/PV. 924, pars. 162–68 and 958, pars. 76–79; *Daily Express,* 7 October 1960.

7. H/R Debates, 1960–61, 1:201; *Daily Times,* 29 November 1960, p. 5; *West African Pilot,* 24 November 1960, p. 4.

8. United Nations, *GAOR,* 15th sess., annexes, vol. 2, 20 September–20 December 1960; 7 March–21 April 1961, annex 15 (Doc. A/L. 331/Rev. 1), pp. 62–63; *UN Review* 8(12) (December 1961):6; United Nations, *Annual Report of the Secretary-General,* 16 June 1961–15 June 1962, pp. 8–12; United Nations, *SCOR,* 16th Year, Supplement for October–December 1961, pp. 132–34, 137–38.

9. United Nations, *GAOR,* 15th sess., vol. 2, 1960, pp. 1474–75; pt. 2, 1961, p. 317, par. 113.

10. Ibid., pt. 2, 1961, p. 317, pars. 114–16; pt. 1, vol. 2, 1960, p. 1475, pars. 89–90.

11. Ibid., pt. 2, 1961, p. 317, pars. 115–17.

12. Ibid., pt. 2, 1961, p. 317, par. 118; pt. 1, vol. 2, 1960, p. 1475, pars. 89–90.

13. Ibid., pt. 2, 1961, p. 314, par. 94.

14. Ibid.

15. *UN Review,* May 1961, pp. 5, 35–36; United Nations, *GAOR,* 15th sess., pt. 2, 1961 (Doc. A/PV. 985, pars. 125–38).

16. United Nations, *GAOR,* 15th sess., pt. 2, 1961 (Doc. A/PV. 985, par. 136).

17. United Nations, *GAOR,* 16th sess., vol. 1 (1961) (Doc. A/PV. 1031, p. 343, par. 37).

18. Ibid., par. 44; Doc. A/PV. 1034, par. 8.

19. United Nations, *GAOR,* 16th sess., vol. 1, 1961 (Doc. A/PV 1031, pars. 42–43).

20. United Nations, *GAOR,* 16th sess., 5th Committee (20 September 1961–22 February 1962), p. 85.

21. United Nations, *GAOR,* 15th sess., pt. 1, vol. 2, 1960, p. 1473, par. 72.

22. Ibid., p. 1475, par. 88.

23. United Nations, *GAOR,* 15th sess., 1960–61 Annexes, Agenda Item 85, p. 70 (Doc. A/4711, par. 2): *Report of the UN Conciliation Commission for the Congo, March 20, 1961.*

24. United Nations, *Annual Report of the Secretary-General*, 16 June 1960–15 June 1961, p. 25.
25. Dr. Azikiwe's Speech from the Throne, 29 March 1961, in H/R Debates, 1961.
26. *London Times*, 11 January 1961, p. 10.
27. Interview with Hon Jaja Wachuku, Aba, Nigeria, August 1966.
28. *Africa Digest*, 8(4) (February 1961): 167.
29. *West African Pilot*, 19 December 1960, p. 6.
30. United Nations, *GAOR*, 15th sess., 1960–61, Agenda Item 85, Annexes (Doc. A/4696), p. 65.
31. See United Nations, *GAOR*, 15th sess., 1960–61 (Doc. A/4711 and Add. 1 and 2), *Report of the UN Conciliation Commission for the Congo*, pars. 7–124.
32. Joseph Ileo had split with Lumumba's Movement Nationale Congolais in 1959. Elected president of the Senate in June 1960 against the opposition of Lumumba's party, he had encouraged Kasavubu to oust Lumumba from office and was appointed prime minister by Kasavubu in September 1960. He was ousted by Mobutu and the College of Commissioners immediately, but he became prime minister again in February 1961 and was appointed minister of information in the subsequent Adoula government.
33. United Nations, *GAOR*, 15th sess., 1960–61 (Doc. A/4711 and Add. 1 and 2, pars. 125–47); United Nations, *Annual Report of the Secretary-General*, 16 June 1960–15 June 1961, p. 43.
34. Annex 22 to the report.
35. *Daily Times*, 6 March 1961, p. 3; H/R Debates, 10 April 1961, p. 294.
36. *New Commonwealth*, 40(6) (June 1962), p. 357.
37. *Daily Times*, 19 October 1960.
38. United Nations, *Annual Report of the Secretary-General*, 16 June 1960–15 June 1961, p. 49.
39. United Nations, *SCOR*, 16th Year, Supplement for January–March 1961 (Doc. S/4743), pp. 150–52, which was a telegram dated 22 February 1961 from president of the Republic of the Congo (Léopoldville) to the president of the Security Council.
40. Ibid., Doc. S/4741, pp. 147–48.
41. Letter from the Congolese president referred to in note 39 above.
42. *Daily Times*, 24 March 1961, p. 1.
43. United Nations, *SCOR*, 16th Year, Supplement for January–March 1961 (Doc. S/4752/Add. 3), pp. 199–201, which was a letter dated 5 March 1961 from the president of the Republic of the Congo (Léopoldville) to the secretary-general.
44. United Nations, *Annual Report of the Secretary-General*, 16 June 1960–15 June 1961, p. 39.
45. Ibid.; *Year Book of the United Nations*, 1961, pp. 59–60.
46. O'Brien, *To Katanga and Back*, pp. 122–23.
47. Interview with Dr. Elias at the University of Lagos (Nigeria) in August 1966; United Nations, *Annual Report of the Secretary-General*, 16 June 1961–15 June 1962, p. 1.
48. *Africa Digest*, October 1962, p. 38.

49. "A New Plan for the Congo," *Africa Report*, October 1962, p. 21.
50. United Nations, *Annual Report of the Secretary-General*, 16 June 1962–15 June 1963, p. 2.
51. *West African Pilot*, 13 August 1962, p. 1; *Daily Times*, 17 August 1962, p. 4.
52. *Daily Times*, 21 August 1962, p. 6.
53. *West African Pilot*, 21 August 1962, p. 8.
54. *Daily Times*, 17 August 1962, p. 4; *West African Pilot*, 23 August 1962.
55. "A Federal Government for the Congo? No!" *Daily Times*, 23 August 1962, p. 5.
56. United Nations, *Annual Report of the Secretary-General*, 16 June 1962–15 June 1963, pp. 1–4; *Africa Report*, 7(9) (October 1962):22.
57. United Nations, *Annual Report of the Secretary-General*, 16 June 1962–15 June 1963, pp. 1–4.
58. *Africa Report*, 7(9) (October 1962):22; United Nations, *Annual Report of the Secretary-General*, 16 June 1962–15 June 1963, pp. 1–4.
59. Interview with Dr. Elias at the University of Lagos (August 1966).
60. Report of Defense Minister to the House of Representatives, H/R Debates, 18 April 1961; *Daily Times*, 15 September 1960.
61. *Mr. Prime Minister*, p. 43.
62. *West African Pilot*, 17 September 1960, p. 4.
63. *Daily Times*, 16 September 1960.
64. Editorial, *Daily Express*, 19 October 1960.
65. *UN Review*, January 1961, p. 31.
66. *Daily Express*, 21 September 1960.
67. The USSR did contribute planes, other matériel, and advisers to Lumumba but not under UN auspices.
68. *West African Pilot*, 20 October 1960.
69. H/R Debates, 1960–61, 1:251.
70. For accounts of the major clashes see: United Nations, *GAOR*, 15th sess., 1960–61, Annexes, vol. 2, Agenda Item 85 (Doc. S/4601/A/4682), pp. 60–62; *Royal Nigerian Army Magazine*, 2(3) (May 1962): 45–47, 56–69, 72–77; *The Nigerian Army Magazine*, 1(1) (October 1963): 61–67; H/R Debates, 18 April 1961, pp. 653ff; Richard Lawson, *Strange Soldiering*, pp. 26–40.
71. Details of these activities were recorded in the *Nigerian Army Magazine*, published during the entire period Nigerian troops served in the Congo. The major Nigerian dailies also reported the activities and military engagements in which Nigerian troops were involved. Typical of the guard duties the troops performed were those at Lovanium University, where the Congolese Parliament reconvened and agreed on the formation of Adoula's Government of National Reconciliation; at Kitona, where Tshombe was guarded during his talks with Premier Adoula in December 1961; at Léopoldville, where Katanga members of the Congolese Parliament met their other central government colleagues to negotiate terms of reunification; and again at Léopoldville, where Third Battalion troops prevented Antoine Gizenga, leader of the Stanleyville regime, from being strangled to death by a Léopoldville faction of the Congolese National Army.
72. United Nations, *SCOR*, 18th Year, Supplement for July–September 1963: "Re-

port of the Secretary-General on the Question of Military Disengagement in the Congo (Léopoldville)," pp. 166–78.

73. Ohawady Alily, "Unit Notes," First Battalion, Nigerian Army (1964), copy owned by the author.

74. Lawson, *Strange Soldiering*, p. 18.

75. *Daily Times*, 6 March 1961; H/R Debates, 18 April 1961, p. 651.

76. United Nations, *Annual Report of the Secretary-General*, 16 June 1960–15 June 1961, p. 38; *Federal Nigeria*, 4(7–9) (July–September 1961): 8–9.

77. *West African Pilot*, 10 December 1960.

78. Ibid., p. 1.

79. *Federal Nigeria*, 4(7–9) (July–September 1961): 9.

80. "Nigeria Police on Duty in Léopoldville," *Nigeria Police Magazine*, 10(1) (March 1961): 20.

81. *Federal Nigeria*, 4(7–9) (1961): 9.

82. Press officer, Nigerian Police Force, "The Nigeria Police Congo Operation," 1966, copy given to the author.

83. Reprinted in *The Nigeria Police Magazine*, 9(2) (September 1962): 17.

84. Press officer, Nigerian Police Force, "The Nigerian Police Congo Operation."

85. "Welcome statement by Rt. Hon. Prime Minister on 9 January 1966, on the return of the last police contingent from the Republic of the Congo," mimeographed copy in the collection of the author (n.p.: Press officer, Nigeria Police Force).

86. John Stoessinger, "The United Nations: Financing Peace-keeping Operations," in *Power and Order: 6 Cases in World Politics*, ed. J. G. Stoessinger and A. F. Westin, pp. 140–78.

87. This figure does not include the expenses of individual member states contributing military and police contingents to the United Nations Operations in the Congo. United Nations, *SCOR*, 18th Year, Supplement for July–September 1963 (Doc. A/5567), p. 168, par. 7; United Nations, *GAOR*, 18th sess., 17 September–17 December 1963, Annexes, vol. 2: "Report of the Fifth Committee"; United Nations, *GAOR*, 18th sess., 1963, Annexes, vol. 2, Agenda Item 59: "UN Operation in the Congo: Cost Estimates," pp. 1–11.

88. *UN Review*, April 1962, pp. 20–21.

89. Ibid.

90. United Nations, *GAOR*, 16th sess., *General Assembly Draft Resolution* A/C.5/L. 706 and Add. 1; A/C.5/SR. 903, par. 2, p. 319.

91. United Nations, *GAOR*, 18th sess., Fifth Committee, 1008–1018 meetings.

92. H/R Debates, 29 March 1961, p. 599; 18 April 1961, pp. 654–55.

93. *Africa Digest*, April 1964.

94. Ghana was in a similar predicament. See W. Scott Thompson, *Ghana's Foreign Policy, 1957–1966: Diplomacy, Ideology and the New State*, pp. 128–34; *The Nigerian Army Magazine*, 3 (December 1965): 72; letter to *West African Pilot*, 22 November 1961.

95. Sir Abubakar did call for the expansion of the membership of some organs of the United Nations—the Security Council and the Economic and Social Council—to give Africa its due place and voice within those organs of the world organization.

Chapter 6: Avenues of Policy Implementation: Bilateral Aid
(text pages 119–26)

1. The groups that attempted collective action in the Congo crisis included the Second Conference of Independent African States, Addis Abba, June 1960; the Monrovia Conference of Independent African States, May 1961; and the African Summit in Lagos, January 1962. For details of their efforts see: United Nations, *GAOR*, 15th sess., pt. 1, vol. 2, 1960, p. 1473, par. 71; *Daily Times*, 18 May; 15, 20 June 1961; 17, 30 January 1962; Colin Legum, *Pan-Africanism: A Short Political Guide* (New York: Praeger, 1962), pp. 45–48, and rev. ed. (1965), appendix 5, p. 177; Legum, *Congo Disaster*, pp. 145–47; Nigeria, Federal Ministry of Information, *African Summit in Monrovia;* United Nations, *Report of the UN Conciliation Commission for the Congo*, appendix; *West African Pilot*, 15 May 1961, p. 5; 23 June 1961, p. 3; 30 January 1962; "African Summit in Lagos," *Federal Nigeria* 5(1) (January 1962): 18; United Nations, *Annual Report of the Secretary-General*, 16 June 1961–15 June 1962, p. 21.
2. The U.S. Marshall Plan, Point Four Program, and policy of containment were all aspects of this kind of policy. "With [foreign aid programs] we have an opportunity to influence events in crucial areas of the world. Without them, our power to shape events is drastically diminished," Edmund S. Muskie, then U.S. secretary of state, told the Foreign Policy Association in New York, 7 July 1980 (*New York Times*, 8 July 1980).
3. Soviet aid to the United Arab Republic, Iraq, Guinea, and Algeria during this period was of this type.
4. Quoted in Nigeria, Federal Ministry of Information, *Dawn of Africa*, p. 6.
5. H/R Debates, January 1960, p. 95.
6. Nigeria, Federal Ministry of Information, *Dawn of Africa*, p. 18; see also Nnamdi Azikiwe, "Nigeria's African and Commonwealth Policies," *Federal Nigeria*, 6(7) (1963): 3.
7. See *Daily Express*, 21 September 1960; H/R Debates, 22 November 1961, p. 195.
8. See *Daily Times*, 18 January 1961; *West African Pilot*, 24 January 1961.
9. The officers included the Nigerian governor-general and the regional governors (patrons); Chief Ayo Rosiji (president); M. Bank-Anthony (secretary-treasurer); and Akintola Williams (auditor).
10. See *Daily Times*, 18, 25, 26, 28 January; 1, 6, 11, 14, 16, 18 February 1961;*West African Pilot*, 24 January 1961, p. 2.
11. See *Daily Times*, 15 November 1960, p. 2.
12. Interview with Dr. Robert C. Good (formerly U.S. ambassador to Zambia) at Denver, Colorado, 1967.
13. United Nations, *Annual Report of the Secretary-General*, 16 June 1962–15 June 1963, pp. 14–15.
14. United Nations, *SCOR*, 18th Year, Supplement for July–September 1963 (Doc. S/5428), p. 174, pars. 29–30.
15. See *Daily Times*, 7 December 1961, p. 2; 23 May 1963, p. 16.
16. The Congolese government paid Nigeria great tribute for its role in the police

training program. Two Nigerian diplomats to the Congo told the author that Nigeria's police aid to the Congo would have lasted longer but for the jealousy it provoked among some other African states. Interview, Information Officer, Nigeria Police Force, Lagos.

Chapter 7: Congolese Appraisal of Nigeria's Role
(text pages 127–37)

1. *Nigeria Police Magazine,* 9(2) (September 1962):17; *West African Pilot,* 10 February 1961, p. 6.
2. H/R Debates, 17 April 1961, p. 603.
3. See *West African Pilot,* 7 August 1961, p. 3.
4. See reprints from *Actualités Africaines* in *West African Pilot,* 10 February 1961, p. 6; *Nigeria Police Magazine,* 9(2) (September 1962):17.
5. Reprinted in *West African Pilot,* 4 December 1962, p. 8; *Daily Times,* 14 December 1962, p. 20; 15 December 1962, p. 5.
6. A. B. Oyebode, "Towards a New Policy on Decolonization," in Akinyemi, ed., p. 104; H/R Debates, 1960–61, 1:317.
7. See *Federal Nigeria,* 3(10) (November–December 1960):8; H/R Debates, 1960–61, 1:196–98.
8. *West African Pilot,* 9 August 1961.
9. In a 24 August 1960 cable from Léopoldville to the CIA director, the CIA station officer (Léopoldville) reported: "Anti-Lumumba leaders approached Kasavubu with plan assassinate Lumumba . . . Kasavubu refused agreed saying he reluctant resort violence and no other leader sufficent stature replace Lumumba" (United States Senate, *Alleged Assassination Plots Involving Foreign Leaders: An Interim Report of the Select Committee to Study Governmental Operations with Respect to Intelligence Activities* [Washington: U.S. Government Printing Office, 1975], p. 15).
10. See *West African Pilot,* 10–12, 18 August 1961; *Daily Times,* 10 August 1961.
11. *Daily Times,* 19 February 1962.
12. Reproduced in *Daily Times,* 19 March 1963, p. 6.
13. See *Daily Times,* 4 May 1963.
14. Ibid., 6 May 1963, p. 11.
15. Ibid.
16. Ibid., 9 May 1963, p. 3.
17. Ibid., 8 May 1963.
18. See *Mr. Prime Minister,* p. 203.
19. From July 1964 (when Moise Tshombe was appointed prime minister of the Congo by President Kasavubu) a rebel group, Conseil National de Liberation, struggled to overthrow the central government. In August of that year, after what appeared to be initial success, the rebel group found themselves in difficulties. Consequently they took hostage about 2,000 nationals of the United States and Belgium—countries which had been assisting Tshombe's central government— as negotiating counters to halt advancing columns of the central government

forces closing in on Stanleyville. On 24 November 1964, at the request of Tshombe's government, a Belgian-American parachute operation undertook to rescue the hostages. The task was accomplished, in the process killing thousands of northern Congolese nationals and rousing the vehement anger and protest of several African states.

20. *Daily Times*, 5 December 1965, p. 8.
21. See Kwame Nkrumah, *Challenge of the Congo*, pp. 290–92.

Chapter 8: Conclusion (text pages 138–50)

1. For the UN aspect of the experience see Catherine Hoskyns, *The Congo since Independence*, pp. 476–80.
2. See K. W. J. Post, "Nigerian Pamphleteers and the Congo," *Journal of Modern African Studies* 2(3) (November 1964):305–18.
3. Tshombe was asked by Kasavubu and Mobutu as a gesture of genuine national reconciliation and recognition of economic and political realities, to form the government in 1964, at the end of Adoula's government.
4. See "Zaire: Mobutu under Fire," *Africa Confidential*, 21(14) (2 July 1980): 1–3; "Anti-Mobutu Feeling Swells Among Masses Living in Destitution," *The Wall Street Journal*, 25 June 1980; "A Zaire Dossier," *Africa News* 29 May 1978; C. Young, "Zaire: The Unending Crisis," *Foreign Affairs* (Fall 1978), pp. 169–85; K. Adelman, "Zaire's Year of Crisis," *African Affairs* (January 1978), pp. 36–44.
5. It took the intervention of foreign troops (Moroccans and the French Legionnaires) to rescue the Congo (Zaire) in 1977 and 1978 from invasions of its Shaba Province by about two thousand rebels based in Angola. Tshombe, too, had relied heavily on foreign mercenaries rather than on soldiers of the Congolese National Army to subdue internal rebellion. See "A Zaire Dossier," *Africa News*, 29 May 1978, pp. 5–9; Young, "Zaire: The Unending Crisis," *Foreign Affairs*, 57(1) (Fall 1978): 169–85; Ghislaim Kabwit, "Zaire: The Roots of the Continuing Crisis," *The Journal of Modern African Studies* 17(3) (September 1979): 381–407.
6. For example, the quest for political unity and economic cooperation among African states; the nature of the relationships between African states and their former colonial rulers on the one hand and the superpowers on the other; and the liberation of Southern Africa from Portuguese and white minority regimes.
7. See *Morning Post*, 30 October 1961; A. B. Oyebode, "Towards a New Policy on Decolonization," in *Nigeria and the World: Readings in Nigerian Foreign Policy,* ed. A. Bolaji Akinyemi, pp. 104–7.
8. Nigeria's almost complete isolation from the Eastern bloc of powers during its colonial years was largely responsible for its cautious approach to Warsaw Pact members after Nigerian independence. The prime minister had thought it unnecessary to forget Nigeria's old friends, from whom most of the aid for economic development came. See J. S. Coleman, "The Foreign Policy of Nigeria," in *Foreign Policies in a World of Change,* ed. Black and Thompson, pp. 379–405.
9. See Obafemi Awolowo, *The People's Republic,* p. 35.

10. Ibid., p. 331.
11. See *Daily Times*, 22 June 1960; 15, 28 June 1961.
12. See W. Scott Thompson, *Ghana's Foreign Policy, 1957–1966: Diplomacy, Ideology and the New State*, p. 134.
13. It was not until the overthrow of Gen. Yakubu Gowon's government in July 1975 that Nigeria departed drastically from aspects of the foreign policy tradition established by Sir Abubakar. Notable then was Nigeria's support and recognition of the Popular Movement for the Liberation of Angola (MPLA) government of Angola when the Organisation of African Unity was unable to make up its mind and the major Western powers—the United States, in particular—supported the National Front for the Liberation of Angola and the National Union for the Total Independence of Angola (FNLA and UNITA), opponents of MPLA. Nigeria followed its recognition of the MPLA government with intensive diplomatic efforts that culminated in Organisation of African Unity recognition for the MPLA government. During the civilian administration of President Alhaji Shehu Shagari, however, the pendulum appears to have swung totally back to the Abubakar foreign-policy tradition of caution and low profile. See "Nigeria: Political Realignment," *Africa Confidential* 22(17) (19 August 1981): 1–4.
14. See John de Saint Jorre, *The Nigerian Civil War* (London: Hodder & Stoughton, 1972); Guy Arnold, *Modern Nigeria* (London: Longman, 1977), pp. 135–36; Michael Crowder, *The Story of Nigeria* (London: Faber & Faber, 1978), pp. 260–61.
15. See Akinyemi, ed., *Nigeria and the World*, pp. x–xi. The Murtala Ramat Muhammed and Olusegun Obasanjo administrations, occuring after 1975, were characterized by continuity and change. Most of the changes the two men introduced, however, were essentially those of style, not a fundamental or wholesale departure from the principles established by Sir Abubakar. That Muhammed and Obasanjo were definitely more vigorous and decisive in their prosecution of foreign policy than their predecessors may be attributed to their personalities. The change was certainly facilitated by a phenomenal increase both in the production and price of crude oil and in investment opportunities in a growing economy, which provided Nigeria enormous political leverage in international politics during their tenure.
16. Under Sir Abubakar's low-profile policy Nigeria was required to operate within the consensus of the African Group in the United Nations and later in the Organisation of African Unity; to use quiet diplomacy, that is, minimal or no publicity for Nigerian initiatives; to reject flamboyance on the part of Nigerian diplomats; and to demand no political concessions in return for Nigerian assistance.
17. Mazi R. Ofoegbu and Chibuzo S. A. Ogbuagu, "Towards a New Philosophy of Foreign Policy for Nigeria," in Akinyemi, ed. *Nigeria and the World*, p. 126. These critics forgot that Ghana, as the first sub-Saharan African state to achieve self-rule (April 1957), had had international exposure and experience as an independent state three years longer than Nigeria.
18. For example, see Thompson, *Ghana's Foreign Policy*, pp. 117–61.
19. Nigeria's population ironically carries a disadvantage in international relations: its

population of eighty million (a fifth of the total population of Africa) puts it in a frightening position in relation to smaller African states, causing concern and suspicion among its neighbors. See Guy Arnold, *Modern Nigeria,* pp. 134–35; Akinyemi, ed., *Nigeria and the World,* pp. xiii, 121.

20. Particularly in the Congo. There Nkrumah's policy was a disaster and earned Ghana "the opprobrium of the moderate [African] states and of the Kasavubu-Mobutu regime." Nkrumah lost what he considered to be his own foothold in the vital center of Africa and also the confidence of the West. Thompson, *Ghana's Foreign Policy,* p. 151.

21. Arnold, *Modern Nigeria,* p. 143.

22. Mazi Ray Ofoegbu and Chibuzo S. A. Ogbuagu, "Towards a New Philosophy of Foreign Policy for Nigeria," in Akinyemi, ed., *Nigeria and the World,* pp. 123–24.

Selected References

Nigerian Government Publications

Federal Ministry of Information. *African Summit in Monrovia*. Apapa: Nigerian National Press, Ltd., n.d.

———. *Dawn of Africa*. Apapa: Nigerian National Press, n.d.

———. *Federal Nigeria: Record of Progress and Development,* vol. 3, nos. 1–10 (Jan.–Dec. 1960); vol. 4, nos. 2–12 (Jan.–Dec. 1961); vol. 5, nos. 1–11 (Jan.–Nov. 1962); vol. 6, no. 7 (Oct. 1963); vol. 6, no. 8 (Nov.–Dec. 1963); vol. 7, no. 6 (Nov.–Dec. 1964).

———. "Foreign Policy of the Federation of Nigeria: Statement by the Prime Minister in the House of Representatives," Lagos, 20 August 1960.

———. *Mr. Prime Minister: A Selection of Speeches Made by Alhaji the Right Honourable Sir Abubakar Tafawa Balewa, Prime Minister of the Federation of Nigeria*. Apapa: Nigerian National Press, 1964.

Federation of Nigeria. *Governor-General's Speeches to the House of Representatives, 1952–1961*. Lagos: Federal Government Printer, 1961.

———. *House of Representatives Debates,* 2d sess., vol. 1: 1953.

———. *House of Representatives Debates, Official Report,* vol. 3, Session 1959–60: 5–18 August 1959.

———. *House of Representatives Debates, Official Report,* Session 1960–61: 11–22 Jan., 3–20 August 1960.

———. *House of Representatives Debates, Official Report,* vol. 1, Session 1960–61: 30–31 March, 1, 2, 4–9, 11–14, 16, 19–23, 25–29 April, end of May 1960.

———. *Official Gazette,* 47(20) (14 April 1960), pt. D.

———. *Our Ministers Speak,* Crown Bird Series, no. 24. Lagos: Public Relations Dept., n.d.

———. *Parliamentary Debates,* 1st sess.,1960–61, House of Representatives, vol. 1: 14, 17–19, 21–6, 28–9 November 1960.

———. *Parliamentary Debates,* 1st Parliament, 1961–62, vol. 1: 29–30 March, 1, 4, 8, 10–12 April; 1st Parliament, 2d sess.,1961–62, vol. 2: 13–15, 17–20 April, 20 July, 23, 25–26, 28–31 August, 1–2, 4 September 1961; 15–18, 20–25, 27–31 March, 2–7 April 1962.

_____. *Parliamentary Debates,* 1st Parliament, 3d sess., 1962–63, vol. 1: 21–24, 26–31 March, 2–7 April 1962.

_____. *Parliamentary Debates,* 1st Parliament, vol. 2: 9–14, 16–19 April, 29 May 1962.

_____. *Parliamentary Debates,* 1st Parliament, 4th sess., 1963–64, vol. 2(b): 16–20, 22–27, 29 April, 3 June 1963.

_____. *Parliamentary Debates,* 1st Parliament, vol. 2(a): 27–30 March, 1–6, 8–11 April 1963.

_____. Report by the Ad Hoc Committee of the Nigerian Constitutional Conference Held in Lagos in February 1958.

_____. Report of the Resumed Nigeria Constitutional Conference Held in London in September and October 1958.

_____. *The Economic Survey of Nigeria.* Lagos: Federal Government Printer, 1959.

_____. The Nigeria (Constitution) Order in Council, 1960 (no. 1652 of 1960) in *Supplement to the Official Gazette Extraordinary,* no. 62, vol. 47, 30 Sept. 1960, pt. B.

_____. The Training of Nigerians for the Representation of Their Country Overseas: A Statement of Policy by the Government of the Federation of Nigeria. Lagos: Federal Government Printer, 1956.

_____. *Who's Who of the Federal House of Representatives.* Lagos: Federal Information Service, 1958.

United Nations Publications

United Nations. *Annual Report of the Secretary-General on the Work of the Organization,* 16 June 1960–15 June 1961, supplement no. 1 (A/4800); 16 June 1961–15 June 1962, supplement no. 1 (A/5501); 16 June 1962–15 June 1963, supplement no. 1 (A/5501); 16 June 1963–15 June 1964, supplement no. 1 (A/5801); 16 June 1964–15 June 1965, supplement no. 1 (A/6001).

_____. *General Assembly, Official Records,* 15th sess., pt. 1, Plenary Meetings, vol. 1: 20 Sept.–17 Oct. 1960; vol. 2: 27 Oct.–20 Dec. 1960; 7 March –21 April 1961.

_____. *General Assembly, Official Records,* 15th sess., 1960–61, 15:13 annexes, vol. 2, Doc. A/4682 (S/4601).

_____. *General Assembly, Official Records,* 15th sess., pts. 1, 2, Fifth Committee: Administrative and Budgetary Questions, July 1960–April 1961.

_____. *General Assembly, Official Records,* 15th sess., pt. 2, Fifth Committee, 1961.

_____. *General Assembly, Official Records,* 15th sess., annexes, Agenda 85: The Situation in the Republic of the Congo, 1960–1961.

_____. *General Assembly, Official Records*, 15th sess., supplement no. 2 (A/4494): Report of the Security Council to the General Assembly, 16 July 1959–15 July 1960.

_____. *General Assembly, Official Records*, 4th special sess., annexes, Agenda Item 7, 14 May–27 June 1963.

_____. *General Assembly, Official Records*, 16th sess., Plenary Meetings, vol. 1: 19 Sept.–18 Oct. 1961; vol. 2: 19 Oct.–15 Dec. 1961; vol. 3: 18 Dec. 1961–28 June 1962.

_____. *General Assembly, Official Records*, 16th sess., supplement no. 2 (A/4867): Report of the Security Council to the General Assembly, 16 July 1960–15 July 1961.

_____. *General Assembly, Official Records*, 16th sess., Fifth Committee, Administrative & Budgetary Questions, 20 Sept. 1961–22 Feb. 1962, Doc. A/C 5/SR. 862, pars. 43–45.

_____. *General Assembly, Official Records*, 16th sess., Fourth Committee, Trusteeship, 1961/62, Doc. A/C. 4/SR. 1215, par. 4.

_____. *General Assembly, Official Records*, 17th sess., Plenary Meetings, vol. 1: 18 Sept.–4 Oct. 1962; vol. 2: 5 Oct.–20 Nov. 1962; vol. 3: 21 Nov.–20 Dec. 1962.

_____. *General Assembly, Official Records*, 17th sess., supplement no. 2 (A/5202): Report of the Security Council to the General Assembly, 16 July 1961–15 July 1962.

_____. *General Assembly, Official Records*, 18th sess., Plenary Meeting, vol. 1: 17 Sept.–14 Oct. 1963; vol. 2: 14 Oct.–20 Nov. 1963; vol. 3: 21 Nov.–17 Dec. 1963.

_____. *General Assembly, Official Records*, 18th sess., annexes, vol. 2: 17 Sept.–17 Dec. 1963.

_____. *General Assembly, Official Records*, 18th sess., supplement no. 2 (A/5502): Report of the Security Council to the General Assembly, 16 July 1962–15 July 1963.

_____. *General Assembly, Official Records*, 18th sess., Fifth Committee, Administrative & Budgetary Questions, Summary Records of Meetings, 17 Sept.–16 Dec. 1963.

_____. *Introduction to the Annual Report of the Secretary General on the Work of the Organization*, 16 June 1961–15 June 1962, supplement no. IA (A/5201) (Add. 1).

_____. *Security Council, Official Records*, 15th year, supplement for July, August, September 1960.

_____. *Security Council, Official Records*, 16th year, supplement for Jan., Feb., March 1961.

_____. *Security Council, Official Records*, 18th year, supplement for July–Sept. 1963.

_____. *Security Council, Official Records*, 19th year, supplement for Jan.–

March 1964, Doc. S/54288/Add. 2; supplement for April–June 1964, Doc. S/5784.

_____. *United Nations and the Congo: Some Salient Facts.* 1963.

_____. *United Nations Review.* May 1961, pp. 5, 35–36; Dec. 1961; April 1962, pp. 20–21.

_____. *United Nations Yearbook of International Trade Statistics, 1963, 1964.* New York: 1965, 1966.

_____. *Yearbook of the United Nations, 1961.* New York: UN Office of Information, 1963.

United States Government Publications

Department of Commerce. *Africa: A Growth Market for U.S. Business.* Washington: U.S. Government Printing Office, 1968.

_____. "Overseas Business Reports: Basic Data on the Economy of the Democratic Republic of the Congo (Kinshasa)." OBR 68(6), April 1968.

Department of State. *Bulletin.* 1960–64.

Senate. *Alleged Assassination Plots Involving Foreign Leaders: An Interim Report of the Select Committee to Study Governmental Operations with Respect to Intelligence Activities.* Washington: U.S. Government Printing Office, 1975.

Doctoral Dissertations

Amirie, Abbas. "The United Nations Intervention in the Congo Crisis, 1960–1961: With Special Emphasis on the Political Role of the Late Secretary General, Dag Hammarskjöld." Southern Illinois University, 1967.

Brenneman, Lyle Eugene. "Conflict and Change in the Republic of Zaire: An Analysis of Domestic Factors Leading to Military Rule." The American University, 1976.

Cole, Babalola. "The United Nations Peace-Keeping Operations: The Actions of the African Nations in the Congo." Georgetown University, 1967.

Culp, Wayne Alford. "An Analysis of Congolese Foreign Policy during the Tshombe Prime Ministry, July 1964–October 1965." The American University, 1974.

Gingrich, Newton Leroy. "Belgian Education Policy in the Congo, 1945–1960." Tulane University, 1971.

Hyde, Emmanuel Aryeeguaye. "The Role of Ghana in the Congo Crisis: A Study of a Small State's Involvement in a Postcolonial Problem." University of Pennsylvania, 1971.

Kabwit, Ghislain Claude. "The Evolution of the Congo Foreign Policy 1960–1970: A Case Study in the Determinants Influencing the Making of Foreign Policy." The American University, 1975.

Kalb, Madeleine Jane Green. "The Soviet Union and the Congo: 1960–1962." Columbia University, 1971.

Keliams, Dean R. "United States Policy toward Intervention, with Special Reference to the Congo: 1960–1964." Southern Illinois University, 1966.

King, Mae Coates. "Nonalignment and the United Nations: The Congo Crisis 1960–1961." University of Idaho, 1968.

McNemar, Donald William. "International Law and Internal War: The Congo and the United Nations Model." Princeton University, 1971.

Ohaegbulam, Festus Ugboaja. "The Congo Crisis (1960–June 1964) as a Case Study of the Formative Stages of Nigeria's Foreign Policy." University of Denver, 1967.

Reid, Inez Smith. "Constitutional Development in the Democratic Republic of the Congo." Columbia University, 1968.

Sears, Richard Duncan. "The Political Behavior of African States in the Congo Crisis: July 1960–August 1961." Indiana University, 1970.

Singleton, Francis Seth. "The African States and the Congo Affair: 1960–1965." Yale University, 1968.

Struelens, Michel. "ONUC [United Nations Operations in the Congo] and International Politics." The American University, 1968.

Winkates, James Edward. "The Influence of the United Nations on National Policy: The United States in the Congo Crisis." University of Virginia, 1972.

Books

Abi-Saab, George. *The United Nations Operations in the Congo, 1960–1964*. New York: Oxford University Press, 1977.

Aboyade, Ojetunji. *Foundations of an African Economy: A Study of Investment and Growth in Nigeria*. New York: Frederick A. Praeger, 1966.

Akinyemi, A. Bolaji, ed. *Nigeria and the World: Readings in Nigerian Foreign Policy*. Ibadan: Oxford University Press, 1978.

Akinyemi, A. B. *Foreign Policy and Federalism: The Nigerian Experience*. Ibadan: Ibadan University Press, 1974.

Alexander, Henry Templer. *African Tightrope: My Two Years as Nkrumah's Chief of Staff*. New York: Praeger, 1966.

Aluko, Olajide. *Ghana and Nigeria*. New York: Barnes & Noble, 1976.

Awolowo, Obafemi. *AWO: The Autobiography of Chief Obafemi Awolowo*. Cambridge: Cambridge University Press, 1961.

———. *The People's Republic*. Ibadan: Oxford University Press, 1968.

Azikiwe, Nnamdi. *Zik: A Selection from the Speeches of Nnamdi Azikiwe*. Cambridge: Cambridge University Press, 1961.

Belgian Congo and Ruanda-Urundi Information and Public Relations. *Belgian Congo*. 2 vols. Translated by F.H. and C. Heldt. Brussels, 1959.

Biebuyck, Daniel, and Douglas, Mary. *Congo: Tribes and Parties*. London: Royal Anthropological Institute, 1961.

Black, Joseph E., and Thompson, Kenneth W., eds. *Foreign Policies in a World of Change*. New York: Harper & Row, Publishers, 1963.

Brett, Lionel, ed. *Constitutional Problems of Federalism in Nigeria*. Lagos: Times Press, 1961.

Bretton, Henry L. *Power and Stability in Nigeria*. New York: Praeger, 1962.

Burns, Arthur Lee. *Peace Keeping by UN Forces, from Suez to the Congo*. Princeton: Princeton University Press, 1963.

Calder, Ritchie. *Agony of the Congo*. London: Gollanz, 1961.

Chome, Jules. *Le Gouvernment Congolais et L'O.N.U.: UN Paradox Tragique*. Suivit de texte intégral des deux Rapports Dayal et de la réponse du gouvernment belge, 1961.

_____. *La Crise Congolaise: de l'indépendance à l'intervention militaire belge, 30 juin–juillet*. Brussels: Éditions de "Remarques Congolaises," 1960.

Coleman, J. S. *Nigeria: Background to Nationalism*. Berkeley and Los Angeles: University of California Press, 1958.

Davies, H. O. *Nigeria: The Prospects for Democracy*. London: Weidenfeld & Nicholson, 1961.

Dayal, Rajeshwar. *Mission for Hammarskjöld: The Congo Crisis*. Princeton, N.J.: Princeton University Press, 1976.

Dinant, Georges, *L'O.N.U. Face à la Crise Congolaise*. Brussels: Éditions de "Remarques Congolaises," 1962.

Dumont, Georges H. *La Table Ronde Belgo-Congolaise (Janvier–Fevrier 1960)*. Paris: Éditions Universitaires, 1961.

Epelle, Sam. *The Promise of Nigeria*. London: Pan Books Ltd., 1960.

Ezera, Kalu. *Constitutional Developments in Nigeria*. Cambridge: Cambridge University Press, 1960.

Frankel, Joseph. *The Making of Foreign Policy*. New York: Oxford University Press, 1963.

Georges, Brausch. *Belgian Administration in the Congo*. New York: Oxford University Press, 1961.

Gerard-Libois, Jules. *Katanga Secession*. Madison: University of Wisconsin Press, 1966.

Gordon, King. *The UN in the Congo: A Quest for Peace*. New York: Carnegie Endowment for International Peace, 1962.

Hanna, William John. *Independent Black Africa: The Politics of Freedom*. Chicago: Rand McNally & Company, 1964.

Hartmann, Frederick H. *The Relations of Nations*. 2d ed. New York: The Macmillan Co., 1964.

Hempstone, Smith. *Katanga Report*. London: Faber & Faber, 1962.

Higgins, Rosalyn. *United Nations Peacekeeping, 1946–1967: Documents and Commentary,* pt. 3: "Africa." Oxford: Oxford University Press, 1980.

Hodgkins, Thomas. *Nationalism in Colonial Africa.* New York: New York University Press, 1957.

Hoskyns, Catherine. *The Congo since Independence: January 1960–December 1961.* London: Oxford University Press, 1965.

————. *The Congo: A Chronology of Events: January 1960–December 1961.* Oxford: Oxford University Press, 1962.

Houart, Pierre. *La Pénétration Communiste au Congo: Commentaires et documents sur les événements du juin–novembre 1960.* Brussels: Center de documentation internationale, 1960.

House, Arthur H. *UN in the Congo: The Political and Civilian Efforts.* Washington: University Press of America, 1978.

Hovet, T. *Africa in the UN.* Evanston, Ill.: Northwestern University Press, 1963.

Kanza, Thomas. *Conflict in the Congo: The Rise and Fall of Lumumba.* Baltimore: Penguin Books, 1972.

Kitchen, Helen, ed. *Footnotes to the Congo Story: An "Africa Report" Anthology.* New York: Walker & Co., 1967.

Lawson, Richard G. *Strange Soldiering.* London: Hodder & Stoughton, 1963.

Lefever, Ernest W. *Crisis in the Congo: A UN Force in Action: Studies of U.S. Policy and the UN.* Washington: The Brookings Institution, 1965.

Legum, Colin, ed. *Africa: A Handbook to the Continent.* New York: Praeger, 1962.

————. *Congo Disaster.* London: Penguin Books, 1961.

————. *Pan-Africanism: A Short Political Guide.* Rev. ed. New York: Praeger, 1965.

Lemarchand, Réné. *Political Awakening in the Congo: The Politics of Fragmentation.* Berkeley: University of California Press, 1964.

London, Kurt. *The Making of Foreign Policy: East and West.* New York: J. P. Lippincott Co., 1965.

Lumumba, Patrice. *Lumumba Speaks: The Speeches and Writings of Patrice Lumumba,* edited by Jean Van Lierche. Boston: Little, Brown & Co., 1972.

Mackintosh, J. P. *Nigerian Government and Politics.* London: George Allen & Unwin Ltd., 1966.

Macridis, Roy C., ed. *Foreign Policy in World Politics.* 2d ed. Englewood Cliffs, N.J.: Prentice-Hall, 1962.

McKay, Vernon. *Africa in World Politics.* New York: Harper & Row, 1965.

Martin, Laurence W., ed. *Neutralism and Nonalignment: The New States in World Affairs.* New York: Praeger, 1962.

Marvin, David K., ed. *Emerging Africa in World Affairs*. San Francisco: Chandler Publishing Co., 1965.

Merriam, Alan P. *Congo: Background of Conflict*. Evanston: Northwestern University Press, 1961.

Michel, Serge. *Uhuru Lumumba*. Paris: R. Juilliard, 1962.

Modelski, George. *A Theory of Foreign Policy*. New York: Praeger, 1962.

Morgenthau, Hans J. *Politics among Nations: The Struggle for Power and Peace*. 3d ed. New York: Alfred A. Knopf, 1964.

Niedergang, Marcel. *Tempête sur le Congo*. Paris: Plan, 1960.

Nkrumah, Kwame. *Challenge of the Congo*. New York: International Publishers, 1967.

———. *Africa Must Unite*. New York: Praeger, 1963.

O'Brien, Conor Cruise. *To Katanga and Back: A UN Case History*. London: Hutchinson, 1962.

Odumosu, O. I. *The Nigerian Constitution: History and Development*. London: Sweet & Maxwell, 1963.

Okumu, Washington. *Lumumba's Congo: Roots of Conflict*. New York: I. Oblensky, 1963.

Oliver, E. I. *Nigeria: Economic and Commercial Conditions in Nigeria*. London: Her Majesty's Stationery Office, 1957.

Oyediran, Oyeleye, ed. *Survey of Nigerian Affairs*. Ibadan: Oxford University Press, 1978.

Padelford, Norman J., and Emerson, Rupert, eds. *Africa and World Order*. New York: Praeger, 1963.

Padelford, N. J., and Lincoln, George A. *The Dynamics of International Politics*. 2d ed. New York: The Macmillan Co., 1967.

Phillips, Claude S. *The Development of Nigerian Foreign Policy*. Evanston: Northwestern University Press, 1964.

Post, K. W. J. *The New States of West Africa*. Baltimore: Penguin Books, 1964.

———. *The Nigerian Federal Elections of 1959: Politics and Administration in a Developing Political System*. London: Oxford University Press, 1963.

Ribeaud, Paul. *Adieu Congo*. Paris, 1961.

Rosenau, James, ed. *International Politics and Foreign Policy: A Reader in Research and Theory*. New York: The Free Press of Glencoe, Inc., 1961.

Royal Institute of International Affairs. *Survey of International Affairs 1959–1960*, edited by G. Barraclough. London: Oxford University Press, 1964.

———. *Survey of International Affairs 1961*, edited by D. C. Watt. London: Oxford University Press, 1965.

Schwarz, Frederick O. *Nigeria: The Tribes, the Nation, or the Race—The Politics of Independence*. Cambridge: M.I.T. Press, 1965.

Schwyler, Phillipa D. *Who Killed the Congo?* New York: Devin Adir Co., 1962.

Scott, Andrew M., and Dawson, Raymond H. *Readings in the Making of Foreign Policy*. New York: Praeger, 1961.

Scott, Ian, Sir. *Tumbled House: The Congo at Independence*. New York: Oxford University Press, 1969.

Segal, Ronald. *Political Africa: A Who's Who of Personalities and Parties*. New York: Praeger, 1961.

Sklar, Richard L. *Nigerian Political Parties: Power in an Emergent African Nation*. Princeton: Princeton University Press, 1963.

Snyder, Richard, et al. *Decision Making as an Approach to the Study of International Politics*. Princeton: Princeton University Press, 1954.

Stenmans, Alain. *Les premiers mois de la République du Congo (Léopoldville), 1 juillet–22 novembre 1960*. Brussels: 1961.

Stoessinger, John G., and Westin, Alan F., eds. *Power and Order: 6 Cases in World Politics*. New York: Harcourt, Brace & World, Inc., 1964.

Struelens, Michel. *The United Nations in the Congo: Or O.N.U.C. and International Politics*. Brussels: Max Arnold, Publisher, 1977.

Thiam, Doudou. *The Foreign Policy of African States*. New York: Praeger, 1964.

Thompson, W. Scott. *Ghana's Foreign Policy, 1957–1966: Diplomacy, Ideology and the New State*. Princeton: Princeton University Press, 1969.

Tilman, Robert O., and Cole, Taylor, eds. *The Nigerian Political Scene*. Durham, N.C.: Duke University Press, 1962.

Tournaire, Hélène. *Le Livre noir du Congo*. Paris: Perrin, 1963.

Tully, Andrew. *C.I.A.: The Inside Story*. New York: W. Morrow, 1962.

Urquhart, Brian. *Hammarskjöld*. New York: Alfred A. Knopf, 1972.

Welensky, Sir Roy. *Welensky's 4,000 Days: The Life and Death of the Federation of Rhodesia and Nyasaland*. London: Collins, 1964.

Wells, F. A., and Warmington, W. A. *Studies in Industrialization: Nigeria and the Cameroons*. London: Oxford University Press, 1962.

Young, M. Crawford. *Politics in the Congo: Decolonization and Independence*. Princeton: Princeton University Press, 1965.

Articles and Pamphlets

Adebayo, O. "The Foreign Policy of a Free Nigeria." *West African Pilot*, 23 September 1960.

Ademulegun, S. A. "Congo Diary: The Battle That Never Was." *Daily Times*, 11 August 1961.

Amachree, Godfrey K. J. *International Action in the Congo*. Pamphlet. n.p.: United Nations, 1963.

Anglin, Douglas G. "Nigeria: Political Non-alignment and Economic Alignment." *Journal of Modern African Studies* 2 (July 1964): 247–66.

Awa, Eme. "Nigeria's Foreign Policy: The Need for a Third Force." *Daily Times,* 12 October 1959.

_____. "Nigeria in the Politics of Africa." *West African Pilot,* 17 May 1961.

Awolowo, O. "Organization for African Community." *West African Pilot,* 29 June 1961.

Awoyinfa, Moses. "The Genius of Moderation: The Many Tributes to Alhaji Sir Abubaker Tafawa Balewa." *Daily Times,* 10 January 1962.

Azikiwe, N. "Nigeria in World Politics." *West African Pilot,* 6, 7 August 1959.

_____. "Policy for a Free Nigeria." *West African Pilot,* 22 August 1959.

_____. "The Future of Pan-Africanism." *West African Pilot,* 2, 4 September 1961.

Balewa, Abubakar T. "Nigeria Looks Ahead." *Foreign Affairs* 41(1) (October 1962).

Bavassa, Réné. "What Do You Think of the Nigeria Police?" *The Nigeria Police Magazine* 9 (September 1961).

Coleman, J. S. "The Foreign Policy of Nigeria." In *Foreign Policies in a World of Change,* edited by Joseph E. Black and K. W. Thompson. New York: Harper & Row, Publishers, 1963.

Decraene, Philippe. "The Monrovia Conference." *West African Pilot,* 23 June 1961.

"Epilogue to the Congo Operation." *The Nigeria Police Magazine* 13 (December 1965–January 1966):17–18.

Esin, O. A. "On the Question of Our Foreign Policy." *West African Pilot,* 18 July 1960.

Everwyn, Gerhard. "Which Way in Katanga?" *African Affairs: Journal of the Royal African Society* 61 (April 1962):149–57.

Eyo, Boco E. "The Significance of Nigerian Independence." *West African Pilot,* 9, 13 July 1960.

Ezera, Kalu. "Nigeria's Foreign Policy." *West African Pilot,* 12 July, 6 December 1960.

Frodin, Reuben. "Nigeria and the World Outside." *West Africa Series* 4(4) (Nigeria) AUFS (1961).

_____. "Political Potpourri." *West Africa Series* 4(3) (1961).

_____. "Though Tribe and Tongue May Differ." *West Africa Series* 4(2) (1961).

_____. "An African Corner Stone?" *West Africa Series* 4(5) (June 1961).

Fall, Bernard B. "Education in the Republic of the Congo." *Journal of Negro Education* 30 (Summer 1961):267–76.

Good, Robert C. "Four African Views of the Congo Crisis." *Africa Report* 6 (June 1961).

_____. "Congo Crisis: The Role of the New States." In *Neutralism,* edited by Arnold Wolfers. Washington: Foreign Policy Research, 1961.

Gray, Alan. "Congo Developments." *African Affairs: Journal of the Royal African Society* 62 (January 1963):8–15.

Hastings, Stephen. "The UN in Katanga." *African Affairs: Journal of the Royal African Society* 61 (July 1962):191–200.

Hoffmann, Stanley. "In Search of a Thread: The UN in the Congo Labyrinth." *International Organization* 16 (Spring 1962): 331–60.

Hoskyns, Catherine. "Violence in the Congo." *Transition* 4 (1965).

Ibegbu, F. "Experiences in a Military Detention Camp." *The Nigeria Police Magazine* 9 (September 1961):23–25.

Ita, Eyo. "On the Path of Destiny." *West African Pilot,* 7 November 1959.

Iguh, Thomas. *The Last Days of Lumumba (The Late Lion of the Congo): a Drama.* Onitsha: A. Onwudiwe & Sons, n.d.

———. *Tshombe of Katanga (a Drama).* Onitsha: A. Onwudiwe & Sons, n.d.

James, E. E. "Lessons from Our Congo Success." *The Nigeria Police Magazine* 13 (September–October 1965).

Jesman, Major Czeslaw. "Background to Events in the Congo." *African Affairs: Journal of the Royal African Society* 60 (July 1961):382–91.

Kabwit, Ghislain. "Zaire: The Roots of the Continuing Crisis." *Journal of Modern African Studies* 17(3) (Sept. 1979):381–407.

Kitchen, Helen. "Mutiny in the Congo: The Linchpin Gives Way." *Africa Special Report* 5 (August 1960).

Kraft, Joseph. "The Untold Story of UN Congo Army." *Harper's Magazine,* November 1960.

Lemarchand, Réné. "Patrice Lumumba: A Political Post Mortem?" *Africa Report* 6 (February 1961).

———. "How Lumumba Came to Power." *Africa Special Report* 5 (August 1960).

Mackintosh, J. P. "Nigeria's Foreign Policy." *Journal of Commonwealth Political Studies* 2 (November 1964):207–18.

Morgenthau, Hans J. "The Conduct of Foreign Policy." In *Aspects of American Government,* edited by Sydney Bailey. New York: The Hansard Society, 1950.

Munger, Edwin S. "Conflict in the Congo, Part I: Impressions of an Eyewitness." *Central and South African Series* 8(1), AUFS (1960).

———. "Conflict in the Congo, Part II: External Pressures." *Central and South African Series* 8(2), AUFS (1960).

———. "Conflict in the Congo, Part III: External Pressures." *Central and South African Series* 8(4), AUFS (1960).

Nimier, Benjamin. "African Participants in the UN Force in the Congo." *African Studies Bulletin* 8 (December 1964).

O'Brien, C. C. "Conflicting Concepts of the United Nations." In *Writers and*

Politics, edited by C. C. O'Brien. New York: Pantheon Books, 1965, pp. 195–214.

―――――. "The United Nations, the Congo and the Tshombe Government." In *Writers and Politics,* edited by C. C. O'Brien. New York: Pantheon Books, 1965, pp. 215–22.

Olisha, Okenwa. *The Life Story and Death of Mr. Lumumba.* Onitsha: A. Onwudiwe & Sons, n.d.

Perham, Margery. "A Prospect of Nigeria." *Daily Times,* 28 October 1960.

Post, K. W. J. "Nigerian Pamphleteers and the Congo." *Journal of Modern African Studies* 2 (November 1964).

Robertson, James. "Sovereign Nigeria." *African Affairs: Journal of the Royal African Society* 59 (April 1961):145–54.

Rosenau, James. "Pre-Theories and Theories of Foreign Policy." In *Approaches to Comparative and International Politics,* edited by R. Barry Farrell. Evanston: Northwestern University Press, 1966.

RWAFF (The). *Brief History.* Typed manuscript in the collection of the author, n.d.

Segal, Aaron. "Israel in Africa." *Africa Report* 8 (April 1963).

Sklar, Richard L., and Whitaker, C. S. "Nigeria." In *Political Parties and National Integration in Tropical Africa,* edited by J. S. Coleman and Carl G. Rosberg. Berkeley: University of California Press, 1964.

Sonnenfeldt, Helmut. "Lessons Learned in the Congo: Soviet Strategy in Africa." *Africa Report* 5 (November 1960).

―――――. "Nigeria as Seen from Moscow." *Africa Report* 6 (January 1961): 9–10.

Spencer, John H. "Africa at the UN: Some Observations." *International Organization* 16 (Spring 1962):375–86.

Stephen, Felix N. *The Trials of Lumumba, Jomo Kenyatta and St. Paul.* Onitsha: Njoku & Sons Bookshop, n.d.

Wachuku, Jaja. "Nigeria's Foreign Policy." In *Africa: The Political Pattern,* edited by Millar Maclure and Douglas Anglin. Toronto: University of Toronto Press, 1961.

Williams, David. "Nigeria in the UN." *Daily Times,* 5 October 1960.

Young, M. Crawford. "Congo: Background to Independence." *Transition* 5 (February 1966):34–40.

―――――. "Congo Political Parties Revisited." *Africa Report* 8 (January 1963): 14–20.

Zolberg, Aristide R. "A View from the Congo." *World Politics* 19 (October 1966):137–47.

Periodicals

Africa Digest. 7 (June 1960); 8 (August–December 1960), (April–June 1961); 9 (August 1961–June 1962); 10 (October 1962), (April–June 1963); 12 (August 1964).

Africa Report. 6 (June–July 1961); 7 (October–November 1962).

New Commonwealth. (October 1960):637–40; (February 1961):126–27; (October 1961):668–69.

Nigerian Army Magazine. 1 (October 1963); 3 (1965).

Royal Nigerian Army Magazine. 2 (March 1961); 3 (May 1962).

The Nigeria Police Magazine. 10 (March 1961): 20–23.

The Nigerian Students Voice: Journal of Research, News and Analysis. 3 (January 1966): 51–84.

West Africa. July 1960–1964.

West Africa Review. 31 (September–October 1960).

Index

Abubakar, Sir. *See* Balewa, Sir Abubakar Tafawa

Action Group of Nigeria, 16–17

Addis Ababa (Ethiopia), Conference of African Heads of State and Government at, 135

Adebo, Chief S. O., 115, 117

Adoula, Cyrille: biography, 50, 94–95; and Nigeria, 90, 125, 134–35, 136; as Congolese prime minister, 99, 123–24; and Congo constitutional reviews, 100–101; and U Thant Plan of National Reconciliation for Congo, 103

African states, 4, 119, 141–42, 143, 165n1, 167n6

African Summit, 165n1. *See also* Pan-Africanism

Afro-Asian states, 6. *See also* India

Aguiyi-Ironsi, Maj. Gen. J. T. U.: and UN Operations in the Congo, 52, 110, 127; as successor to Sir Abubakar, 147–48

AID (U.S. Agency for International Development), 123

Albania, 98

Alily, Capt. Ohawady, 110

Alliance des Bakongo, 40

Amachree, Godfrey, 96, 117

American Committee for Aid to Katanga Freedom Fighters, 37

Anglo-American block, 78, 79, 84. *See also* Great Britain; United States

Awolowo, Chief Obafemi, 79–81

Azikiwe, Dr. Nnamdi, 6, 15, 136

Balewa, Sir Abubakar Tafawa, 112–14; and African states, 6, 73, 116; assessed, 13, 130, 142; foreign policy of, 15, 17, 18–19, 72, 73–75, 78, 83–84, 118, 120, 146–49, 164n95, 168n16; and Great Britain, 17; biography, 53–54, 60, 145, 147–48, 168n13, 168n16; criticism of, 55–56, 64–66, 130–31, 148–49; and the Congo crisis, 53–65, 69, 77–78, 91, 107–8; and the United Nations, 63–64, 69, 164n95; and Congolese authorities, 134, 135–36

Bandung Conference (1955), 6

Baudouin (king of Belgium), 28

Bavassa, Réné, 113

Belgium: interests in Congo, 2, 3, 139, 166n19; intervention in Congo, 21, 32–33; colonial policy in Congo, 24, 25–29; officers in Congolese police and army, 31–32; support of Tshombe, 34–35, 139

Bello, Sir Ahmadu, 145–46
Benin (formerly Dahomey), 71
Bolikango, Jean, 26
Bomboko, Justin, 50, 98, 100, 132–33
British Commonwealth Relations Office, 14
Brussels Round Table Conference (1960), 29, 30
Bunche, Dr. Ralph, 45, 51, 139

Cameroon, 71
Canada, 101, 104–5
Casablanca group, 135
Centre d'Études des Problèmes Sociaux Indigènes, 25
Chad, 71
CIA (U.S. Central Intelligence Agency), 40; implicated in murder of Lumumba, 48
Cold war, 119; impact on Congo crisis, 1–3
Colonialism. *See* Belgium; Neo-colonialism
Confédération des Associations du Katanga, 33, 36, 37
Conference of African Heads of State and Government (at Addis Ababa, Ethiopia), 135
Congo, Democratic Republic of the (now Zaire), 20, 133; geography, 5–6, 23, 57; crisis in, 21, 24, 32–33; and rest of Africa, 39; police training program, 112, 165n16; since end of the UN Congo mission, 140–41, 167n5. *See also* Belgium; Force publique; *names of Congolese officials;* Nigeria; United Nations
Congo Conciliation Commission (United Nations), 91–92, 95–96
Congo Relief Fund, 121–22, 165n9

Congo Republic (Brazzaville), 71
Conseil National de Liberation, 166n19
Coquilhatville (city, now Mbandaka, Democratic Republic of the Congo), 121; Congolese summit conference at, 49
Courrier d'Afrique, (Léopoldville), 133
Czechoslovakia, 98

Dahomey (now Benin), 71
Davies, Chief H. O., 101–2
Dayal, Ambassador Rajeshwar, 88, 89, 92, 94, 97, 127, 139
Decolonization, Belgian approach to, 28–29. *See also* Belgium
Deputies, Chamber of (Democratic Republic of the Congo), 41

Edet, Louis O., 111
Eisenhower, Dwight D., 21
Elias, Dr. T. O., 59, 82, 100–105, 117
Equator province (Democratic Republic of the Congo), 23
Ethiopia, 70. *See also* Addis Ababa

Fagbenro-Beyioku, Chief O. A., 106–7
FAO (United Nations Food and Agricultural Organization), 110
Federal Constitution (1960) of Nigeria. *See* Nigeria: Federal Constitution (1960)
Federal system of government: in Congo, 42, 101
Force publique (Congo): mutiny of, 20, 21, 29–32; discontent of, 30–31; irresponsibility of, 141, 167n5
Ford Foundation, 123

Foreign aid, 95; and political strings, 119–20; as instrument of foreign policy, 119, 165n2, 165n3
Foreign policy formulation, 72. *See also* Nigeria: develops foreign policy principles
Foster, Maj. Gen. N. L., 108
France, 3, 4

Gabon, 71
Gardiner, Robert K.: envoy to Kasavubu, 98–99; and modernization of Congolese army, 123–24
Geiger, W., 100–101
George, Mrs. S., 121
Ghana: Congo policy of, 70; on Congo delegation to United Nations, 86–87; rivalry with Nigeria, 83; police from, in Congo, 112; UN troops from, 129
Gizenga, Antoine, 48, 49, 98
Good, Robert C., 70–71
Gordon, King, 35
Gowon, Gen. Yakubu, 148, 168n13
Great Britain, 3–4, 17, 70. *See also* Nigeria: independence of
Guinea, 70, 129

Hammarskjöld, Dag: on crisis, 24, 43; role in crisis, 43, 48, 97, 106, 111, 139; death of, 51, 139
Hodgkin, Thomas, 27

Ileo, Joseph, 41, 95, 162n32
"Independence constitution" (Nigeria). *See* Nigeria: Federal Constitution (1960)
India: interests in Congo, 39; and Congo constitutional review, 101, 104–5. *See also* Dayal, Ambassador Rajeshwar

Italy, 100–101
Ivory Coast, 71

James, E. E., 125
Janssens, Lt. Gen. Emile, 31, 32

Kalonji, Albert, 23, 37, 38, 128
Kamina (air base), 5, 32, 97, 99
Kasai province (Democratic Republic of the Congo), 23, 38; deployment of Nigerian troops in, 108
Kasavubu, Joseph: and Congo constitutional crisis, 21, 40–41, 49; and United Nations, 21, 47, 86–87, 92, 100, 127; implicated in Lumumba assassination, 131–32, 166n9; overthrown by Mobutu, 137, 140
Katanga province (now Shaba province, Democratic Republic of the Congo): secession, 21, 33–37; geography, 23, 34; and UN Operations, 51–52; self-determination for, 90; deployment of Nigerian troops in, 108
Khrushchev, Nikita S., 21, 88
Kisangani. *See* Stanleyville
Kitona (city, Democratic Republic of the Congo): agreements at, 51–52
Kivu province (Democratic Republic of the Congo), 23; deployment of Nigerian troops in, 108

Lagos (Nigeria): telecommunications link with Léopoldville, 133; Summit Conference of African states, 134
Lagos *West African Pilot,* 106, 131–32
Legum, Colin, 35

Léopoldville (now Kinshasa, capital of Democratic Republic of the Congo): headquarters of UN Congo Operations, 99; telecommunications link with Lagos, 133

Léopoldville province (Democratic Republic of the Congo), 23; deployment of Nigerian troops in, 108

Liberia, 70

Libya, 70

Lihau, Marcel, 100

Loi fondamentale (interim Congolese constitution), 34; and Congo constitutional crisis, 40–41; replacement recommended, 95, 100

London *Daily Telegraph,* 4

London *Economist,* 56

London *Observer,* 5–6

London *Times,* 92

Lovanium University, 49, 50, 99, 123

Lumumba, Patrice: on Katanga secession, 21; relations with Force publique, 30–31; and Congo constitutional crisis, 40; and United Nations, 40, 42–43, 94; and Soviet Union, 42; arrest and assassination of, 48, 94; and Nigeria, 86, 87, 88, 126, 128, 129, 140; and Joseph Ileo, 162n32

Lumumbists, 128–29

Madagascar (formerly Malagasy Republic), 71

Matadi (city, Democratic Republic of the Congo), 32–33

Mbandaka. *See* Coquilhatville

Medical aid, 121

Michel, Serge, 40

Mobutu, Joseph Marie (now Mobutu Sese Seko): "authenticity drive" by, 7; seizure of Congolese government, 21; and Congo constitutional crisis, 31, 41; and UN Operations in the Congo, 127; and Nigeria, 133–34, 137; and Nkrumah of Ghana, 137; since end of UN Congo mission, 140–41, 167n5; and CIA, 155n60

Monrovia (Liberia) Conference of Independent African States, 165n1

Monrovia group, 135

Morgenthau, Hans J., 76

Morocco, 70, 129

Moumie, Felix, 40

Movement Nationale Congolais, 37, 39

Mpolo, Maurice, 48

Muhammed, Murtala Ramat, 168n15

Munongo, Godefroid, 48, 51

Muslim Confederation, 145

Nasser, Abdul, 136

National Council of Nigeria and Cameroons, 16, 76–77

NATO powers, 42, 47

Neocolonialism, 4, 33

Nigeria, 145–46; and Congolese relations, 5, 6, 121, 128, 129, 133, 136; Federal Constitution (1960, the "independence constitution"), 8–9, 68, 73; develops foreign policy principles, 9–14, 15–16, 146–47, 168n13, 168n15, 168n16; independence of, 14–16, 53, 54; and the Congo crisis, 58, 59, 61, 62, 63–71, 74–80, 100–105, 115, 116, 127, 128,

164n94; African policy of, 66, 69, 88, 119, 126, 131, 136, 137, 143; domestic policy of, 79, 80, 81, 83, 85–91, 131, 145, 148, 160n29, 160n31, 163n71; and the United Nations, 86, 87, 88, 90–91, 108–11, 114–15, 128–29, 140, 163n71; foreign policy of, 116–17, 143–44, 167n8; and bilateral aid, 119–26, 121, 165n16; and Tshombe, 128, 129, 136–37, 167n3; and the United States, 137, 166n19; role in UN mission assessed, 144–45. *See also* Nigeria Police Force

Nigeria Police Force, 111–14

Nkrumah, Kwame, 137, 148–49, 169n20

Nonaligned states, 124, 137, 167n3

Northern People's Congress, 16

Nwokedi, Francis, 54, 96–99, 117

Obasanjo, Olusegun, 168n15

O'Brien, Conor Cruise, 99

Ogundipe, Brigadier B. A. O., 110

Ogunsulire, O., 76, 131

Oki, T. A. B., 96

Okito, Joseph, 48

O.K. Jazz Band, 132–33

Okoye, F., 125

Okwu, B. C., 107

Organisation de l'armée secrète, 37

Organization of African Unity, 142

Osadebay, Chief Dennis C., 68, 128

Osakwe, Albert, 76

Owen, David, 113

Pan-Africanism, 15, 54, 122, 144; "practical," in Congo, 141–42, 167n6

Pan-Africanists, 54, 82

Platonism, 27

Poland, 98

Quadri, Rowland, 100–101

Rand (South Africa) *Daily Mail,* 29

Rhodesia, Northern and Southern (now Zambia and Zimbabwe), 36

Rikhye, Lt. Gen. Indrajit, 127

Robertson, Sir James, 13

Rockefeller Foundation, 123

Roman Catholic Church, 26

Second Conference of Independent African States (Addis Ababa), 165n1

Sendwe, Jason, 35

Senegal, 71

Sese Seko, Mobutu. *See* Mobutu, Joseph

Shaba province. *See* Katanga province

Shagari, Alhaji Shehu, 148, 168n13

Slim, Mongi, 44

Smith, Ian, 70

Somalia, 70

South Africa, Republic of, 36–37, 142

Soviet Union, 33, 39, 42, 98, 119, 165n3

Stallard, Peter, 75

Stanleyville (city, now Kisangani, Democratic Republic of the Congo), 99, 121

Sudan, 70, 129

Sule, Maitama, 120

Switzerland, 100–101, 104–5

Tananarive (capital, Madagascar), 49, 96

Thant, U, 36, 50–52, 97, 102–3, 125, 139

Togo, 70
Treaty of Friendship, 33
Tshisekedi, Etienne, 113
Tshombe, Moise: criticism of, 4,
    34; and Katanga secession, 21,
    33, 34–35, 36, 51–52, 129–30,
    136, 137, 140, 166n19, 167n3;
    biography, 33–34, 137, 140,
    167n3; and reconciliation, 34,
    101, 104–5; on Lumumba, 35;
    and the United Nations, 51–52,
    104, 127, 129–30
Tunisia, 70, 129

UNESCO (United Nations Educa-
    tional, Scientific, and Cultural Or-
    ganization), 110
Union Minière du Haut Katanga, 36
Unitary form of government, 35,
    39, 40, 42
United Arab Republic (now Egypt),
    70
United Nations: Operations in the
    Congo, 33, 43–47; Security
    Council, 44, 51, 87; Congo Ad-
    visory Committee, 45, 85, 90,
    91, 95, 114, 160n2; "Congo
    Club," 45, 85, 160n3; Congo
    Conciliation Commission, 47, 48,
    91–96, 156n71; and developing
    nations, 85; used by Nigeria,
    85–91, 116–18; finances, 86,
    114–15, 164n87; General Assem-
    bly debates, 86–91; objectives of
    member states in Congo crisis,
    138–39; mission in Congo as-
    sessed, 138–40. *See also* Ham-
    marsjköld, Dag; *names of
    individual agencies; names of in-
    dividual nations;* Thant, U
United States, 3, 4, 38–39, 119,
    123, 165n2
Upper Volta, 71

Van Horn, Maj. Gen. Carl, 45

Wachuku, Jaja, 117; views on Nige-
    ria's role in Congo crisis, 6, 74,
    77, 81, 82, 95, 133; views on
    Congo crisis, 56, 57, 60, 61, 86,
    87, 88–89, 90, 95, 134; and UN
    work, 66–67, 92–94, 96
Warsaw Pact, 38
Weiss, Herbert F., 35
Welensky, Sir Roy, 57, 70
WHO (World Health Organization),
    109, 110, 121

Zaire. *See* Congo, Democratic Re-
    public of the
Zambia (formerly Northern Rho-
    desia), 36
Zimbabwe (formerly Southern Rho-
    desia), 36